Novatian of Rome and the Culmination of Pre-Nicene Orthodoxy

Princeton Theological Monograph Series

K. C. Hanson, Charles M. Collier, D. Christopher Spinks,
and Robin Parry, Series Editors

Recent volumes in the series:
Linda Hogan
Religion and the Politics of Peace and Conflict

Chris Budden
Following Jesus in Invaded Space: Doing Theology on Aboriginal Land

Jeff B. Pool
*God's Wounds: Hermeneutic of the Christian Symbol of
Divine Suffering, Volume One: Divine Vulnerability and Creation*

Lisa E. Dahill
*Reading from the Underside of Selfhood:
Bonhoeffer and Spiritual Formation*

Samuel A. Paul
*The Ubuntu God: Deconstructing a South African Narrative
of Oppression*

Jeanne M. Hoeft
*Agency, Culture, and Human Personhood: Pastoral Thelogy
and Intimate Partner Violence*

Ryan A. Neal
*Theology as Hope: On the Ground and Implications
of Jürgen Moltmann's Doctrine of Hope*

Scott A. Ellington
Risking Truth: Reshaping the World through Prayers of Lament

Novatian of Rome and the Culmination of Pre-Nicene Orthodoxy

James L. Papandrea

☞PICKWICK *Publications* · Eugene, Oregon

NOVATIAN OF ROME AND THE CULMINATION
OF PRE-NICENE ORTHODOXY

Princeton Theological Monograph Series 175

Copyright © 2011 James L. Papandrea. All rights reserved. Except for brief quotations in critical publications or reviews, no part of this book may be reproduced in any manner without prior written permission from the publisher. Write: Permissions, Wipf and Stock Publishers, 199 W. 8th Ave., Suite 3, Eugene, OR 97401.

Pickwick Publications
An Imprint of Wipf and Stock Publishers
199 W. 8th Ave., Suite 3
Eugene, OR 97401

www.wipfandstock.com

ISBN 13: 978-1-60608-780-0

Cataloging-in-Publication data

Papandrea, James L.

    Novatian of Rome and the culmination of pre-Nicene orthodoxy / James L. Papandrea.

        xiv + 170 p. ; 23 cm. —Includes bibliographical references and index.

    Princeton Theological Monograph Series 175

        ISBN 13: 978-1-60608-780-0

        1. Novatianus. 2. Church history—Primitive and early church, ca. 30–600. I. Title. II. Series.

BR65 P25 2011

Manufactured in the U.S.A.

To my sons
Richard James and John Paul

"What could be more fortunate
than the old man who will declare to everyone who will listen
that he has been surpassed in benefits by his son[s]?"

—Seneca, *Benefits* 38

Contents

Preface / ix

1. The State of Christology before the Mid-Third Century • 1
   The Age of Apostolic Fathers and Apologists • 1
   The Age of the Theologians • 15
   The State of Christology before Novatian • 42

2. Novatian: His Life and Historical Context • 47
   The Church in Rome • 47
   Novatian the Priest and Theologian • 55
   Novatian the Schismatic • 58
   Novatianists after Novatian • 69

3. Novatian: Master of Doctrine • 73
   The Problem of Christian Monotheism • 73
   Novatian's Interpretation of Philippians 2:6–11 • 74
   Kenosis and the Life of the Divine Word • 84
   The Relationship of the Father and Son: Dynamic Subordination • 96
   Novatian's Trinity Anticipates Nicaea and Constantinople • 106
   Novatian's Christology Anticipates Ephesus and Chalcedon • 110

4. Novatian's Ongoing Legacy • 121
   Western Theologians Who Show Evidence of Influence from Novatian • 123
   Eastern Theologians Who Show Evidence of Influence from Novatian • 128
   Between Two Thieves • 132
   Conclusion • 140

   Appendix: Outline of Doctrinal Terms • 143

   Other Works by the Author • 157

   Bibliography • 159

   Subject Index • 167

Preface

The Background and Sources for This Book

AS A DOCTORAL STUDENT, I STARTED WORKING WITH NOVATIAN AS a dissertation topic in part because I found in him a fascinating and brilliant character of the early church, about whom relatively little had been written. It seemed like unexplored territory. Of course I came to find several serious studies of his life and work, but in comparison to the more well-known patristic figures the fact remained (and remains to this day) that most scholars who address Novatian at all do so only as a brief mention within the broader context of surveys of pre-Nicene theology, and then only to scratch the surface. It has been my intention from the time I wrote my dissertation,[1] through its publication,[2] and a follow-up chapter in a festschrift for Dennis E. Groh,[3] to the completion of this book, that I could somehow bring to the surface a deeper understanding of (and appreciation for) Novatian, and make his thought more accessible to the student of the early church. In addition to my own work, the main studies on Novatian are by D'Ales[4] and DeSimone.[5]

As far as primary sources, Novatian's theology is understood almost entirely from his one doctrinal treatise, labeled *De Trinitate* (*On the Trinity*). We also have a few ethical treatises that come from the time after his schism, during which Novatian wrote as a bishop, despite the fact that he had no legitimate see.[6] The other primary sources that contribute to our understanding of Novatian and his times include

---

1. Papandrea, "'Between Two Thieves': The Christology of Novatian as 'Dynamic Subordination.'"

2. Papandrea, *Trinitarian Theology of Novatian*.

3. Papandrea, "Between Two Thieves: Novatian of Rome and Kenosis Christology," in Kalantzis and Martin, eds., *Studies on Patristic Texts and Archaeology*.

4. D'Alès, *Novatien*.

5. DeSimone, *Treatise of Novatian*.

6. The treatises are *De Spectaculis* (*On the Spectacles*), *De Cibis Iudaicis* (*On Jewish Foods*), and *De Bono Pudicitiae* (*On the Benefit of Purity*, sometimes called *In Praise of Purity*).

the letters of Cyprian of Carthage,[7] a few letters written by Novatian on behalf of the Roman church,[8] and an assortment of contemporary and later commentaries on Novatian's significance, usually related to the schism that followed his election as a rival bishop of Rome. These include the legitimately elected bishop Cornelius's condemnation of him and Dionysius of Alexandria's letter to him, both preserved in Eusebius's *Ecclesiastical History*.[9] Novatian is also mentioned by Pacian of Barcelona,[10] Ambrose of Milan,[11] Epiphanius of Salamis,[12] Jerome,[13] and others. Novatian gets a sympathetic mention in Socrates's history of the church.[14] Finally, two anti-Novatianist documents require mention. The first is the anonymous *Ad Novatianum* (*To Novatian*), a letter written to Novatian himself, possibly by Pope Sixtus II in about 257 CE, though some have argued that it was written by Cornelius.[15] The second is *Contra Novatianum* (*Against Novatian*), also anonymous, but possibly written in the 370s by Ambrosiaster.[16]

Novatian has continued to hold a fascination for me, not only as an important figure of church history, but as one who made a great

---

7. Most especially letters 6, 8, 27–28, 37, 41, 44–60, 68–69, 72–74.

8. Letters numbered 30, 31, and 36 in the corpus of Cyprian's correspondence. Novatian's authorship of letter 31 is in doubt, though it seems to be a response to Cyprian's letter 28. Cf. Cyprian, *Epistle* 55.5 for Cyprian's acknowledgment of Novatian's authorship of letter 30. Following the precedent set by DeSimone, the letters of Novatian will be referred to as *Epistles* 1, 2, and 3, respectively, with the corresponding number from Cyprian's correspondence in parentheses.

9. Eusebius, *Ecclesiastical History* 6.43 (Cornelius), 6.45, 7.7–8 (Dionysius).

10. Pacian (Pacianus) of Barcelona (310–391 CE), *Epistles* 1–3, written to the Novatianist Sympronius (*Ad Sympronianum*).

11. Ambrose of Milan (339–397 CE), *On Penance* (sometimes called *On Repentance*) 1.3, 3.14.

12. Epiphanius of Salamis (310–403 CE), *Panarion* 59.

13. Jerome, *Illustrious Men* 70; *Apology in Answer to Rufinus* 2.19; *Epistle* 10.2, 42.1.

14. Socrates Scholasticus, *Ecclesiastical History* 1.10, 5.10, 7.7. Socrates has been accused of being a Novatianist, most especially by Philostorgius in his own history of the church, which is preserved in summary by Photius of Constantinople. Photius himself was an Arian (Eunomian) and, like many of his predecessors (including Eusebius), confuses Novatian with Novatus. See Philostorgius 4.28f, 8.15. Philostorgius also erroneously thought Novatian had come from Phrygia, a misconception probably caused by a confusion or conflation of the Novatianists with the Montanists.

15. Harnack, "Novatian." Cf. *Ad Novatianum* (*To Novatian*) 7.

16. Gregory, "Essay *Contra Novatianum*," 566.

positive contribution to the development of doctrine, and yet at the same time held a potentially damaging ecclesiology. I see in him aspects of myself, some with which I'm comfortable, others not so much. I consider Novatian one of the great cloud of witnesses who cheers me on as I run the race of faith, but who also (I hope) prays for me that I don't make some of the same mistakes he made. May we be zealous for our faith, but not to the point of making enemies out of our fellow children of God.

The Methodology of This Book

Before turning to Novatian himself, it is important to survey the development of Christology and Trinitarian theology up to the point of the mid-third century. Chapter 1 will trace the trajectory of thought through the post-New Testament period, from the apostolic fathers and apologists to the major theologians of the late second and early third centuries. The purpose is twofold: to understand Novatian's influences, and to see how he both accepted and advanced aspects of Christology and theology from his predecessors. To do this, we will look at the previous theologians with Novatian in mind (and to some extent from his vantage point), intentionally focusing on those who either influenced him or those whom he corrects (explicitly or implicitly).[17] In other

17. The reader may notice that Origen is not included as an influence on Novatian. While Origen and Novatian were contemporaries, there is no evidence that they ever met, corresponded, or that either one had read the other's works. In fact, Novatian and Origen seem completely ignorant of each other's works. As it will become clear through the pages below, comparing Origen's *On First Principles* 1.2.8–9, 4.1.31–32; *Commentary on John* 20.153–55; *Against Celsus* 4.15, 6.15; and *On Prayer* 15.2 with Novatian's *On the Trinity* shows no similarity of thought, especially with regard to the way the two interpreted Phil 2:6–11, the most important passage for Novatian. For Origen, the *kenosis* is one of glory, not power, and he would not have accepted that the divine nature of Christ was circumscribed in the incarnation. See also Origen, *Commentary on Matthew* 29. Also, while Origen acknowledged a human rational soul in Christ, he did not believe that this rational soul had free will, so he could not have agreed with Novatian on the voluntary nature of the subordination of the Son to the Father. Eusebius of Caesarea did say that Origen had once visited Rome (cf. also Jerome, *Illustrious Men* 61) and had even corresponded with Fabian of Rome, *Ecclesiastical History* 6.15, 6.36, however the lack of similarity of thought, or indeed mention of the other writer in each theologian's documents, argues against doctrinal influence, let alone a meeting between Novatian and Origen. As I will argue below, Rufinus's Latin translation of Origen's *On First Principles* may show some connection to Novatian's concept of eternal generation in *On the Trinity*, however the connection is more likely that Novatian influenced Rufinus's post-Nicene doctoring of the text than

words, since it would be impossible to fully explore the thought of the likes of Irenaeus and Tertullian within the scope of this book, I will highlight those aspects of their thought which will be important for understanding Novatian's own Christology and his understanding of the Trinity.

After bringing the development of Trinitarian doctrine up to the middle of the third century, we will take stock of the historical, social, and political context of Novatian's church in Rome. I will tell the story of Novatian's life, such as we can reconstruct from the primary sources, filtering out the rumors spread by his enemies who were out to discredit him.[18] Once the stage is set we will examine Novatian's *On the Trinity*, a commentary on the rule of faith that demonstrates Novatian's understanding of the Trinity, and shows that in his explanation of Christology he was both the spokesperson for the church of Rome in the mid-third century and ahead of his time.[19] I will bring in the ethical treatises and letters where relevant, but for the most part everything we know about Novatian the theologian is in *On the Trinity*.[20] Finally, in the last chapter, we will see some ways in which Novatian influenced later theology and how both his doctrinal thought and his life story are relevant for the church today—the latter if only as a lesson in what not to do.

Acknowledgments

I would like to take this opportunity to thank the people who contributed to this book in indirect ways: my first professor of church history,

---

that Origen influenced Novatian. See Chin, *Rufinus of Aquileia*, 630. In the end, the christological conclusions of Novatian and Origen are so different that it is most likely that neither one of them read the other, let alone were influenced by the other's writings. If there are similarities between the two, the most we could say is that they came to similar conclusions independently.

18. For a complete treatment of the spurious as well as the more trustworthy accounts of Novatian's life, see Papandrea, *Trinitarian Theology of Novatian*, 5–42.

19. The doctrine of the Trinity and the development of Christology are so interdependent in the pre-Nicene period that I find it unnecessary, and in fact artificial and unhelpful, to make a strict distinction between them. If the reader finds that sometimes it sounds like I believe it's really all Christology in the end, so be it.

20. All English translations of primary sources are the author's translations from Greek and Latin. For a complete translation of Novatian's *On the Trinity*, see Papandrea, *Trinitarian Theology of Novatian*, 367–472. The author's translation of the entire *De Trinitate of Novatian* can be found online at www.Novatianus.info.

James E. Bradley; my dissertation advisors, Dennis E. Groh and Robert Jewett; my colleagues, especially George Kalantzis and Stephanie Perdew VanSlyke; my students and discussion partners, especially Carol Korak and my research/teaching assistant Julie Schubring. Thank you for the ways you helped me, challenged me, for all your patience, and for your friendship.

1

The State of Christology before the Mid-Third Century

The Age of the Apostolic Fathers and Apologists

BEFORE WE CAN LOOK AT THE WRITERS WHO PRECEDED AND INFLUenced Novatian, it must be acknowledged that the early church produced a variety of interpretations of Scripture and of the life of Christ, including alternatives to what would come to be called orthodoxy. These alternatives came to be labeled "heresies," a word that implies that they were deviating, or separating, from the church of the apostles. While it is not the case that these alternatives ("heresies") preceded orthodoxy, nevertheless it is true that in some sense, the *clarification* of orthodoxy is a response to heresy. Therefore, it is necessary to briefly mention the two major groups of alternative interpretations to which the orthodox writers were responding, and outline the theological/christological options as they were in the second century. Although there was a significant amount of diversity within each of these two major heresy groupings, and although the groupings themselves are somewhat artificial (constructed as labels for the losers of the debates), nevertheless Novatian and others like him saw these groups as the extremes, on the fringes of the church, with orthodoxy as a "middle way" between the extremes.

Ebionites

The word *Ebionites* means "the poor ones," and they called themselves this because they believed they were following Jesus by imitating his poverty and humility. The early Christian writers saw the Ebionites as the legacy of the so-called Judaizers of Paul's letters in the New Testament.[1] They were probably mostly Jewish Christians who were uncomfortable with the idea of the divinity of Christ as it was being expressed in Christian worship, perhaps worrying that such a belief implied the worship of two Gods. Therefore Ebionites maintained that Jesus was a mere man, perhaps a prophet, or anointed like the heroes of the Old Testament, but not the divine Son of God. Some said he was an angel, but still a created being, and therefore they rejected the idea of a divine nature in Christ. As a prophet, Jesus received the Holy Spirit for the first time at his baptism. However, he was only temporarily indwelt by the Spirit, who left him alone on the cross (Mark 15:34/Matt 27:46). The resurrection of Christ, then, would not be a bodily resurrection, but would be interpreted as a metaphor for eternal life. Thus the Ebionites affirmed the humanity of Christ, but denied his divinity. For the Ebionites, salvation was primarily by obedience to the Jewish law. Some tended toward asceticism. Interestingly, this belief also had implications for the Eucharist. Since they did not believe that the blood of Jesus had any atoning significance, they seem to have rejected the use of wine in the Eucharist.

Docetics and Gnostics

At the other end of the spectrum from the Ebionites were the Docetics and Gnostics, who affirmed the divinity of Christ, but to varying degrees denied his humanity. Just as the Ebionites were most likely Jewish Christians, the Docetics and Gnostics were primarily Gentile Christians, former pagans, for whom it was never a priority to limit the number of gods to one.[2] In the New Testament we can already see that there were certain "false teachers," who denied the real flesh of Christ (1 John 4:2–3). The earliest expression of this is called *Docetism*, from

---

1. Ignatius, *Letter to the Ephesians* 7.2; *Letter to the Magnesians* 8.1; *Letter to the Philadelphians* 6.1. Ignatius refers to the Ebionites as "the uncircumcised preaching Judaism," which implies that at least some of the Ebionites he knew of were Gentiles.

2. The use of the term "pagan" is admittedly somewhat anachronistic, since it did not have the current use until later in the church's history. The term refers to the people who live in rural areas outside the cities, who (after the Christian population became a majority in the urban areas) were said to be the only ones who still held on to the old mythologies. As used at that time, the term had a pejorative connotation, and was certainly an exaggeration, however it is used here simply to refer to those inhabitants of the Roman Empire who were neither Jewish nor Christian.

the Greek verb meaning "to seem" or "to appear." Docetics, as they are called, believed that Jesus only *appeared* to be a real human, but was in reality a phantom. This was based on an extreme form of dualism that assumed that only what belongs to the spiritual realm is good, and anything that belongs to the physical world is inherently evil. Therefore Docetics reasoned that the divine Christ could not become flesh, since flesh was of the material world and evil. They also reasoned that the Creator of this material world could not be the same good God that Jesus called his Father. The most famous proponent of docetism was Marcion, who would eventually be excommunicated from the church at Rome and start his own movement known later as the Marcionites. They taught that there were (at least) two gods, and the God of Jesus was a better, higher God than the Creator in the Old Testament. Salvation, for them, meant being rescued from this world and its "inferior god." This led Marcion and his followers to reject the Old Testament, and any part of the New Testament that connected Jesus to the God or the prophets of the Hebrew Bible.

Eventually, a form of docetism evolved called *Gnosticism* (from the Greek word *gnosis*, meaning "knowledge").[3] Gnostics taught that Jesus had not come to bring salvation, but secret knowledge. Part of this "knowledge" was the belief that we are all divine, and therefore we do not need forgiveness or salvation, per se, what we need is illumination, that is, to be enlightened as to our own divinity. Based on these teachings, Docetics and Gnostics rejected the idea of a future resurrection (2 Tim 2:17–18). For them, the resurrection of Christ would have been interpreted as a mystical vision in which Christ shed the appearance of his humanity to reveal his real (non-human) self. Gnostics rejected the church's baptism as an image of dying and rising with Christ, and they created their own baptisms. They rejected the church's Eucharist since they did not believe that Jesus had a real flesh and blood body. Some (ironically, like the Ebionites) had their own eucharistic rituals that substituted water for the wine (because they believed Jesus had no blood), but others refused to participate in any Eucharist.[4] Many of them rejected marriage, even creating a second baptism that was meant

---

3. Generally speaking, all Gnostics were also Docetics, but not all Docetics were Gnostics, since they did not all subscribe to the teachings of secret knowledge. For this reason, Marcion was a Docetic but not a Gnostic.

4. Ignatius, *Letter to the Smyrnaeans* 6.1–2.

to symbolize a mystical marriage. Some distanced themselves from the world by a life of extreme asceticism. Others chose to disregard the physical world with a lifestyle of extreme promiscuity.

The Gnostics eventually separated themselves from the mainstream church. They evolved into a wide variety of secret societies with elaborate mythologies based on a syncretism of Christianity with paganism and astrology. Gnosticism was never one organized religion, and in fact it is misleading to talk about it as one movement. It was really many different teachers with a diverse following, creating widely divergent groups, each with their own versions of the Gnostic myths. Some even allowed that Jesus might have had a tangible body, however they would have separated this tangible Jesus (who was nevertheless not really human) from the concept of the divine Christ, as if Jesus and Christ were two distinct entities.

With the Ebionites on one side, maintaining that Christ was human, but not at all divine, and the Docetics and Gnostics on the other side, teaching that Christ was divine but not really human, the Christology of the apostolic fathers and apologists was built around the affirmation of both the divine and the human natures in Christ.[5]

Ignatius of Antioch (c. 50–110 CE)

Ignatius was bishop of Antioch in Syria at the beginning of the second century. He had been arrested during a time of persecution and was being taken to Rome where he would eventually be martyred, in about 110 CE. Along the way, he wrote letters to several churches, which provide some of the first glimpses of early Christology after the New Testament.

Against docetism (which he calls "strange doctrines," and "antiquated myths"), Ignatius maintains that the birth of Christ proves his true humanity.[6] Also, his suffering on the cross shows the reality of his flesh, since if he were divine only, he could not suffer.[7] Against Ebionite Christology (which he understood as the legacy of the Judaizers of the Pauline letters), Ignatius asserts the divinity of Christ by calling Jesus

---

5. For example, see Irenaeus, *Against Heresies* 4.6.7.

6. Ignatius, *Letter to the Ephesians* 7.7, 18.2, 19.1; *Letter to the Magnesians* 8.1, 11; *Letter to the Trallians* 9.1–2, 10.1; *Letter to the Smyrnaeans* 1.1–2, 2.1, 4.2, 5.2. See also Hurtado, *Lord Jesus Christ*, 330.

7. Ignatius, *Letter to the Magnesians* 11; *Letter to the Trallians* 9.1–2; *Letter to the Smyrnaeans* 1.1–2. The Docetics would have argued that, in fact, he did not suffer.

"God," and by describing him as eternal.[8] He clearly affirms both natures of Christ against the two opposite heresies by emphasizing the dual lineage of Jesus—that he is Son of Mary (or Son of Man/Son of David) in his humanity and Son of God in his divinity.[9] For Ignatius, the resurrection of Christ is the perfect picture of his two natures, since the resurrection was both spiritual (divine) and physical (human).[10] However, what seems to be just as important for Ignatius is the fact the "heretics" are also schismatic. In almost every one of his letters, he criticized these groups for holding separate meetings (cf. 1 John 2:19), without the authority of the local bishop.[11]

Virtually everyone would have agreed that part of the very definition of divinity was *immutability*, the conviction that it would be against the nature of God to change, and therefore any change would necessarily disqualify a being as divine.[12] The Ebionites reasoned that since Jesus changed (started out as a baby and grew up, Luke 2:52),

---

8. Ignatius, *Letter to the Ephesians* 7.2; *Letter to the Magnesians* 8.1; *Letter to the Philadelphians* 6.1. Ignatius refers to the Ebionites as "the uncircumcised preaching Judaism."

9. Ignatius, *Letter to the Ephesians* 7.2, 18.2, 20.2; *Letter to the Smyrnaeans* 1.1; *Letter to Polycarp* 3.2.

10. Ignatius, *Letter to the Smyrnaeans* 12.2.

11. Ibid., 5.2–3; *Letter to the Magnesians* 6.2, 7.1; *Letter to the Trallians* 2.2, 3.1; *Letter to the Smyrnaeans* 8.1–2; *Letter to the Philadelphians* 2.2, 3.3, 7.2. Ignatius emphasized his belief that there is no salvation outside the church, and defined the church as those in communion with the bishops.

12. For example, see Theophilus, *To Autolycus* 1.4, 2.4; and Augustine, *On the Trinity* 1.2, where Augustine says that whatever is eternal must also be immutable. The logic of immutability was that in order for God to be perfect, he must be eternally perfect, or else the possibility would exist that God progressed to perfection from imperfection, or worse, that God could digress from perfection to imperfection. Any change in God would therefore imply something less than perfection. In addition, the possibility of change also would imply the possibility of decay and eventual non-existence. In other words, mutability would imply an end and/or a beginning to the existence of the mutable being in question. Therefore, immutability is understood as interdependent with eternality. To put it another way, whatever can change can also die. Since God cannot die, God cannot change. It was also assumed that suffering was a form of change, so that for God to be immutable, he must also be *impassible*, incapable of suffering. This presented a problem for Christology since it was obvious that Christ suffered, yet he was also worshipped as divine. The solution of the apologists was to mark the distinction between the two natures by saying that only the human nature suffered, while the divine nature remained impassible, and immutable. Cf. Ps 102:26–27, Mal 3:6, Heb 13:8.

he therefore could not be divine. In fact, they extended the concept of progress in Jesus to moral progress, believing that he achieved perfection, rather than believing that he was sinless by nature. On the other extreme, Docetics and Gnostics reasoned that since Christ was divine, he must be immutable and therefore could not have been human or had a real human body. Their presuppositions, and their apparent unwillingness to accept the paradox of a Christ who is both divine and human, led them to an "either/or" approach. Ignatius advanced the Johannine response to docetism by making a distinction between the divine and human natures in Christ, so that the divine nature remained immutable, while the human nature was born, grew, ate and drank, suffered and died. While the alternative christologies maintained that Jesus must be *either* divine *or* human, Ignatius held to the conviction that he is both. Yet the two natures are not separate as in the Gnostic separation of Jesus and "the Christ." It would not be acceptable to say that the divine nature is called Christ and the human nature is called Jesus, since this would imply only a temporary connection between the two. For Ignatius, Jesus Christ is the one product of the incarnation, in which the divine Word *became* human—not just united with humanity, or indwelt humanity, but *became* human.[13] In the incarnation, the invisible one became visible, the intangible one became tangible and the immutable one suffered for our sake.[14] The point is that both alternative christologies (both "heresies") represent a kind of dualism that rejected any real connection between the divine and human. Orthodox Christology, in the other hand, would emphasize a unity between the human and divine in the person of Christ, that then becomes the point of contact between God and humanity.

Justin Martyr (c. 112–165 CE)

Sometimes known as Justin of Neapolis, the appellation "Martyr" is of course not his last name, but rather describes his fate. Justin is the typical example of a second century apologist—the philosopher who

---

13. Note that this language of *becoming* will also be applied to the Eucharist, so that just as the Word became flesh in the incarnation, the bread and wine become the flesh and blood in the sacrament of communion.

14. Ignatius, *Letter to Polycarp* 3.2. This is not really an early expression of *communicatio idiomatum*, but simply an expansion on the phrase, "the Word became flesh" (John 1:14).

found Christianity to be the most convincing philosophy. Probably born between 110 and 114 CE, Justin was a Greek from Flavia Neapolis in Samaria. At a time when many philosophers were experimenting with various forms of monotheism, Justin explored as many different philosophical systems as he could, looking for something to which he could devote his life.[15] He was initially intrigued by the church's interpretation of Jesus as the fulfillment of Old Testament prophecies. When he examined the lives of Christians, he was impressed with their high moral standards. He was finally converted in about 130–132 CE, when he witnessed the bravery of Christian martyrs who were willing to die rather than give up their beliefs.[16] He would eventually follow in their footsteps. After moving to Rome, he taught Christianity as a philosophy, until the teachers of other philosophical schools conspired to have him arrested and eventually executed. He died by beheading outside the city walls of Rome in 165 CE.

Justin's most important writing is his First Apology (*I Apology*), which was written as an open letter to the emperor Antoninus Pius in the 150's CE. He also wrote a shorter Second Apology (*II Apology*), as well as an apology for a Jewish audience called *Dialogue with Trypho*, and a treatise defending the Pauline concept of resurrection against a philosophical view of the afterlife as the existence of disembodied souls (*On the Resurrection*). Typical of Christian philosophers, Justin was attracted to the idea of Christ as the *Logos* of God (John 1:1), since it incorporated a Christianized version of what was to them a familiar concept.[17] Justin taught that the *Logos* is the wisdom and rationality of God, and since humans are created in the image of God, human reason is like the seed of the *Logos* planted in the human mind.[18] For Justin, this is a result of the fact that it is the *Logos* who is the agent of creation, and he has infused humanity with his own rational creativity.

Justin taught that the *Logos* interacted with humanity before his incarnation and these interactions can be seen in the Old Testament.

---

15. See Hippolytus, *Refutation of All Heresies* 1.2, 4.43. Hippolytus believed that the philosophers had gotten their version of monotheism from a strain of Egyptian religion that worshipped the sun.

16. Justin Martyr, *II Apology* 12.

17. Hurtado, *Lord Jesus Christ*, 642–43.

18. Justin Martyr, *II Apology* 8, 13. Cf. *I Apology* 32. Justin calls the seed of the *Logos* the *logos spermatikos*. See Grillmeier, *Christ in Christian Tradition*, 1:91–92.

Since it was assumed that, "no one can see God and live," (Exod 33:20, cf. 1 Tim 6:16), Justin reserved for God the Father alone the divine attributes of transcendence (such as immutability, impassibility, invisibility and omnipresence), as well as the conviction that God cannot be *circumscribed* (confined by time and space). This allowed him to explain appearances of God in the Old Testament as visitations of the pre-incarnate *Logos*.[19] Although the *Logos* is divine, and is therefore invisible and uncircumscribable by nature, his distinction from the Father means that it is *possible* for him to be visible, and to be localized in space.[20] This will become typical of orthodox Christology in the second and third centuries. Virtually all of Novatian's predecessors will describe the Old Testament appearances of God as appearances of the pre-incarnate *Logos*, especially when he is called the "angel of the Lord," and this "angel" is treated as divine by accepting worship, or by making promises as God (cf. Gen 18).[21]

Justin Martyr continues the discussion that was begun in the Johannine writings surrounding the interplay between the unity and distinction of the Father and the Son. For him, the Father and Son are one in divinity, in fact the *Logos* is the very divine power of the Father, extended from the Father, and never separated from him.[22] Therefore

---

19. Justin Martyr, *I Apology* 63; *Dialogue with Trypho* 56–60, 127.1–2. See Hurtado, *Lord Jesus Christ*, 576. The *Shepherd of Hermas*, though it may reflect an Ebionite Christology, nevertheless explains the common understanding of God as uncircumscribable, which is that God "contains all things, but is himself alone uncontained." *Shepherd of Hermas* 26.1.

20. Some modern writers have placed too much emphasis on the distinction between Father and Son in Justin Martyr. See, for example, Turner, *Patristic Doctrine of Redemption*, 38. Justin's distinction does not go beyond the Johannine, and does not constitute subordinationism, let alone a "lesser divinity" or a "second god." If one is looking for precedents for Arius, they are more to be found in Theophilus of Antioch than in Justin Martyr.

21. See for example, Irenaeus, *Demonstration of the Apostolic Preaching* 32. This is not to be confused with so-called angel Christology, which is a form of Ebionite Christology that denies the pre-existence of Christ. Orthodox Christology affirms the divinity of the *Logos*, while Ebionite angel Christology assumes that the pre-incarnate Angel-Christ is a created being.

22. Justin Martyr, *Dialogue with Trypho* 61, 128. Cf. also *I Apology* 6, 33. In this, Justin anticipates the one essence of Irenaeus and the one substance of Tertullian, however Justin does not use the language of essence or substance. He talks about the divine essence in terms of divine power (*dunamis*), but his language is imprecise, as sometimes it sounds like he believes the Father and Son have (or are) two divine powers,

the Father and Son are also united in all divine activity, thus Justin affirms the concept that would later be called *inseparable operation*.[23] On the other hand, the Father and Son are not one and the same, but are distinguished as two in number.[24] Justin further described the divine relationships in terms of an "order" or hierarchy in which the Father takes first place, the Son takes second place and the Holy Spirit third place.[25] However, he does not have the same well-defined distinction between the Son and the Holy Spirit as he has between the Father and the Son. In fact, there are times when Justin blurs the distinction between the *Logos* and the Holy Spirit, to the point of speaking of them as though they are the same, and the only difference is the incarnation.[26] This probably comes from the conviction that it is the Holy Spirit who inspired the prophets, though it is also the *Logos,* or *Word* of God that they preached. This would prove typical of the proponents of *Logos* Christology. They often seem to equate the Holy Spirit with the pre-incarnate Christ, as if there is little difference between the Spirit and the *Logos* before the incarnation.[27] This demonstrates the very real belief in the divine nature of Christ (and implies as much about the Spirit), however it lacks the full distinct personhood of both Son and Spirit that would be required for later orthodoxy.

---

and at other times it sounds like he believes the Father and Son share one divine power. He probably locates divine power in the essence as an attribute of divine substance, as Tertullian did, rather than as a property of each divine person. This is typical of *Logos* Christology and would be later refined by Novatian's *kenosis* Christology, in which Novatian locates divine power in the person (as a personal property) such that each divine person has his own divine power. See Hurtado, *Lord Jesus Christ*, 646.

23. Justin Martyr, *Dialogue with Trypho* 56. Inseparable operation affirms that all three divine persons are involved in all divine activity. Ignatius of Antioch had hinted at this as well, as part of an argument for the unity of the church. See Ignatius, *Letter to the Magnesians* 7.

24. Justin Martyr, *Dialogue with Trypho* 56, 62, 128–29. See Hurtado, *Lord Jesus Christ*, 643, 647.

25. Justin Martyr, *I Apology* 13, 60.

26. Ibid., 33, 36.

27. Ignatius, *Letter to the Ephesians* 7.2. Cf. also Justin Martyr, *Dialogue with Trypho* 61, and II Clement 9.5.

Athenagoras (dates unknown, fl. 170's CE)

Athenagoras was an Athenian philosopher turned Christian apologist, whose conversion was said to be the indirect result of Paul's preaching in Athens (Acts 17:34). According to tradition, he had set out to refute Christianity, especially Paul's understanding of the resurrection of the body, from a philosophical point of view. However, when he actually read Paul's letters for himself, he was convinced and converted. We have two documents from him, *A Plea for the Christians*, written to the emperor Marcus Aurelius and his son Commodus in about the year 177 CE and *On the Resurrection of the Dead*, an explanation and defense of Paul's theology of the resurrection body against the philosophical position he himself had formerly held. The latter document is heavily influenced by Justin's treatise of similar name.

Athenagoras was indirectly a student of Justin Martyr and so he takes his Christology from Justin and expands on it. Like Justin, he believed that philosophy was good, but it could only bring one so far, since human reason was flawed. The only reliable source of truth is revelation and the ultimate manifestation of God's revelation is the divine *Logos*.[28] The *Logos* is the agent of creation and is the "mind and rationality of God."[29] Following his predecessors, Athenagoras of course believed that the *Logos* was pre-existent, but he also clarified that this pre-existence is eternal. However, he stops short of saying that the Son is eternally *distinct* from the Father, since he implies that in eternity past the *Logos* existed only as the mind of God, until such time as he "came forth" from within the Father to be an extension of the will of God, as an idea is an extension of a person's mind. Therefore for Athenagoras, the Son of God is eternally pre-existent, since he never came into being from non-being, yet he is not eternally *distinct* from the Father as a numerically distinguished rational entity.[30] Athenagoras wrote:

> He was the first to come forth from the Father, but not as if he were created, for from the beginning God, who is eternal Mind, had within himself the Logos, who is eternal Word.[31]

---

28. Athenagoras, *Plea for the Christians* 7.
29. Ibid., 4, 10.
30. Ibid., 10.
31. Ibid., My translation.

Athenagoras calls the Father "God" and he calls the Son "God," but he does not call the Holy Spirit "God." The Spirit is an "emanation from God," using the analogy of a beam of light from the sun.[32] The unity of Father, Son and Holy Spirit is described in terms of divine power, while the distinction between the them is described as an "order" (hierarchy), or an "arrangement of distribution."[33] Athenagoras is a bit clearer than Justin in describing the persons as "united according to power," (there is only one divine power) though he still did not describe the Trinity in terms of a shared "essence."[34] What this means is that it had yet to be clarified that the unity of persons in the Trinity is more than just a functional unity (power as activity), but is also an ontological unity (power as essence, the very being of God). This ontological unity will have to wait until Irenaeus to be explicitly stated.

Theophilus of Antioch (c. 115–188 CE)

Born around 115 CE, Theophilus was bishop of Antioch in Syria from 168 or 169 CE until his death, probably in 188 CE. This is the same see occupied by Ignatius sixty years earlier. His only extant work is a compilation of three letters written to a pagan named Autolycus. Known collectively as *To Autolycus*, the letters were written in the 180's CE. In these letters, Theophilus tried to convince Autolycus of the truth of Christianity and that the life and ministry of Jesus Christ was the fulfillment of ancient prophecies. In the process, Theophilus was the first writer (that we know of) to attempt to coin a term to express God as three in one, calling God a divine "Triad" (in Greek: *Triados*).

---

32. Ibid. It is interesting to note how Athenagoras describes the "movement" of the Holy Spirit, flowing out from God, and returning back again. This is an early anticipation of the doctrine of *reciprocity*, also called *circumincessio*, or *perichoresis*.

33. Ibid., 10, 12.

34. Ibid., 24. At least one English translation uses the word "essence" in this passage, however this is an anachronism. Athenagoras did not use the word *ousia*, and therefore he did not anticipate the language of Tertullian or the later Greek fathers, as the use of the word "essence" in the translation would suggest. Like Justin, the unity is in the one power (*dunamis*). It is interesting to note that Athenagoras compared the Father and Son to the Emperor and his son/heir, implying a kind of "ontological" equality where the son carries the authority of the father (the Emperor) yet with a hierarchy of authority in the relation between the two. In this, he almost stumbles on Novatian's later solution to the problem of unity and distinction of the Father and the Son.

When the apologists read the New Testament, they saw three phases (for lack of a better term) in the life of the divine Word: Pre-existence (before the birth of Jesus), Incarnation (the life of Jesus) and Exaltation (after the ascension of Jesus). Theophilus divided the first phase into two, essentially making four phases. In his first phase, the Word was *in* the Father, as the Father's wisdom, but (like Athenagoras had implied) not as distinct from the Father, only "being his own mind and thought."[35] Theophilus said, ". . . at first, God was alone, and the Word was in him."[36] Theophilus called this the *Logos endiathetos*, or the "internal Word."

In Theophilus's second phase, the Word was *with* the Father. The point at which the Word goes from being *in* the Father (as a thought in the Father's mind) to being *with* the Father (as distinct from the Father) is the point when the Word is "spoken forth" or "emitted" from the Father.[37] After the Word was emitted and distinct from the Father, then the Word can be said to be *with* the Father, which Theophilus called the *Logos prophorikos*, or the "emitted Word."[38] It is interesting to note that Theophilus goes out of his way to clarify that after the Word (or wisdom) of God is emitted, God the Father is not without his own wisdom, though this is not explained further.[39] The point at which the Word is

---

35. Theophilus, *To Autolycus* 2.22. See Grillmeier, *Christ in Christian Tradition*, 111.

36. Theophilus, *To Autolycus* 2.22. Cf. Tatian, *Address to the Greeks* 5. Tatian, writing perhaps a decade earlier than Theophilus, also makes the distinction between the Word *in* the Father, and the Word *with* the Father. For Tatian, this proves the unity of the Father and Son, therefore both Tatian and Theophilus diminished the distinction in order to safeguard the unity. Since we cannot date these documents precisely, it is not possible to determine whether there was any direct influence of Tatian on either Athenagoras or Theophilus. See Grillmeier, *Christ in Christian Tradition*, 111.

37. This is the result of following primarily the philosophical understanding of the *logos*. Philo of Alexandria understood the *logos* as being both the mind of God and internal to God, and at the same time a distinct divine personification. See Philo, *On Dreams* 1.227–30. However, for Philo, both conditions of the *logos* exist at all times. Apologists such as Theophilus turned these two conditions into two chronological stages, in which the *Logos* goes from being *in* the Father to being *with* the Father. The problem is that this movement from *in* to *with* constitutes a change in the *Logos*, which compromises divine immutability. Theophilus may not have been directly influenced by Philo, but could have inherited this concept from Tatian. Those who stayed on the path of Tatian and Theophilus in the third and fourth centuries became Adoptionists and Arians.

38. Grillmeier, *Christ in Christian Tradition*, 111.

39. Theophilus, *To Autolycus* 2.22. Cf. Tatian, *Address to the Greeks* 5. In both Tatian and Theophilus, it is not clear whether divine power is a property of each person of

emitted is described as the point when the Father "begets," or generates, the Word.[40] It is important to emphasize, however, that before this generation, the *Logos* has no personal distinction from the Father. After the Word was generated, the Word became the Father's counselor, specifically as the agent of creation and the inspiration of revelation and prophecy.[41]

Although Theophilus does not mean to say that the Word of God was mutable, let alone created, he does define the "begetting," or generation, of the Word as an *event* that begins a new phase of the Word's existence as distinct from the Father.[42] This does imply that there is a change in a *Logos* that goes from *endiathetos* (in the Father) to *prophorikos* (with the Father), and furthermore it implies a beginning to the existence of the Word *as distinct from the Father*.[43] Therefore, while Theophilus still accepts the immutability of the *Logos* on principle, he has inadvertently given later Adoptionists a precedent, in that he described what could only be seen as a change in the *Logos*. The "emission" or as it was called in the second century, "procession" of the *Logos* would later be used to describe a beginning in the *Logos* such that be-

---

the Trinity, or whether (like Justin and Athenagoras) divine power is an attribute of the divine substance. However it seems clear that for Theophilus, divine wisdom is a personal property, so that each person of the Trinity has his own distinct wisdom. This is necessary for the Father to retain wisdom after the *Logos* is spoken forth, however before the *Logos* is emitted from the Father, there is no clear distinction between the Father's wisdom and the *Logos*.

40. Theophilus, *To Autolycus* 2.3. See also Tatian, *Address to the Greeks* 5.

41. As "wonderful counselor" (Isa 9:6), the apologists understood the *Logos*, not only as the counselor of humanity, but also as the Father's *consigliere*. The *Logos* is the one to whom the Father speaks when he says, "Let *us* make humanity in *our* image." See Irenaeus, *Demonstration of the Apostolic Preaching* 55.

42. Theophilus's language will influence later theologians such as Tertullian, who will continue to understand the generation (or begetting) of the Word as an event at, or just prior to, creation. For Tertullian, Thought *becomes* Word at the Word's generation, and this is the point at which the Son becomes equal to the Father, because before this point the Son was not distinct. Tertullian still has the problem that his system implies a change in the divine *Logos*, leaving the *Logos* mutable. Novatian will make the shift from seeing generation as an event to seeing it as an eternal state of being. Even though Novatian will continue to use Theophilus's language of the Word "emitted" at creation, Novatian will call this proceeding, not begetting. This will allow him to understand generation as an eternal state of being, because the eternally generated Word is an eternally distinct divine person.

43. Theophilus, *To Autolycus* 1.4, 2.3–4.

gotten could be defined as *created*. The problem for later orthodoxy is compounded in that before the generation of the Word, understood by Theophilus as an event, the *Logos* (Son of God) was not a distinct divine person, so it would seem that God was not always triune, but *became* triune, which not only implies a change in the *Logos*, but also in the Trinity—a change that would seem to compromise divine immutability.

Following his predecessors, Theophilus did not make a clear distinction between the Holy Spirit and the emitted Word before the incarnation. Both are described by the apologists as an extension from the Father, and the word, "procession" could be used for the "extending out" of either one. For example, the inspiration of the Old Testament prophets is said to be both the Holy Spirit and the *Logos prophorikos*. And while the *Logos* is described as the wisdom of God, the Trinity is described as "God, his Word and his wisdom," thus using the concept of divine wisdom also for the Holy Spirit.[44] An explicit distinction is made, therefore, only between the Father on one hand and the Word/Wisdom/Spirit on the other. This is in fact typical of the second century, since the divinity of the Holy Spirit was not yet a point of major debate. In the second century, the important point was that the Father cannot be localized in one place (he is uncircumscribable), but the Word/Wisdom/Spirit can be "extended" from the Father into the human realm, making the Old Testament theophanies and especially the incarnation possible.[45]

Theophilus had taken the three phases of the life of the divine Word from the New Testament and expanded them into four phases: Internal Word, Emitted Word, Incarnate Word and Exalted Word. This system was not to catch on however, since it negates the eternal distinction between Father and Son (they are not distinct in the first phase) and it implies a change in the *Logos* that compromises divine immutability. Although Theophilus's conception was acceptable by second century standards, it would be refined in the third century, and by the fourth century the refined version would be necessary to refute Arianism, since Theophilus's precedent actually provided fuel for the Arian fire. Eventually, the definition of orthodoxy would require the doctrine of *eternal generation*, which includes both the *eternal distinc-*

---

44. Ibid., 2.15.
45. Ibid., 2.22. Cf. Irenaeus, *Against Heresies* 2.1.2.

tion of the Son from the Father, and the clarification that the generation of the Son from the Father is not an event (that implies a change), but rather an eternal state of being. Therefore, from Novatian's perspective, Theophilus's attempt at explaining Christ falls short because in his desire to emphasize the unity of the divine Triad, he blurs the distinction between the three divine persons: between the Father and Son before the generation of the Son and between the Son and the Holy Spirit after the generation of the Son.[46]

The Age of the Theologians

As we come to the end of the second century and the beginning of the third, we make the transition from the apologists to the theologians. Whereas the apologists were also philosophers who used philosophy in an attempt to persuade non-Christians that the church was not a threat to the Empire, the theologians turned their attention inward toward a Christian audience, using Scripture to refute heresy within the church. Thus it will be helpful to take a brief aside to survey the two major heresy groups of the late second and early third century.

Adoptionism

As we enter the age of the theologians, the legacy of the Ebionites is adoptionism. Like the Ebionites, Adoptionists accepted the humanity of Christ, but denied his divinity. They were concerned that the doctrine of the Trinity as it was being expressed in the church compromised monotheism, since to them the worship of Christ seemed to imply two Gods. Their solution was to affirm the *monarchy* (oneness) of God by emphasizing the separation (i.e., the difference) between the Father and Son, claiming that the Father alone is divine. In other words, God is *one* because Jesus Christ is not God (i.e., not divine). Adoptionism is so called because of the belief that Jesus Christ was the Son of God only by adoption; that he was essentially just a human who had earned God's favor through perfect obedience. To the Adoptionists, Jesus was

---

46. In Theophilus, this blurred distinction is compounded by the fact that his concept of "persons" in the Trinity is based on a Greek term that was used for the theatrical mask, the same description that would be used later by Modalists. See Theophilus of Antioch, *To Autolycus* 2.22.

the first human to achieve moral perfection. As a reward for this, he was adopted by God to be his son (cf. Ps 2:7).

It is important to understand the role that adoption played in Roman society, and especially in the succession of emperors. When an emperor wanted to choose his successor, he could legally adopt a man, even if that man was an adult. The adoption would create a legal heir for the purpose of the transfer of power. The Adoptionists understood Jesus as having received his power (in Greek, *dunamis*) from the Father through a kind of adoption, which they believed took place at his baptism (cf. Mark 1:11 and parallels).[47] Because of their emphasis on the monarchy of God, and the assumption that Christ received his power at his baptism, Adoptionists are sometimes referred to as *dynamic monarchians*.

A third-century bishop of Antioch, Paul of Samosata (c. 200–275 CE),[48] openly denied the divinity of Christ, and tried to put a stop to the worship of him, specifically the singing of hymns in praise of Christ.[49] According to his opponents, he would not "acknowledge that the Son of God came down from heaven."[50] In other words, whereas Novatian and his predecessors described the incarnation as a *descent* (Phil 2:6–8), adoptionism is a Christology of *ascent*, the elevation of a mere human to an exalted status based on merit. This means that the Adoptionist Christ is not an incarnation, in which "the Word became flesh," (John 1:14); it is the result of an indwelling of the *Logos*. In fact, for Paul of Samosata, the *Logos* was not substantially pre-existent, but was believed to be merely the personification of the will of God.[51] In this, he could be said to have followed some of the apologists, such as his predecessor

---

47. Beryllus of Bostra had taught that Christ did not have a divinity of his own, but was indwelt with the Father's divinity. See Eusebius, *Ecclesiastical History* 6.33. Beryllus had also denied the pre-existence of the *Logos*.

48. Novatian and his predecessors were not directly responding to Paul of Samosata, however he is included here to demonstrate the point to which adoptionism evolved in the third century. No doubt there were others during the time of the theologians who were proponents of an Adoptionist Christology much like Paul of Samosata. In addition, Paul's Christology is important for understanding Arianism, and the orthodox response to it.

49. Eusebius, *Ecclesiastical History* 7.27–30. See also Malchion, *In the Name of the Synod of Antioch Against Paul of Samosata*.

50. Malchion, *In the Name* 3.

51. Eusebius, *Ecclesiastical History* 7.30. See also Malchion, *In the Name*.

at Antioch, Theophilus, who had appeared to diminish the distinction between the Father and the Son before the Son's generation. Paul was eventually accused of heresy and deposed from the church of Antioch.

Modalism

Modalism is the opposite of adoptionism, since it affirms the divinity of Christ, but it assumes a unity of Father and Son that results in an implied denial of his humanity. However, it is the legacy of docetism and gnosticism only in the sense that it results in a diminished human nature in the person of Christ. The Gnostics eventually separated from the church, so gnosticism did not evolve into modalism, though any Docetics or Gnostics who remained in the church would certainly have leaned toward a modalist understanding of the Trinity.[52] Ironically, modalism is also the opposite of docetism in the sense that it is based on philosophical monism, which led the Modalists to see the Trinity as one, but not really three.

As Hippolytus admitted, the Modalists (like the Adoptionists) were motivated by a desire to protect monotheism.[53] They perceived the doctrine of the Trinity as a threat to the oneness of God, and their desire to preserve the oneness, or *monarchy* of God, means that they are also called *monarchians*. However, the Modalists solved the problem by coming to the opposite conclusion as the Adoptionists. For the Adoptionists, God is one because Jesus is not divine. For the Modalists, on the other hand, God is one because Jesus is the Father.[54] They taught that the Father had become the Son in the incarnation. Thus the Modalists were determined to emphasize the unity of God, but to the point of diminishing the distinction between the Father and the Son.

---

52. This is not to imply that gnosticism was gone from the church by the time of the theologians. Irenaeus's primary target was gnosticism.

53. Hippolytus, *Against Noetus* 2. There is some debate over the authorship of the documents attributed to Hippolytus. It is not within the scope of the present book to cover this debate, however it is assumed that even if all of the documents cited are not by (the same) Hippolytus, they do come from the same school of thought, and represent the bridge from Tertullian to Novatian.

54. In modalism, God is one because Jesus was simply the Father in disguise. This diminishes the humanity of Christ, since divine immutability would prevent the Father from taking on real humanity in the incarnation. Therefore the modalist Christ was divine, but not truly human.

In other words, not only are the Father and Son *one*, they are one and the same.

Therefore the Modalists proposed a Trinity that was three in name only, the distinction of persons limited to a chronological or functional distinction. The three manifestations of God were interpreted as three "masks" that the one God wears, depending on when God was acting (Old Testament, New Testament, church age) or what God was doing (creating, saving, inspiring, etc.). But these distinctions were more perceived (from the perspective of humanity) than real. In fact, the distinctions between the persons of the Trinity were reduced to labels of "job description," or *mode* of activity, so that the one God is called the Father when he is the Creator, called the Son when he is the Savior and called the Holy Spirit when he is the Sanctifier.[55] Hence the name *modalism*, and therefore the Modalists are also sometimes called *modalistic monarchians*. Against this distinction of function, Novatian and his predecessors maintained that there is a real distinction between persons that is defined by the relationships between them, but not by time or function. The doctrine of inseparable operation would clarify that all three persons of the Trinity are at work in all divine activity. Thus in reality all three are always Creator, all three are always Redeemer, and all three are always Sanctifier.

We will see the three most famous modalist teachers as the opponents of our theologians. Praxeas (possibly a pseudonym) was a modalist and persecutor of the Montanists, whom Tertullian would use as his foil in explaining his concept of the Trinity. Noetus of Smyrna was a modalist teacher who came to Rome, and became a thorn in the side of Hippolytus. As we will see, Hippolytus would accuse Noetus of putting the Father on the cross, a concept called *patripassionism*, which became another name for modalism. Finally, Novatian will oppose Sabellius in his *On the Trinity*. In fact, modalism would eventually come to be named after Sabellius, and be called *Sabellianism*. Before we can come to these, though, we will begin with Irenaeus. Although his

---

55. The problem with defining the persons of the Trinity by function (such as in the recasting of the Triune name as "Creator, Redeemer, Sustainer") is that it implies that the Father is not also Redeemer, and the Son is not also Creator (cf. John 1:3). Modalism also implies that the one God can only be one person of the Trinity at a time, the name depending only on the task at hand.

main opponent was still gnosticism, Iraneaus is nevertheless the first of the theologians.

Irenaeus of Lyons (c. 125–202 CE)

Whereas the apologists had written primarily to an audience outside the church, the theologians were writing to a Christian audience, to respond to and refute the alternative Christologies emerging within the church.[56] Christian apology was as important as ever with the expansion of persecution across the empire, but as time went on, it also became important to write theological treatises that would interpret and clarify the apostolic documents that were becoming the Christian canon. Irenaeus is considered the first true theologian (since the apostles) because he turned away from philosophy, supporting his arguments from Scripture. In fact, Irenaeus was skeptical of philosophy and believed that the use of philosophy led to heresy (primarily gnosticism).

Irenaeus was born between 120 and 130 CE and flourished in the last two decades of the second century. He came from Asia Minor, possibly Smyrna, and may have been a student of Justin Martyr. He was sent to Gaul by the bishop Polycarp of Smyrna to assist the bishop of Lyons. True to his name, Irenaeus worked as a mediator with the bishop of Rome in the controversy over the Montanists. He was away in Rome when a wave of persecution came to Lyons in 177 CE. The bishop of Lyons was martyred, and Irenaeus was elected to succeed him.

There are two extant works by Irenaeus. His shorter work is *Demonstration* [or *Proof*] *of the Apostolic Preaching*. Here Irenaeus described the three persons of the Trinity according to an analogy of anointing. In this analogy, the Father is the Anointer, the Son is the Anointed One, and the Spirit is the Oil of Anointing. More important, Irenaeus advanced the understanding of the Trinity beyond Justin and Athenagoras when he stated that the oneness of the Trinity is a unity of *essence* (i.e., an ontological unity, which in the case of God is a unity of divinity itself), rather than simply describing the unity in terms of divine power.[57] This is our earliest version of the doctrine of *consubstan-*

---

56. Certainly some of Clement of Alexandria's writings were written for a Christian audience, though I consider him among the apologists. It is also true that many of the apologists' writings (especially documents such as Justin's *Dialogue with Trypho*) were probably read by more Christians than non-Christians.

57. Irenaeus, *Demonstration of the Apostolic Preaching* 47.

tiality—that the persons of the Trinity are of one and the same essence, or divine substance. This concept will be an important part of later orthodoxy, as a counter to the separation of Father and Son inherent in adoptionism.

The distinction between the persons is described by Irenaeus as an "economy" (or hierarchy) of revelation, in which the Spirit reveals the Son and the Son reveals the Father.[58] Put another way, the Father gives to the Son what the Son gives to the Spirit and the Spirit gives to the church. There seems to be an assumption here of a hierarchy of transcendence, in an inverse relationship to "approachability." The Father is the most transcendent, and is therefore unapproachable. The Father can only be approached though the Son. Thus it was not God the Father, but the *Logos*, who spoke to Adam in the garden, to Abraham by the oaks of Mamre, and to Moses in the burning bush.[59] However, it was the Holy Spirit who spoke through the prophets.[60] Therefore, with Irenaeus, we finally get a clearer distinction between the pre-incarnate *Logos* and the Holy Spirit. It was the *Logos* who appeared in the Old Testament theophanies, but it was the Holy Spirit who inspires revelation. This was probably based on the distinction that only the *Logos* would be incarnate and visible.[61] For Irenaeus, the visibility of the Son was based on the incarnation, even though it could be retroactively applied to Old Testament appearances. Thus the distinction between the *Logos* and Spirit was described such that the Son of God is the Word and the Holy Spirit is the Wisdom.[62] Even so, "the Spirit manifests the Word . . . but the Word articulates the Spirit," demonstrating that while the persons of the Word and the Holy Spirit are distinct, their works are unified.

---

58. Ibid. For Irenaeus, the "economy" is simply the order or hierarchy within the Trinity. The "economy" describes the "threeness" of God, while the "monarchy" describes the oneness.

59. Ibid., 2, 12, 44, 51.

60. Ibid., 49.

61. Irenaeus, *Against Heresies* 3.16.6. While this may seem like a modalist distinction between the Son and the Spirit, it really has more to do with the incarnation as applying only to the Son. For Irenaeus, the Father is invisible, but the Son is the invisible becoming visible, the impassible becoming passible. The Holy Spirit is apparently also necessarily invisible, and so it is only the Son who could be visible, tangible, and circumscribed within creation.

62. Irenaeus, *Demonstration of the Apostolic Preaching* 5.

Here we have a further hint of the doctrine of inseparable operation, the conviction that the persons of the Trinity never act individually.

Irenaeus's longer work is *Against Heresies*, written about 185 CE. It is primarily a refutation of the various forms of gnosticism that had existed by that time. He critiques the Gnostics, saying that they teach that God is unknowable and yet claim to know God's secrets, when in fact the opposite is true—no one but the Son can know the Father's secrets and yet we can know the Father through the Son. Irenaeus argued against a Docetic rejection of the Old Testament by showing how Christ could be found there. First of all, any time there seems to be an "internal" conversation of God, it is said to be a conversation among the persons of the Trinity.[63] For example, "The Lord said to my Lord, 'Sit at my right hand . . .'" (Ps 110:1) is understood as a statement by the Father to the Son. "The Lord rained down fire and sulfur from the Lord on Sodom and Gomorrah" (Gen 19:24) is interpreted as saying that the pre-incarnate Christ is also the agent of judgment, working the Father's punishment on the sinful cities. And of course, "Let us make humanity in our image . . ." (Gen 1:26) is a conversation between the Father and the *Logos*.[64] Second, he followed the lead of the apologists in seeing the pre-incarnate *Logos* in the Old Testament appearances of the angel of the Lord, based on the assumption that "no one can see God and live" (Exod 33:20; 1 Tim 6:16).[65] Irenaeus also argued that the *Logos* as agent of creation demonstrates that the Creator God of the Old Testament is one and the same God as the Father of Jesus Christ.[66] Therefore, Christ did not come to reject or cancel the Old Testament, but rather to fulfill it. He did not come to bring secret knowledge, but grace. Finally, Irenaeus argued from the concept of apostolic succession to refute the Gnostic idea of secret knowledge. If Jesus had taught anyone the secrets of God, it would have been his closest disciples, who were the predecessors of the bishops. These apostles would have passed the secrets on to their own disciples and successors, who would have passed them on to later generations. Therefore, if there were any such secret knowledge,

---

63. Irenaeus, *Against Heresies* 3.6.1.
64. Cf. Theophilus, *To Autolycus* 2.18.
65. Irenaeus, *Against Heresies* 1.19.2, 4.10.1.
66. Ibid., 2.31.1, 4.32.1. In book 4, chapters 28 and 32, Irenaeus describes the Christian Scriptures as the "New Testament," becoming the first writer to use this term.

the current bishops (of whom Irenaeus himself was one) would know about it.[67]

The incarnation is all-important for Irenaeus. The incarnation is the pivotal event in human history, when (against docetism) the *Logos* became human. Since it is the flesh of the human that engages in sin, Christ must become true flesh in order to be the savior of humanity.[68] If Christ were not human, but came in the appearance of a human only, then he has deceived humanity, making him a liar—and then why should anyone believe what he taught?[69] While the *Logos* had appeared to humanity before, the incarnation was the definitive revelation of the *Logos*.[70] In the incarnation, Christ recapitulates the failures of human history, but correcting and reversing them.[71] This is based on the apostle Paul's connection of Christ and Adam (Rom 5:12–18; 1 Cor 15:21–22).[72] Christ is the new Adam who succeeds where the first Adam failed. He also reverses the failures of God's chosen people Israel. For example, Israel gave in to the temptation to worship the golden calf in the desert, but Christ did not give in to temptation in the desert. For Irenaeus, the incarnation of Christ is both the fulfillment of the promise of a messiah for Israel and the fulfillment of the promise to Abraham that the nations would be blessed. In his humanity, as the Son of David, Christ was the One who came to be in solidarity with humanity, and as such would reconcile humanity to God. In his divinity, as the Son of

---

67. Ibid., 2.9.1, 3.2–3. Apostolic succession was tentatively proposed by Clement of Rome, and to a lesser extent by Ignatius, though Irenaeus seems to be the first one to treat it as a "doctrine." Like Ignatius and others, Irenaeus criticized any groups who held "unauthorized meetings," meaning without the sanction of the bishop. Gnostics apparently responded to Irenaeus's critique with their own version of apostolic succession, saying that Jesus handed down the secret knowledge through Matthias or James. Cf. Hippolytus, *Refutation of All Heresies* 5.2.

68. Irenaeus, *Against Heresies* 2.22.4. See also Grillmeier, *Christ in Christian Tradition*, 103.

69. Irenaeus, *Against Heresies* 3.18.7.

70. Grillmeier, *Christ in Christian Tradition*, 103.

71. Irenaeus, *Demonstration of the Apostolic Preaching* 99. See also *Against Heresies* 4.2.2, 3.32.1.

72. Although Irenaeus is often given credit as the originator of "recapitulation," he is following the lead of New Testament writers such as Paul. Justin Martyr also used this interpretive technique to a certain extent. Cf. *Dialogue with Trypho* 100. After Irenaeus, it would become a standard technique of the early Christian exegete. Cf. Tertullian, *On the Flesh of Christ* 17.

God, he was able to be what previous sons of God could not—perfectly obedient to God.

Irenaeus criticized the idea that the *Logos* first existed *in* the Father only (like a thought in the Father's mind), though he never mentioned Theophilus of Antioch by name.[73] He called it a Gnostic concept, apparently because the way the apologists described the generation of the *Logos* reminded him of the Gnostic mythologies, with their gods begetting other gods through cosmic procreation. It seems that for Irenaeus, the full and equal divinity of the Son requires an eternal distinction of the Son from the Father, in order to clarify that there was no beginning to the existence of the *Logos*.[74] While he does not explore the implications of this, he has (perhaps unknowingly) hinted at the doctrine of *eternal generation*, since he seems to instinctively know that Son of God must be, not only eternal, but eternally distinct from the Father in his personhood.

Irenaeus also explained that divine immutability necessarily implies *divine simplicity*. The divine is described as "simplex," which means that God does not have "parts" that can be separated, since such separation would imply the possibility of degradation, or *corruptibility*, which is of course a form of change.[75] Therefore because of divine simplicity, generation ("begetting") implies that what is generated must be of the same essence as the one who generates.[76] Thus the Father and the Son

---

73. Irenaeus, *Against Heresies* 2.12.5, 2.13.8, 2.28.4–6, 4.20.3. Both Tatian and Theophilus seem to have gotten this lack of distinction between the Father and the pre-incarnate *Logos* from philosophy (possibly Philo of Alexandria) rather than gnosticism. However, it is interesting to note that Irenaeus accused Tatian of becoming a Gnostic after the death of Justin Martyr, and while there is no conclusive evidence for this in the extant writings of Tatian, other early authors seem to have followed Irenaeus's lead in lumping Tatian in with the Gnostics. Cf. Epiphanius of Salamis, *Panarion* 46.

74. Irenaeus, *Against Heresies* 2.30.9, 4.20.3. Irenaeus says that the Son coexists *with* the Father eternally. By rejecting Theophilus's distinction between the *Logos in* the Father and the *Logos with* the Father, he anticipates Novatian. Irenaeus said that the *Logos* was always *with* the Father, Novatian would later say that the *Logos* was always *in* the Father. In both cases, there is a rejection of a change in the status of the *Logos*, however Irenaeus simply transferred the blurred distinction to the Holy Spirit. Therefore, Irenaeus is still a *Logos* theologian, while Novatian will advance to the next phase in the development of doctrine, *kenosis* Christology.

75. This is explained well by Novatian, *On the Trinity* 4.4, 5.5–6, 6.9. Novatian says that divinity requires simplicity and immutability, or divine perfection is called into question.

76. Irenaeus, *Against Heresies* 2.17.3–7. Irenaeus is arguing against a Gnostic un-

(and, by implication, the Spirit) must be consubstantial. This prevents us from speaking of the Father, Son, and Holy Spirit as three "parts" of God, as if they could be separated. All of this together leads back to the doctrine of inseparable operation, that all three persons of the Trinity are always unified in all divine activity. Therefore, in both the being and the activity of God as Trinity, there is an essential unity. At the same time, there is distinction between the persons of the Trinity, the most important manifestation of which is the incarnation.

As I have indicated above, heretics and orthodox alike would have agreed that the very definition of divinity includes the concepts of immutability and impassibility.[77] In other words, God (by definition) cannot change, which means that God cannot suffer, since suffering is a kind of change. Therefore, the Ebionites and Adoptionists had argued that because Christ suffered, he could not be divine. The Docetics and Gnostics had argued that because he was divine, he could not have suffered. Irenaeus's response was that the incarnation is the answer to the paradox—though he is divine, he became human so that he could suffer (cf. 1 Cor 1:23–24).[78] When the Word became flesh, the immutable became mutable and the impassible became passible.[79] To be more specific, it is only the human nature of Christ that is mutable and passible, however Irenaeus cautions against naming the divine nature "Christ" and the human nature "Jesus," separating Jesus from Christ, as some of the Gnostics did.[80] He maintains that it is incorrect because it divides the one person of Jesus Christ into two. It is more correct to say that both the name "Jesus" and the title "Christ" refer to the whole person of the Word of God who became flesh and who is both divine and human.

---

derstanding of the generation of *aeons*, in which one *aeon* is said to suffer. He argues that a passible *aeon* could not be generated from impassible deity.

77. For example, see Theophilus, *To Autolycus* 1.4, 2.3–4, cf. 2.22. Certain aspects of Gnostic mythology would be an exception to this rule in the sense that their broadened concept of divinity allowed some of the *aeons* to be thought of as begotten (with a beginning) or enduring suffering.

78. Hultgren and Haggmark, eds., *Earliest Christian Heretics*, 8–10.

79. Irenaeus, *Against Heresies* 3.18.3, 3.19.3.

80. Ibid., 3.9.3, 3.11.7. Note that Irenaeus also says that Christ did not descend on Jesus at his baptism, but the Holy Spirit descended on the whole person of the Word of God, human and divine. It was not that the Christ anointed Jesus, but that the Holy Spirit anointed Jesus Christ.

Both extreme alternatives essentially denied a real incarnation.[81] Docetics and Gnostics (and to a certain extent Modalists) conceived of a Christ who came into the world without flesh, while Ebionites and Adoptionists preached a Jesus who was a mere human and therefore not the divine Son of God, though perhaps temporarily indwelt by the *Logos* or the Holy Spirit.[82] For Irenaeus, Jesus Christ is not an elevated man, but the result of the descent of the *Logos*, who became a true human with real flesh. The implication for soteriology, as Irenaeus points out, is the fact that salvation can only occur by divine intervention, and since the Ebionite/Adoptionist Christ is not divine, he lacks the ability to save.[83] At the same time, the savior must also be human in order to reconcile humanity to the Father.[84] In order to be the savior, specifically the savior of humanity, the Son of God has to be both divine and human.[85]

Tertullian (c. 145–225 CE)

Quintus Septimius Florens Tertullianus was born around 145–150 CE and lived into the 220s.[86] He is the first theologian of the third century, the first to write in Latin, and the one who coined the Latin term *Trinitas* for the Trinity. For the latter two reasons he is called the father of Latin theology. Tertullian was from Carthage, in North Africa. It is often assumed that Tertullian had been a lawyer, since the terminology that he would use to describe the Trinity was said to have come from Roman law.[87] However, even if the terms do come from Roman legal use, a law career would not have been required for him to understand and use the terms, and therefore we cannot say for sure what his first career was. He became a Christian in about 185 and was married shortly

---

81. Ibid., 3.11.3, 3.20.4, 5.19.2.

82. Ibid., 3.20.4.

83. Ibid., 3.20.3, 4.33.4. For the incarnation as descent, see *Demonstration of the Apostolic Preaching* 64.

84. Irenaeus, *Against Heresies* 5.14.3.

85. Ibid., 4.6.7. In making this point, Irenaeus anticipates Anselm of Canterbury's *Cur Deus Homo?*

86. For an excellent summary of Tertullian's life, see Dunn, *Tertullian*, 3–11. For a more detailed treatment, see Barnes, *Tertullian*.

87. Eusebius, *Ecclesiastical History* 2.2.4.

thereafter.[88] He may have become a priest in Rome in the early 190s, when he began a prolific writing career, heavily influenced by Irenaeus.[89]

Tertullian never became a bishop. Apparently, around the turn of the third century, he had a falling out with the church in Rome when he began to associate with the Montanists, a charismatic movement within the church that called themselves the "New Prophecy."[90] This group was being suppressed by some bishops because the Montanist claim to charismatic authority was perceived as a threat to the developing hierarchy.[91] If Tertullian had been in Rome, he must have left Rome at this time and gone back to Carthage where he associated with the Montanists there. Although many of his writings were written during his time with the Montanists, his Christology would not only be acceptable to the mainstream church, but in many ways would help define orthodox doctrine.[92]

For our purposes, Tertullian's three most important works are *Against Marcion*, *Against Praxeas*, and *On the Flesh of Christ*. Written half a century after Marcion, *Against Marcion* lumps all Docetics, Marcionites, and Gnostics together and responds to them all at once.

88. At this time, priests were not required to be celibate. The earliest known mandate for the celibacy of clergy is the Synod of Elvira, Spain, in about 305 CE. This was based on an existing practice, but was not universally followed, hence the need for the synod's mandate. By the end of the fourth century, celibacy for clergy was becoming the norm in the West, based on the tradition that one had to "fast" from sexual intercourse for twenty-four hours before receiving the Eucharist. Since priests celebrated Mass every day, that left them no time to have a consummated marriage. Tertullian's marriage would not have prevented him from becoming a priest, though it does cause one to speculate that he may have been initially drawn to Christianity because of the influence of his future wife.

89. Recent scholarship questions whether Tertullian was ever ordained, or indeed whether he was ever in Rome. See Dunn, *Tertullian*, 3. He does seem to have at least visited Rome, as he mentions it in *On the Apparel of Women* 1.7. As to the question of whether he was ordained, he seems to speak as a priest at some points, and as a lay person at other points, though this could be explained if he had been a priest at Rome, but had given up the ordained ministry when he came back to North Africa and associated with the Montanists there.

90. Some have argued that Tertullian's document *On the Pallium* shows a rejection of all things Roman, however there is much speculation here, especially if Tertullian had never been ordained in the first place.

91. There is also the possibility that some Montanists leaned toward modalism. See Hippolytus, *Refutation of All Heresies* 8.12. Cf. Epiphanius of Salamis, *Panarion* 48. However, it is unlikely that the Montanists of Tertullian's day were Modalists, since Tertullian himself wrote against modalism.

92. Dunn, *Tertullian*, 9.

In this document, as in *On the Flesh of Christ*, Tertullian is concerned to demonstrate the true humanity of Christ against docetism.[93] At the same time, he affirms the divinity of Christ as well, saying that to deny one nature or the other would leave one with half a Christ.[94]

In *Against Praxeas*, Tertullian addresses the otherwise unknown Praxeas as his antagonist, in order to explain his concept of the Trinity. All we know about Praxeas is that he was a modalist who was critical of the Montanists. It has been suggested that the name Praxeas might be a pseudonym standing in for one of any number of candidates, and some have even suggested one of the bishops of Rome. However, it is more likely that this Praxeas was simply an anti-Montanist whose Christology happened to leaned toward modalism. This gave Tertullian a literary vehicle for attacking an enemy of the New Prophecy while explaining his understanding of the Trinity.

It was in *Against Praxeas* that Tertullian developed the Trinitarian language that would eventually become standard for the Western, Latin-speaking church. Apparently borrowing from Roman legalese, Tertullian settled on two important terms, *persona* and *substantia* (in English: *person* and *substance*). In Roman law, a *persona* was not simply any person, but specifically a legal entity—someone who can own property. At one time in Roman law, a woman was not a *persona* because she could not own property.[95] This was corrected by the time of Tertullian, but it was not until the church was legalized in the fourth century that the church itself became a *persona* with the right to own property. The point is that the term *persona*, while it does not necessarily imply a human person, does refer to a distinct "personal" entity.[96] Tertullian used this term to describe the Father, Son, and Holy Spirit as three *personae*, or "persons."[97] Therefore, the Father, Son, and Holy Spirit are the three

---

93. Tertullian, *On the Flesh of Christ* 16. Note that Tertullian clarified that Jesus retains his humanity even after the ascension, pointing out that the human nature of Christ is not temporary.

94. Ibid., 5.

95. Slaves were also not considered *personae*. See Bethune-Baker, *Meaning of Homoousios*, 70.

96. Osborn, *Tertullian*, 132–33. Osborn defines *persona* as a "distinct individual existence." See also Bethune-Baker, *Meaning of Homoousios*, 70–74.

97. Note that in this context "persons" is not the equivalent of "people," so that it would not be correct to say that there are three "people" in the Trinity.

persons of the Trinity, the term "person" describing the "threeness," or the distinctions within the Trinity. Against modalism, which only allowed for a chronological or functional distinction of names based on mode of operation, Tertullian argued for an ongoing distinction of concurrent persons, with descriptions of the distinctions of persons not based on function or on human perception of divine activity, but based on the internal relationships within the Trinity.

The term *substantia*, in Roman law, referred to any property that could be owned.[98] In other words, a *substance* had a legal status as belonging to some *person*. Tertullian used this term to describe the oneness, or the unity, of the Trinity.[99] The three persons of the Trinity share one substance, almost like three owners who share one property. That "property," or that substance, is divinity itself. However, we have to be careful not to hear a modern concept of "substance" when we hear the word *substantia*. It does not necessarily imply a physical, material, or tangible substance. A substance can be non-tangible (as in the case of intellectual property).[100] In the context of the Trinity, of course, the substance of divinity is spiritual, or non-material. Technically speaking, the three persons of the Trinity do not *share* divinity, as if divinity is something separate from themselves that they *have*, rather each person of the Trinity *is* divinity itself.[101] Therefore, what they share is their very being (or as Irenaeus had said, their *essence*), which is divine. Tertullian also seems to equate the substance of divinity with divine power, so that the three persons of the Trinity are said to share "a common divine power."[102] The fact that the Father, Son, and Holy Spirit are all of the same divine substance, yet without removing the distinction between the persons as the Modalists did, is the doctrine of *consubstantiality*. In this, Tertullian has accepted Irenaeus's comment that the Father and Son are the same essence, and expanded it.[103] Tertullian wrote:

---

98. Bethune-Baker, *Meaning of Homoousios*, 21–23, 65–70. Contemporary scholarship rejects a strictly legal interpretation of the term *substantia*, however the English word, "property," with its range of meaning, is still useful for understanding the sense of *substantia*. See Osborn, *Tertullian*, 131–32.

99. Tertullian, *Against Praxeas* 25. See also Tertullian, *Apology* 21.12.

100. Osborn, *Tertullian*, 132. As Osborn points out, Tertullian called the gospel, "the substance of the New Testament." See Tertullian, *Against Praxeas* 31.1.

101. Augustine would later make this clear in *On the Trinity* 5.

102. Kearsley, *Tertullian's Theology of Divine Power*, 54.

103. Irenaeus, *Demonstration of the Apostolic Preaching* 47.

> These three [persons] are one, but not one and the same, so that when [Jesus] said, "I and the Father are one," he meant a unity of substance, not a numerical singularity.[104]

Tertullian's understanding of the single substance of divinity was necessitated by the concept of divine simplicity.[105] Since God is simplex, he cannot be divided into "parts"—even three parts—without compromising the oneness of God. Although Tertullian did give in to the temptation to speak of Christ as "part of" God on one or two occasions (since it is clear that there is more to God than Christ and Christ is not all there is to God), the indivisible unity of the three persons should prevent us from using this kind of language. Tertullian says that the Son of God is an extension of the Father's divinity, like rays of light from the sun, yet without any division in God, since the rays of light can never be separated from their source.[106] Therefore, the divinity of the Son is the same divinity as the divinity of the Father, which ensures that the Son is no less divine than the Father.[107] There can be no degrees of divinity, for if there were, that would compromise divine simplicity. Furthermore, the fact that the Son is generated ("begotten") from the Father means that his divinity is the same as the Father's. In other words, generation necessarily requires that the one who is generated be of the same substance as the one who generates.[108] Therefore the unity of the three persons of the Trinity is an ontological unity on the level of being itself, not simply a unity of cooperating wills (obedience) as the Adoptionists taught.

The consubstantiality of the Father and Son also confirms for Tertullian two important doctrines. The first is the doctrine of inseparable operation: that all three persons of the Trinity participate in all divine activity.[109] While modalism allowed only a distinction of names between the persons of the Trinity that was defined by function or activity, the predecessors of Novatian were coming to the conclusion

---

104. Tertullian, *Against Praxeas* 25. My translation.
105. Grillmeier, *Christ in Christian Tradition*, 119.
106. Ibid., 120.
107. Ibid., 119.
108. Tertullian, *On the Flesh of Christ* 18; *Against Praxeas* 8. As we have seen, Tertullian is following Irenaeus on this point.
109. Tertullian, *On the Flesh of Christ* 14.

that this distinction was not legitimate. To call the Father the Creator and the Son the Redeemer implies that the Son is not Creator and the Father is not Savior, and therefore it negates inseparable operation.[110] The second important doctrine that comes from consubstantiality is the doctrine of *appropriation*, which affirms whatever can be said of one person of the Trinity must be said of the other two persons, as well as of the whole Trinity.[111] We have not seen this concept before, except as it is hinted in the New Testament documents (cf. 1 Cor 12:4–6), though it follows from the others. As we will see, there are a few important exceptions to the doctrine of appropriation that are necessary to maintain the distinction of persons, including the fact that the Father and the Holy Spirit cannot be said to have been incarnate. However, this is balanced by inseparable operation, which means that it is still true that the Father and the Holy Spirit were actively involved in the incarnation.

On the other hand, Tertullian does envision an order, or hierarchy, within the Trinity that follows from Irenaeus's concept of the "economy." While the unity of the Trinity is ontological (a unity of substance), the distinction between persons is relational, though Tertullian follows Irenaeus in describing the distinction in terms of visibility/invisibility: the Son can be visible, while the Father cannot.[112] While this may sound on the surface as though the distinction is based on human perception, the order of persons within the Trinity is actually a hierarchy of internal relationships of sender and messenger in which the Father sends the Son, making the Son the Father's messenger, or "angel."[113] In turn, the Holy Spirit proceeds from the Father through the Son.[114] This order is based on the fact that even though the Son and the Spirit are the same

---

110. Therefore the contemporary trend of recasting the Trinitarian formula as "Creator, Redeemer, Sustainer" or something similar is actually a form of modalism. Against this trend, it must be maintained that all three persons of the Trinity are Creator, all three persons are Savior and all three persons are Sustainer/Sanctifier.

111. Tertullian, *Against Praxeas* 17.

112. Irenaeus, *Demonstration of the Apostolic Preaching* 47. See also Grillmeier, *Christ in Christian Tradition*, 119, 122. Like the other *Logos* theologians, Tertullian believed that any divine activity in the Old Testament that was visible or localized had to be a manifestation of the Son, not the Father. See Kearsley, *Tertullian's Theology of Divine Power*, 58.

113. Tertullian, *On the Flesh of Christ* 14. Angelos is simply the Greek word for "messenger."

114. Tertullian, *Against Praxeas* 2.4.

divinity as the Father, their divinity is derived (like rays from the sun) from the Father, who is the First Cause and ultimate Source of all being.[115] Therefore, this is a hierarchy of relationships between the persons of the Trinity, not one of relationships between different persons of the Trinity and humanity, or of divine activity.[116] It is also not a hierarchy of divine substance. A hierarchy of perception or activity only would be modalism, and a hierarchy of substance would be adoptionism.

Tertullian affirms that Jesus Christ is the second person of the Trinity and that his divine nature is the same divinity as that of the Father and the Holy Spirit. However, the second person of the Trinity is also one person with two substances, divine and (after the incarnation) human.[117] Tertullian argued for the full humanity and full divinity of Christ, against the alternatives that denied or diminished one or the other.[118] Like the apologists before him, Tertullian especially emphasized the real humanity of Christ against docetism, implying that what is not assumed cannot be redeemed.[119] Tertullian pointed to Philippians 2:6–8 as one passage that demonstrated both the humanity and divinity in Christ.[120] As the "form of God," he is divine and as the "form of a servant/likeness of a man" he is human. Both natures are also demonstrated in the birth of Christ, which Tertullian described by saying, "in

---

115. Ibid., 9, 14. Cf. Clement of Alexandria, *Exhortation to the Greeks* 5.

116. Grillmeier, *Christ in Christian Tradition*, 51–52. See also Osborn, *Tertullian*, 126–27, 129, 137–38.

117. Tertullian, *On the Flesh of Christ* 5. Within the person of Christ, the two substances are generally called "natures," though the meaning is the same.

118. See Tertullian, *Against Marcion* 20; *Against Praxeas* 7, 27; *On the Flesh of Christ* 4–5, 16. Note that the human nature remains even after the ascension of Christ. The Son does not go back to being divine only after the ascension, but remains both divine and human. See also Irenaeus, *Against Heresies* 4.6.7. By "full" humanity or divinity, I mean "undiminished." Therefore, even though some Gnostics and Modalists would speak of a tangible body of Christ, nevertheless he was not fully human. By the same token, some Adoptionists (including later Arians) would speak of a qualified divinity acquired by Christ, which would not be a divinity on the level of the Father. "Full" divinity implies divinity equal to the Father.

119. Tertullian, *On the Flesh of Christ* 4, 10; *Against the Valentinians* 26. Cf. Irenaeus, *Against Heresies* 2.22.4; and Novatian, *On the Trinity* 10.6.

120. Clement of Alexandria had hinted at this dual use of the passage, which would become so important for Novatian. See Clement of Alexandria, *Exhortation to the Greeks* 1, where he refers to Phil 2:6–7 to demonstrate the divinity of Christ, and *The Instructor* 3.1, where he refers to Phil 2:7 to demonstrate the humanity of Christ.

this man God was born."¹²¹ Here Tertullian envisioned a unity between the two natures that allowed him to say that the divine *Logos* was circumscribed in the womb of Mary, anticipating the tradition of calling Mary *Theotokos*, or Mother of God.¹²² Yet Tertullian also states that both natures retain their own distinctiveness, so that the union of the two natures neither creates a third nature, nor diminishes either of the natures.¹²³ The two natures are, "united but not confused, in one person, Jesus, God and human . . . the property of each substance is preserved."¹²⁴ In this balance of unity and distinction between the natures, he anticipates the later clarification known as the *hypostatic union*.¹²⁵ Thus the incarnation implies a *personal* (in Greek: *hypostasis*) union of the two natures in Christ, that is, a union on the level of his very personhood, yet without compromising the individual integrity of the two natures, since the divine nature must remain immutable. In other words, just as the unity of Father and Son is more than a unity of will (obedience of the Son to the Father), so the union of the divine and human in the person of Christ is also more than a union on the level of the will (the submission of his humanity to his divine nature, or the cooperation of the human will with the divine will).¹²⁶

---

121. Tertullian, *On the Flesh of Christ* 17. For Tertullian, the most important aspect of Phil 2 was that it demonstrated Christ's humanity against Marcionite docetism. See Tertullian, *Against Marcion* 5.20. Marcion, on the other hand, interpreted the "likeness" of humanity in Phil 2 as a similarity, but not a real identity. For Marcion, "form" was synonymous with "likeness" (as similarity), while for Tertullian, "form" meant substance. To be in the "form of God" was interpreted by Tertullian and Novatian as highlighting Christ's divine nature and equal divinity with the Father, while to be in the "form of servant/likeness of a man" meant a real humanity.

122. Tertullian, *On the Flesh of Christ* 19, cf. 17.

123. Tertullian, *Against Praxeas* 27; *On the Flesh of Christ* 13. See Osborn, *Tertullian*, 142.

124. Tertullian, *Against Praxeas* 27. My translation.

125. On the other hand, Tertullian is so concerned to protect the distinction of the two natures against modalism that he rejects the possibility of *communicatio idiomatum*, or the communication of idiomatic properties between natures. Hippolytus follows Tertullian in this rejection, but Novatian will find a way to maintain the distinction and avoid the confusion of natures, while allowing the communication of properties.

126. Note that for Tertullian, Christology and Trinitarian theology are not two different things, they are an integrated and dynamic approach to understanding how Jesus Christ is "God with us," the divine intervention promised by the prophets. What modern scholars might call two disciplines (Christology and the doctrine of the Trinity) are for Tertullian completely interdependent.

Tertullian's use of the terms *substantia* and *persona* allowed him to balance the unity and distinction of the persons of the Trinity. His critique of modalism was that its understanding of the relationship of the three persons had too much "monarchy" (unity) and not enough "economy" (distinction/hierarchy).[127] One can only assume that he would have had the opposite critique of adoptionism, that it had too wide a gap between the Father and the Son, to the point where all unity (and indeed the concept of Trinity itself) is lost.

Tertullian also saw an affinity between the way modalism distinguished between the persons of the Trinity by name only and the way divine concepts were personified as the names of deities in Gnostic mythology, as if modalism was a veiled form of gnosticism. He further criticized the polytheism inherent in gnosticism, saying that it negates omnipotence, since any belief system that has more than one god must necessarily limit the sphere of influence of each god to accommodate the others.[128] Although Tertullian's immediate successors did not always follow his lead in the use of precise Trinitarian terminology, by the fourth century Tertullian's description of the Trinity would become standard for the western church.[129] Therefore, Tertullian's genius and contribution to the church cannot be overestimated.

However there was one area in which Tertullian's Christology had not yet developed to the point where it could provide the foundation for later orthodoxy. Following the apologists such as Theophilus of Antioch, Tertullian still saw the generation of the Word as an *event* that took place at (or just before) creation.[130] Therefore, while he believed

---

127. Tertullian, *Against Praxeas* 9. Note that for Tertullian, the economy is *within* the monarchy. In other words, even though Tertullian rejects modalism, there is still a priority of oneness over "threeness," in which the unity of God is like an umbrella, under which the hierarchy exists.

128. Tertullian, *Against Marcion* 1.3.

129. However, when it came to finding agreement on Greek terms to use as equivalents for *persona* and *substantia*, the confusion lingered well into the fifth century. In the east, different writers continued to use different terms to mean the same things, and sometimes the same terms to mean different things. Augustine noted the confusion, especially when translating Greek documents into Latin. The Latin word *essentia* was coined to translate the Greek *ousia* (essence) in an attempt to avoid confusion.

130. Tertullian, *Against Praxeas* 5–6, see also 7–8, 19. For Tertullian, the generation of the Word is the same as the "procession" of the Word. Tertullian wrote, "He became also the Son of God, and was begotten when he proceeded forth from him." Tertullian, *Against Praxeas* 7; *I Apology* 21.

that the *Logos* was eternally pre-existent and coeternal with the Father, he did not describe the *Logos* as eternally distinct from the Father.[131] Tertullian accepted the assumption of *Logos* Christology, that at the generation of the Son, the *Logos* goes from being a thought in the mind of God to the Word emitted from God. In fact, he said that it was not until the generation of the Son that the Son becomes equal to the Father, since equality requires distinction.[132] The problem with this for later orthodoxy is that this understanding of generation implies a change (from *in* the Father to *with* the Father) that would seem to compromise divine immutability, or at least call into question the eternal nature of the distinction between persons. Irenaeus had already criticized this change, saying that the Son was eternally *with* the Father. However, it will not be until Novatian that generation is clarified as an eternal *state of being* rather than an *event*. At that point, we will have a true doctrine of *eternal generation*, which will be necessary to refute Arianism, the fourth century's version of adoptionism.

Hippolytus (c. 170–236 CE)

Hippolytus is a bit of an enigma and there is serious debate over whether the writings attributed to him are actually all by the same person. He was probably born about 170 CE, and wrote his primary works in the 220s. For our purposes, it is enough to look at two writings that serve as the bridge from Tertullian to Novatian. They are *Against Noetus* and *Refutation of All Heresies*.[133]

---

131. However, see Brent, *Hippolytus and the Roman Church*, 255–56. Brent believes that Tertullian did understand a full personal distinction between the Father and Son before the incarnation, based on *Against Praxeas* 13. While it is true that Tertullian describes the distinction before the incarnation, this does not extend back before creation, at which time the Word "proceeded" from the Father and became distinct from him. In *Against Praxeas* 7, Tertullian says, "He became also the Son of God, and was begotten when he proceeded forth from him."

132. Tertullian, *Against Praxeas* 7. See Kearsley, *Tertullian's Theology of Divine Power*, 54–57, and Osborn, *Tertullian*, 124. Since Tertullian follows the likes of Theophilus in understanding the generation of the *Logos* (the "begetting") as the "speaking forth" or "emitting" of the Word of God, it is therefore an event which takes place at (or shortly before) creation so that the *Logos* can be the agent of creation. Thus the distinction between Father and Son begins with the Son's generation.

133. Most scholars today seem to believe that these two documents could not have been written by the same person. My own conclusion is that, even if they are not from the same author, they are from the same school of thought and from the same time

According to the traditional story, Hippolytus was a priest in Rome during the time that Zephyrinus (199–217 CE) and Callistus (217–222 CE) were the bishops. Hippolytus was critical of these bishops and accused them of modalism, eventually writing *Against Noetus* as a way to confront what he perceived as heresy in the bishops, since he thought the bishops should have been more critical of Noetus.[134] However, the "modalism" of Zephyrinus and Callistus was probably just the remnants of *Logos* Christology, in which the terms "Jesus" and "God" were interchangeable and the pre-incarnate Christ could be confused with the Holy Spirit.[135] Specifically, there is no evidence that the Roman bishops equated the Father and the Son, or diminished the Son's human nature. In any case, the bishops' emphasis on the unity of the Trinity apparently caused Hippolytus to react by leaning in the other direction, emphasizing the distinction between the Father and Son to the point where Callistus accused him of worshipping two Gods.[136] Hippolytus

---

period, occupying the theological space between Tertullian and Novatian. The differences between the two documents can be attributed to a development of thought over the time between the writings, as well as a possible difference in intended audience. Note that Dunn says the same regarding Tertullian. Dunn, *Tertullian*, 8. That being the case, their relevance is as a predecessor of, and possible influence on, Novatian. For a survey of the debate, see Brent, *Hippolytus and the Roman Church*, 204–7, 217, 238, 249, 257. Note that Brent believes *Against Noetus* represents a concession to modalistic tendencies in the bishops of Rome, and that it was written after *Refutation of All Heresies*. He sees a development from *Refutation of All Heresies* to *Against Noetus* in two ways: he believes *Refutation of All Heresies* represents a more primitive, "binitarian" theology, while *Against Noetus* is Trinitarian because it has a more fully developed pneumatology. But he thinks *Against Noetus* has made a concession to modalism by compromising the personal distinction of the pre-incarnation *Logos*. See pp. 208–11, 213–14, 257. This is based on his assumption that Callistus of Rome was a modalist (and that Noetus was simply a more extreme modalist). See pp. 211, 213, 240, 257. However, there is not enough evidence of what Callistus actually taught to make this assessment. As I will argue, I do not think that Callistus was a modalist, nor that *Against Noetus* makes concessions to modalism. *Against Noetus* is an anti-modalist document through and through.

134. In his description of Noetus, who was said to have come from the East (as was said of most heretics), Hippolytus explained that Noetus's modalism was based a form of monism applied to the Trinity. Modalism's monistic Trinity may have been a reaction against the dualism and polytheism inherent in docetism and gnosticism. See Hippolytus, *Refutation of All Heresies* 9.2–5.

135. Ibid., 9.12,18.

136. Hippolytus, *Refutation of All Heresies* 9.6–7. The proof of the orthodoxy of Zephyrinus and Callistus is that Sabellius was excommunicated.

apparently set up his own school in opposition to Callistus and he seems to have been treated as a bishop by his followers. Eventually, if the *Refutation of All Heresies* is in fact by Hippolytus, he considered himself a bishop and a rival of Callistus.[137] One has to keep in mind, however, that the limitation of one bishop per city was not necessarily universally accepted and may have been a relatively new phenomenon in the larger metropolitan areas like Rome.[138] In reality, Hippolytus may have been the leader of a Greek-speaking school in Rome, or perhaps the bishop of a smaller town near Rome. In any event, in 235 CE, when persecution led to the arrest and exile of church leaders, there were two Roman leaders sent to the mines of Sardinia: the bishop Pontian, and Hippolytus. Hippolytus died in Sardinia, probably in 236, but his body was taken back to Rome, where he was buried.[139] Later tradition tried to reconcile Hippolytus by saying that he was actually bishop of the smaller city of Portus outside of Rome, however there is no early evidence of this.[140]

Hippolytus, writing in Greek, followed Theophilus in calling God a "Triad" (*Triados*).[141] He explained the Trinity as one power with an "economy" (order/hierarchy) of "threefold manifestation."[142] The Father alone is the First Cause and the ultimate Source of all existence, yet the *Logos* is the same divine essence and coeternal with the Father.[143]

137. The author of *Refutation* complained that Callistus was admitting to communion some whom he had excommunicated. See *Refutation of All Heresies* 9.7.

138. Brent, *Hippolytus and the Roman Church*, 453–56.

139. According to tradition, Hippolytus and Pontian were buried in Rome on the same day, though in different catacombs. See ibid., 257. Brent thinks that the tradition was created after the fact to indicate a reconciliation between the two.

140. In 1551 archaeologists discovered a statue that many believe is of Hippolytus, and which seems to assume that he was a bishop. It was at this time that speculation began that perhaps Hippolytus was bishop of Portus, or some other smaller city within Rome's metropolitan authority. In spite of the lack of early evidence, it is entirely possible. See ibid., 3–203, 234–35.

141. Hippolytus, *Against Noetus* 14.

142. Ibid., 3, 8, 11, 14. Thus Hippolytus followed Tertullian in speaking of the unity of the Trinity in terms of "one power." However, see Brent, *Hippolytus*, 212, where Brent argues that one of the differences between *Against Noetus* and *Refutation of All Heresies* is on the issue of the economy. I maintain that the difference in argument can be accounted for on the basis of the different opponents (Modalists versus Gnostics, respectively).

143. Hippolytus, *Refutation of All Heresies* 10.28–29; *Against Noetus* 11; *Expository Treatise against the Jews* 7. See also *On the Holy Theophany* 7, however the authorship

The Holy Spirit is to be worshipped along with the Father and the Son, however sometimes Hippolytus falls back into older ways of describing the Spirit that confuse the Holy Spirit with the pre-incarnate or post-ascension Christ.[144]

In describing the unity of the Trinity, Hippolytus made a statement that appears to be an early move toward the doctrine of *reciprocity* (in Latin: *circumincessio*; in Greek: *perichoresis*), which was an attempt to explain the balance of unity and distinction in the Trinity by a spatial analogy. The three persons of the Trinity are each always oriented toward the unity of the Trinity, sometimes even describing the unity as "movement toward" the Trinity by the three persons who are nevertheless not distinguished spatially.[145] Hippolytus said, "The hierarchy [*economy*] is a harmony that is oriented back toward the one God, for God is one."[146] Just as Tertullian had said that the economy is "within" the monarchy, Hippolytus also makes the hierarchy subservient to the oneness, the distinction secondary to the unity. We will see the further development of the concept of *circumincessio* in Novatian, however for now the important thing to note is that even the very existence of the three persons of the Trinity is oriented toward the unity of the one God.

Of course Hippolytus also knew that there was a necessary distinction between the persons that was required to avoid modalism. Apparently, Noetus had argued on the basis of John 14:8–9 that the Son is just another name for the Father.[147] Hippolytus responded with a grammatical argument based on the tension between John 10:30 and John 14:28. Jesus said, "the Father and I are *one*," but he did not mean, "the Father and I are *the same*," since he also said, "the Father is greater than I."[148] Therefore, "the Father and I are one," describes the unity of the Trinity, while "the Father is greater than I," describes the distinction

---

of this document is questionable. In any case, by now the one essence of the Trinity is assumed. See also Origen, *On First Principles* 1.2.10–11; 4.1.30.

144. Hippolytus, *Against Noetus* 12, 16. Note that Osborn said the same about Tertullian. Osborn, *Tertullian*, 134.

145. Ayres, *Nicaea and Its Legacy*, 246. Here Ayres defines the doctrine, though it is not recognized as such until found in the writings of later theologians.

146. Hippolytus, *Against Noetus* 14. My translation.

147. Ibid., 7. Also probably John 10:30; see Novatian, *On the Trinity* 28.2–4.

148. Hippolytus pointed out that Jesus said, "The Father and I *are* one." He did not say, "The Father and I *am* one." The plural form of the verb "to be" points to the plurality in the Trinity and the distinction between Father and Son.

between persons, so that here in Jesus's own words we have a balance of unity and distinction that both affirms monotheism and allows for the worship of Christ.

The main difference between the Father and the Son, then, is that the Father cannot be circumscribed (localized in time and space) while the Son can be. This is based on the consensus of previous writers that the Father could not be visible (Exod 33:20) and therefore any Old Testament appearances of God must be the pre-incarnate *Logos*. Unlike Tertullian, however, Hippolytus maintained that it is only the human nature of Christ that can be circumscribed and visible.[149] He assumes that uncircumscribability is part of the nature of divinity, therefore since the divine nature of Christ is the same divinity as the Father, even Christ's divine nature could not be circumscribed. He explained that this is because Christ's divine nature is infinite, while his human nature is finite. He also pointed out that circumscribability assumes movement, since one who is localized in one time and place must necessarily move from place to place.[150] Since he saw motion as a form of change, Hippolytus reasoned that divine immutability would be compromised if one said that the divine nature could be circumscribed.[151] Therefore, circumscribability is the opposite of omnipresence, which Hippolytus also assumed was part of the very definition of divinity. However, all of this forces him to speculate that before the incarnation the pre-incarnate *Logos* must have taken on some temporary tangible created physicality in order to appear to the Old Testament patriarchs.

Hippolytus follows the apologists who understood the pre-existence of Christ to have two "phases." In the first phase, the *Logos* is the wisdom or reason of God, like a thought in the Father's mind.[152] He quotes Theophilus (at first God was alone) but then corrects him, or tries to redeem him, saying that though God was alone, he existed "in plurality."[153] But like his predecessors, Hippolytus's *Logos* does not have

---

149. Hippolytus, *Against Beron* 1–3. The authorship of this document is questionable, but it does reflect Christology consistent with Hippolytus.

150. Novatian made this same argument in *On the Trinity* 12.7. However, like Tertullian, Novatian accepted the circumscribability of the Son's divine nature. Novatian also pointed out that Sabellianism makes the Father circumscribed.

151. Hippolytus, *Against Beron* 1–2.

152. Hippolytus, *Refutation of All Heresies* 10.29. See also *Against Noetus* 10–11.

153. Hippolytus, *Against Noetus* 10–11.

a *distinct* personal existence before he was generated.[154] Generation is described as an event that took place when the *Logos* was extended out from the Father to be the agent of creation.[155] This generation, or "begetting," results in the *Logos* going from being the reason or wisdom *in* the Father, to being the counsel and power of God, *with* the Father.[156] The Son of God is generated as power from power, but this creates a problem (which Novatian will correct) in that the Word was not yet the Son before this generation.[157] This means that the distinction between Father and Son does not exist until the generation of the Son.

Therefore, up to and including Hippolytus, apologists and theologians alike assumed what could be argued was a practical modalism in eternity before the generation of the Son, and the generation itself was understood as an event that occurred for the purpose of creating the universe. However this creates two major problems for later orthodoxy: it (unintentionally) implies that before the generation of the Son, the Father was not a Father (since the *Logos* was not yet Son), and therefore God was not really a Trinity; and it further implies that there was a change within God at the time of generation (the First Cause became the Father as the *Logos* became the Son and God became a Trinity), which compromises divine immutability. In the absence of clear biblical texts that could help refine the logical implications of this, it was not considered a heresy at the time, yet it did create a precedent for some of the alternative Christologies of the fourth and fifth centuries.

For Hippolytus, therefore, there are really two "processions" of the *Logos*. The first is at his generation, the second is at his incarnation.[158] This will be important for Novatian, because it will set the stage for him to separate generation from the concept of procession (making generation an eternal state of being), leaving the concept of procession

---

154. Like Tertullian, Hippolytus saw the *Logos* as having a distinct personal existence before the incarnation, but not before his procession from the Father. Cf. Brent, *Hippolytus*, 208–10.

155. Hippolytus, *Against Noetus* 10–11, 17.

156. Ibid., 10–11.

157. Ibid., 11, 15, 16. Hippolytus follows Tertullian in describing the generation of the Son as a ray of light from the sun, or as water from a fountain. There is a distinction, yet one cannot easily show where the source ends and the emission begins. The point is that there is never a separation that would compromise the unity. This anticipates the Nicene language of "God from God, Light from Light . . ."

158. Hippolytus, *Against Noetus* 17.

as a description of the Son's agency at creation. And while the term "procession" as a descriptor of the Son will not stand the test of time (it will later come to be used of the Holy Spirit), Novatian will use it to turn Hippolytus's two processions into three, so that rather than see the procession of the *Logos* as first generation and then incarnation, Novatian will be able to talk about the generation, *then* the procession (at creation) and then the incarnation. This will allow him to conceive of generation, not as an event, but as an eternal state of being.

Hippolytus believed that the incarnation of Christ was the key to understanding the Trinity. For him, the incarnation was an embodiment of the *Logos* that temporarily concealed his divine glory (John 17:5) and allowed him to be visible, providing the one concrete distinction between the Father and the Son.[159] But this embodiment was more than simply the divine nature putting on a garment of flesh, as some of the apologists had described it. Since his main objective was arguing against Gnostics and Modalists, Hippolytus was motivated to demonstrate the full humanity of Christ.[160] In fact, Hippolytus made a point to emphasize that Jesus Christ did have a human rational soul, a conviction that may have allowed the western church to avoid some of the controversy that the east would endure over the perceived diminished humanity of teachers like Apollinarius and Eutyches.[161]

Therefore, Hippolytus was concerned to emphasize the distinction between the two natures of Christ as another way to refute modalism.[162] In other words, he recognized that the christological byproduct of mo-

---

159. Hippolytus, *On the Holy Theophany* 4. The authorship of this document is questionable, but the point made here is consistent with Hippolytus's thought as expressed in *Refutation of All Heresies* and *Against Noetus*. See also Hippolytus, *Against Beron* 2.

160. Grillmeier, *Christ in Christian Tradition*, 115.

161. Hippolytus, *Against Noetus* 17. However, note that some scholars have ascribed elements in *Against Noetus* to later additions at the time of the fourth or fifth century debates. See Brent, *Hippolytus*, 224f. See also *Against Beron* 8. However, the authorship of this document is in doubt. It is interesting to note that Origen also maintained a human mind (rational soul) in Christ, but without the possibility of sin. Origen had apparently anticipated the fear of Apollinarius, that with a human mind and will Christ might have given in to temptation, but instead of removing the human mind from Christ he simply stated that Christ could not have sinned. Thus Origen has given Christ his human will, yet it is not free. See Origen, *On First Principles* 1.2.5, 4.1.31.

162. That Hippolytus anticipates elements of the Chalcedonian definition, see Brent, *Hippolytus*, 238.

The State of Christology before the Mid-Third Century   41

dalism was a diminished humanity in Christ, which could be refuted with adequate articulation of the differentiation between the natures. As we have seen, Hippolytus taught that the divine nature of Christ remained omnipresent while the human nature was localized, so therefore his concept of the distinction between the two natures extended to a separation of circumscribability. This led him to reject the earliest hints of the doctrine of *communicatio idiomatum*, which he saw in his rival Callistus.[163] Callistus had taken Tertullian's unity of substance seriously, so that he had apparently said that even though the Father is impassible, the Father "suffered along with" the Son in his passion and death.[164] In other words, Callistus was implying that in the suffering of the human nature of Christ, the divine nature of Christ, which is the same divinity as the Father, could somehow feel empathy for human suffering without undergoing the change that would be entailed in actual suffering.[165] For Hippolytus, this seemed like *patripassionism*, putting the Father on the cross.[166]

At the same time, Hippolytus did follow Tertullian in describing the unity of the two natures of Christ in ways that anticipated the concept of the *hypostatic union*. The human and divine natures in Christ were united, yet without confusion or change.[167] The union is a personal union, an "indissoluble union of the two (natures) in one person (*hypostasis*).[168] In a passage that combines the unity of natures (using terms of "uniting" and "mixing") while maintaining distinction between human and divine (mortal/power, corruptible/incorruptible, weak/mighty), Hippolytus wrote:

163. Hippolytus, *Refutation of All Heresies* 9.7. See also *Against Beron* 1, 5–6, 8.

164. Hippolytus, *Refutation of All Heresies* 9.7, 10.23. See also *Against Beron* 1. Note that Callistus may also have had an early version of *circumincessio* (*perichoresis*). Although Hippolytus accused Callistus of modalism, he admitted that Callistus was somewhere in the middle between Sabellius (modalism) and Theodotus (adoptionism). It could be argued that Callistus was closer to the middle way than Hippolytus, and that Hippolytus's separation of the two natures anticipated later Nestorianism.

165. As we will see, this concept will be fleshed out in Novatian.

166. Hippolytus, *Expository Treatise against the Jews* 4.

167. Hippolytus, *On Christ and Antichrist* 4; *Against Beron* 1, 5–6.

168. Hippolytus, *Against Beron* 1–2. The authorship of this document is questionable. Admittedly, if this document is not by Hippolytus, the attribution of the *hypostatic union* to him becomes harder to demonstrate, however since we have already seen this in Tertullian, it is not unlikely to find it in Hippolytus.

> He saves perishing humanity by uniting our mortal body with his own power, mixing the corruptible with the incorruptible, the weak with the mighty.[169]

In some ways, Hippolytus summarizes the conclusions of his predecessors, and he anticipates some important aspects of later orthodoxy while resisting others. For the most part, he is the last theologian in the West to hold on to those aspects of *Logos* Christology that would be considered limitations from the perspective of Nicene orthodoxy.

The State of Christology before Novatian

The Christology of the second century and into the early third century can be characterized as *Logos* Christology. This Christology emphasized the *Logos*, who is incarnate as Jesus Christ. This assumes Christ's pre-existence, as well as the conviction that he is the agent of creation. Therefore the *Logos* is also the rational principle behind creation itself, as well as the mediator between Creator and creation.[170] The *Logos* Christology of the second century goes beyond the first century by explicitly affirming what the first-century writers seem to have assumed—that Christ is not just pre-existent, he is *eternally* pre-existent. He did not come into being from nothing, but has always existed. The apologists experimented with the idea that in his pre-existent state the *Logos* of God existed first as an internal Word, or thought, in the mind of God (*in* the Father), then after he was generated he existed as the emitted Word, spoken forth (*with* the Father). This made the generation of the Son an *event*, before which the Son existed eternally, but not as an eternally *distinct* divine person, distinguished from the Father.

Logos Christology reinforced the belief in the pre-incarnate life of the Word by seeing Christ in the Old Testament. This was in part to emphasize the continuity between the testaments, against a docetic/Marcionite rejection of the Old Testament. More important, an assumption of the utter transcendence of God the Father led to the assertion that the first person of the Trinity could never be visible, which in turn led the apologists and early theologians to identify Old Testament appearances of God as the pre-incarnate Christ.[171] Especially theoph-

---

169. Hippolytus, *On Christ and Antichrist* 4. My translation.
170. Ayres, *Nicaea and Its Legacy*, 303.
171. Hurtado, *Lord Jesus Christ*, 575.

anies of the "angel of the Lord" (Gen 16:7–14; 22:11–18; Exod 14:19–20; 23:20–21; Ezek 1:26–28; 8:2–4) were interpreted as appearances of the Son, not the Father, since "no one can see God and live" (Exod 33:20).[172]

The *Logos* was also seen as the inspiration behind the law and prophets and was often identified with personified divine wisdom.[173] However, in the apologists this sometimes blurred the distinction between the Son and the Holy Spirit, since it was unclear whether they thought the prophets spoke by the inspiration of the Holy Spirit or by the *Logos*.[174] Also, it is sometimes difficult to distinguish between a blurred distinction and the beginnings of a doctrine of inseparable operation.[175] Some also blurred the distinction between the post-ascension Christ and the Holy Spirit (possibly based on John 16:7). Therefore, while *Logos* Christology attempts to define the distinction between the Father and the Son, it sometimes does so at the expense of the distinction between the Son and the Spirit.

Logos Christology affirms the incarnation as the pivotal event in human history and salvation. As understood by Novatian and his predecessors, the incarnation was unacceptable to both Ebionites and Adoptionists on one side, as well as Docetics/Gnostics and Modalists on the other, since neither extreme could accept the idea of a God who becomes human, let alone suffers death (1 Cor 1:22–24). Against both extremes, the apologists affirmed that the incarnation was neither a prophetic indwelling nor a phantasmal visitation, but it was a voluntary

---

172. Hurtado, *One God, One Lord*, ch. 4. This interpretation was shared by Philo of Alexandria, who said that the *logos* was an extension of the power of God into the visible realm.

173. For example, see Melito, *Homily on the Passover* 7. The apologists treated the law (the word of God in the Old Testament) as though it *was* the pre-incarnate Word of God, and saw Christ (the living Word) as the embodiment of the law.

174. It is not always clear when the word "spirit" is used as a noun versus an adjective, so at times it is difficult to know exactly what the author means by using *Logos* and spirit terminology in ways that make them sound synonymous. One has to keep in mind that in the ancient documents, certain conventions that might have been helpful, such as capitalization of words that refer to the divine, were not used.

175. Cf. Melito, *Homily on the Passover* 96. Melito, in writing of the death of Jesus, says, "God was murdered." This could sound like modalism, however he did not say, "The Father was murdered." It is, rather, to be seen as an early expression of inseparable operation. In addition, it is an affirmation of the divinity (and consubstantiality) of the second person of the Trinity.

humiliation of the divine Word.[176] The redeemer's descent (humiliation and suffering) leads to humanity's ascent (salvation).

In general, neither of the extreme alternatives could accept the miraculous birth of Jesus: the Ebionites and Adoptionists could not accept it because it was miraculous, the Docetics could not accept it because it was a real physical birth. And while Modalists and some Gnostics would have accepted the idea of a tangible body of Jesus, and therefore did allow the idea of the birth of *Jesus* (as opposed to "the Christ"), they nevertheless interpreted the person of Jesus/Christ as not fully human. Neither extreme could accept the bodily resurrection of Jesus for similar reasons; the Ebionites and Adoptionists because it was a resurrection, the Docetics and Gnostics because it was the resurrection of a body. But the apologists emphasized that the bodily resurrection of Jesus was a window into the reality of the two natures of Christ, and ultimately our only hope of our own resurrection.[177]

The two natures of Christ were affirmed in the second century, with the title "Son of Man" applied to the human nature and "Son of God" to the divine nature. The apologists, however, clarified that any change (mutability) or suffering (passibility) that is seen in Christ can be attributed only to the human nature and not to the divine nature.[178] So while the Ebionites and Adoptionists assumed that since God must be immutable and impassible, Christ could not be divine; and the Docetics and Gnostics (and possibly the Modalists) assumed that since Christ was divine, he must have been immutable and impassible, the apologists and theologians who influenced Novatian explained the mutability and passibility of Christ by the distinction between the two natures. In other words, the Ebionites and Adoptionists would draw the line of immutability between the Father and Son. The Docetics/Gnostics and Modalists would draw the line of immutability between God (the

---

176. Irenaeus, *Demonstration of the Apostolic Preaching* 69.

177. Cf. Melito, *Homily on the Passover* 47, 100.

178. Sometimes the apologists speak of the incarnation as the *Logos* "putting on" flesh, rather than becoming flesh. This imprecise language could give the impression that the human nature of Christ is only a "garment" of flesh and not a full human nature. While this is not what the apologists meant, it did set the stage for some later writers to speculate on the unity of the two natures in a way that diminished the humanity of Christ and therefore created the same soteriological problem as docetism—Christ can only save what he becomes and if he does not become fully human, how can he be the savior of humanity? Cf. Melito, *Homily on the Passover* 8, 66.

Father/Son) and humanity. Those who would be called orthodox drew the line right down the middle of Christ himself, between the divine and human natures. However, the *Logos* Christology of the apologists, with its imprecision of language that left the Son of God without a distinct existence in a phase of life prior to his generation, or blurred the distinction between the divine nature of Christ and the Holy Spirit, may have actually opened the door for the modalism of the third century.

It was Tertullian who took the baton from Irenaeus and greatly advanced the church's understanding of the Trinity by giving the Latin West the language that would become standard for talking about God. However, Tertullian was still in the camp of *Logos* Christology, in fact the language of *Logos* Christology would linger long after the theologians had moved beyond its limitations.[179] It would not be until Novatian that third century theology would come to an apex, with what we will call *kenosis* Christology. In *kenosis* Christology, the church (especially in the west) will have come to a doctrine of the Trinity that would be the foundation for later orthodoxy.

Taken all together, *Logos* Christology, as both an apologetic response to the opponents of the church, as well as a refutation of heretical alternatives within the church, can be summarized as follows:

- The *Logos* is God's reason and wisdom, and is the inspiration for the prophets and the written word of God.
    - The *Logos* is one and the same with the pre-incarnate Christ, who can be seen in the theophanies of the Old Testament.
    - Human rationality is created in the image of the *Logos*.
- Whereas the Ebionites and Adoptionists affirmed Jesus's humanity, but denied his divinity; and the Docetics, Marcionites, Gnostics, and Modalists affirmed his divinity but denied his full humanity, *Logos* Christology affirms both the full humanity and full divinity—the two natures—of Christ.
- Whereas Ebionites and Adoptionists rejected New Testament passages that affirmed the divinity of Christ; and Docetics and Gnostics rejected New Testament passages that described Christ as human (as well as those that connected Christ to the Old Testament), the theologians accepted the apostolic documents

179. Osborn, *Tertullian*, 134.

as authoritative, refusing to ignore either side, operating on the conviction that both were true.[180]

- Whereas both extremes generally rejected the miraculous birth and bodily resurrection of Jesus, *Logos* Christology emphasized the incarnation as the divine Word becoming human, which allowed Christ to be able to be born, grow, suffer and die, and understood the resurrection as a real, physical, bodily resurrection.
- Salvation requires both divine intervention and human representation.
  - Ebionite/Adoptionist Christology is human effort without divine intervention (apart from the giving of the law), which necessarily leads to a form of self-salvation, or salvation by personal discipline.
  - Gnostic and modalist Christology is divine intervention without human representation, which in the case of gnosticism turns out to be a salvation by knowledge, available only to a select few.
  - *Logos* Christology acknowledges both divine intervention, in the descent of the divine *Logos*, and human representation, in the incarnation and passion of the human nature of Christ.
- Both extremes envision a Jesus who is not unique among humanity.
  - For the Ebionites and Adoptionists, Jesus is not unique because he is essentially a mere human.
  - For the Docetics and Gnostics, Jesus is not unique because all humans are in some sense divine.
  - *Logos* Christology understands Jesus as both one of us and unique among us, because he is fully human but also uniquely one with the Father.
- It is assumed by *Logos* Christology that it is appropriate to worship Christ, and in fact, worshipping Christ *is* worshipping God. However the worship of the three persons of the Trinity does not compromise monotheism because of consubstantiality, divine simplicity, and inseparable operation.

---

180. Hippolytus, *Against Noetus* 3.

2

Novatian: His Life and Historical Context

The Church in Rome

The Sociopolitical Context

THE CHURCH NOVATIAN KNEW WAS A PERSECUTED CHURCH. IT WAS a misunderstood and mistrusted community that was seen as antisocial by those outside of it. Of course, what was perceived as antisocial by those on the outside was held with conviction as countercultural by those on the inside. Bishops and theologians (including Novatian) wrote with urgency against Christian participation in such staples of Roman society as the games and shows of the arenas and theaters. These "spectacles" often included elements of pagan worship, and some of the athletic games were performed in the nude, forcing spectators to engage in what Novatian seemed to consider a kind of "ocular adultery."[1]

It is clear from the ongoing arguments against participation in the games and shows that not all Christians agreed with Novatian and others who had a stricter moral conscience about participation in Roman society. If they did, it would make treatises like Novatian's *On the Spectacles* unnecessary. However, ever since Paul's discussion of whether Christians should eat meat that had been sacrificed to idols (1 Cor 8), Christians had caught the attention of their neighbors by refusing to participate in certain aspects of Roman culture. There are stories of rumors that circulated about the church, rumors of cannibalism based on a misunderstanding of the Eucharist, and rumors of incestuous marriages, based on a misunderstanding of the way Christians called each

---

1. Novatian, *On the Spectacles* 4, 6, 8. Novatian says that we are forbidden to watch whatever we are forbidden to do.

other (including their spouses) *brother* or *sister*.² Therefore the refusal to participate in Roman society (especially those aspects of the culture which were thought to hold the empire together and guaranteed the protection of the gods) combined with these rumors, led the Romans to see Christians as legitimate scapegoats in their midst. In fact, the refusal to worship the pantheon of Greco-Roman deities brought the charge of "atheism" on the Christians.

In the year 64 CE, fire broke out in the city of Rome, and destroyed a significant section of the city. The fact that the emperor Nero (reigned 54–68) was planning to build a new palace in just that section of town led to rumors that the emperor himself had ordered the fire to be started to clear away the wooden tenements and storehouses to make room for his new "Golden House." Sometime between Claudius's expulsion of Jews in about 52 CE and the fire of 64, the Romans had begun to understand that Christianity was becoming something separate from Judaism.³ Thus the new movement was seen with suspicion, and became a convenient scapegoat to deflect the blame for the fire away from Nero.⁴ While Nero's persecution was short-lived and limited to the city of Rome, and technically the Christians were accused of the crime of arson, it set a precedent for later emperors and provincial governors to follow.⁵

Ultimately, the issue of persecution would come down to a test of loyalty, a competition for the affection of the people, in which Caesar would tolerate no rival (cf. John 19:12–15; Acts 17:5–8). By the end of the first century, the emperor Domitian (reigned 81–96 CE) appar-

---

2. See Athenagoras, *A Plea for the Christians* 3; and Tertullian, *To the Nations* 1.7.

3. When Claudius expelled the Jews from Rome, he did not know the difference between Jews and Christians. Both Christian and non-Christian Jews were expected to leave the city (cf. Acts 18:2). Claudius's reason for this was perceived fighting among Jewish leaders, but was probably actually conflict between Christians and non-Christian Jews. See Suetonius, *Life of Claudius* 25.4. The expulsion of Jews from Rome had the effect of leaving the church in Rome without its Jewish leaders, and the now all-Gentile church was left to find its own way for a time without the benefit of those who knew the tradition and foundation of the faith. This may have been the occasion for the writing of the Gospel of Mark.

4. Tacitus, *Annals* 15.44 (cf. Sulpicius Severus, *Chronicle* 2.29); Suetonius, *Life of Nero* 16.2.

5. Eusebius, *Ecclesiastical History* 2.25. It was during Nero's persecution of the church in Rome that both Paul and Peter were martyred.

ently encouraged the persecution of Christians.[6] Domitian had taken the tradition of emperors claiming divine titles to its logical conclusion. Whereas Tiberius (reigned 14–37 CE) had been called *dominus* (lord), Domitian demanded to be called *dominus et deus* (lord and god).[7] The concept of Christ as King, with its gospel of a Kingdom (or empire) of God, would have been perceived as a threat against the empire of the Romans. In practice, the provincial governors would have had the authority to persecute the church, based on the precedent of Nero, or they may choose to leave the church alone, as long as they could maintain the peace.[8] This explains why some Christians might be executed (especially in Rome) and others, like the apostle John, might only be exiled to an island prison such as Patmos.

By the early second century and the reign of the emperor Trajan (reigned 98–117 CE), it was no longer the case that a crime such as arson, or other antisocial behavior, was needed to convict a Christian.[9] In a letter to the emperor, the provincial governor, Pliny the Younger, asked for advice about how to deal with the Christians in his province.[10] As a result of this correspondence, the emperor and governor agreed that simply the admission of being a Christian was worthy of capital punishment. Therefore, the most important development from the first persecution under Nero was that now the very name of Christian was a crime, associated with "sacrilege and treason."[11] As Trajan advised,

---

6. Tertullian, *Apology* 5; and Eusebius, *Ecclesiastical History* 3.17, 4.26.

7. The book of Revelation in the New Testament was written at this time. The so-called number of the beast (666, in Rev 13) is a reference to the emperor Domitian and his blasphemy against God by the use of divine titles. See Papandrea, *Wedding of the Lamb*, 15–27.

8. De Ste. Croix, "Why Were the Early Christians Persecuted?" 11–16. The governor's first priority would be to keep the peace, therefore if the populace demanded action against the Christians, the governor could not afford to ignore them, however if Christians and non-Christians were living in peace then the governor could look the other way. Of utmost importance would be to prevent mob uprisings, such as happened in 177 CE in Lyons and Viennes. This would attract unwanted attention from the emperor.

9. Tertullian, *Apology* 2–4.

10. Pliny the Younger, *Epistle* 10.96-97 (includes Trajan's rescript). See also Eusebius, *Ecclesiastical History* 3.33.

11. Tertullian, *Apology* 10. Some have argued that the charge assumed in the Pliny correspondence was actually illegal assembly, however see Sherwin-White, "Early Persecutions," 206–8. Christians could and did gather legally as *collegia*, so the charge

however, Christians were not to be sought out, nor were anonymous accusations to be trusted. A Christian was only convicted of the charge on his or her own admission, and a simple renunciation of the faith (sometimes with a curse against Christ, just to be sure) was all that was required for acquittal.

Sacrifice to the traditional gods had already been used as a test of religious conformity.[12] Now it became a test of loyalty to the emperor. Participation in the imperial cult, which may have meant nothing more than an oath of loyalty to the emperor or a prayer of dedication added to an offering of incense or libation, became the litmus test for a good Roman. Based on this precedent, in the year 167 CE, the emperor Marcus Aurelius (reigned 161–180 CE) issued an imperial edict ordering sacrifices as a sign of loyalty. This edict was not specifically directed at Christians, since it appears Marcus Aurelius was not aware of any reason why a person could not be a Christian and also make the required sacrifices.[13] However, in 202 CE the emperor Septimius Severus (reigned 193–211 CE) issued an edict that, as far as we can tell, specifically mentioned Christians and outlawed conversion to Christianity.[14]

---

was based on suspicion of illegal activity associated with membership in the church (such as the supposed cannibalism), and possibly also based on the same law that outlawed Druidism (because of human sacrifice), as well as a *senatus consultum* of 16 CE against the practice of magic. Early understanding (or misunderstanding) of the eucharistic rite may have led to charges of sorcery. If there were another crime associated with the persecution, then simply renouncing the faith would not be enough for one to go free. See Barnes, "Legislation against the Christians," 37, 48.

12. See Josephus, *Wars of the Jews* 7.3.3, especially sections 46, 50–51. See also De Ste. Croix, "Why Were the Early Christians Persecuted?," 20.

13. Barnes, "Legislation against the Christians," 40. There are references in third and fourth century sources that Marcus Aurelius was seen as possibly even sympathetic to the church. See Tertullian, *Apology* 5; and Eusebius, *Ecclesiastical History* 5.5.

14. Historia Augusta, *Life of Septimius Severus* 17.1. The edict itself is not extant, and although some have argued against the reliability of the Historia Augusta on this point, the existence of the edict fits the history better than its fabrication. For example, it would be difficult to explain the martyrdoms of Perpetua and Felicitas without such an edict. For the argument, see Barnes, "Legislation against the Christians," 40. Severus was also working with a precedent of a law against Jewish proselytism form the reign of Antoninus Pius (reigned 138–61 CE). The impetus for the edict of 202 CE seems to be Severus's travels to the eastern empire, during which he encountered the church in Alexandria, which was attracting many converts. This apparently made Severus perceive the church as a threat to the stability of the empire. For an opposing view on the edict, see Dunn, *Tertullian*, 17. Dunn does not accept the account of the edict, based on favorable mention of Severus in Tertullian's *To Scapula*. However, this document has an

The advance that this edict made over prior precedent was that now Christians could be sought out, such as was the case with Perpetua and Felicitas in North Africa, the father of Origen in Alexandria, and possibly also Irenaeus, bishop of Lyons.

Thus in the mid-third century the stage would be set for the first systematic, empire-wide persecution of the church. The last piece of the puzzle was put into place in 212 CE when Caracalla (reigned 211–217 CE) made all inhabitants of the empire Roman citizens. Presumably done for reasons of taxation, it would now be impossible for provincials to escape the enforcement of an imperial edict aimed at testing their loyalty.

In the year 249 CE, when the emperor Decius came to power, he inherited the throne of an empire that, on the one hand, had just celebrated the millennial anniversary of its capital city, but on the other hand, was facing a severe economic recession coupled with prolonged war with the Persians and the potential collapse of its borders under pressure from nomadic tribes ("barbarians") from the north and east. Decius's solution was to promise a return to the glorious golden age of the empire, based in part on renewed devotion to the traditional Roman gods. To that end, an edict was issued that demanded all inhabitants of the empire make a sacrifice to the Romans' highest god, Jupiter, in the name and honor of the emperor.[15] To the Christians, this would have amounted to both idolatry (including participation in the imperial cult, which would have implied the worship of a human being) as well as apostasy. As we will see, however, that did not necessarily mean that all Christians resisted complying with the edict.

There were two aspects of Decius's edict that meant he was going beyond his predecessors to instigate the first truly full-scale persecution in the empire.[16] First, everyone had to sacrifice. Simply claiming not to be a Christian, or even taking an oath to the emperor or cursing Christ would not be enough. One had to participate in pagan sacrifice, and a receipt, called a *libellus*, was required to prove compliance. One was

---

apologetic agenda, arguing that it is not in Rome's best interest to persecute the church. Therefore, it would not have supported Tertullian's purpose to do anything other than praise Severus.

15. Knipfing, "*Libelli* of the Decian Persecution," 353–54. The edict is not extant, therefore it is assumed that Jupiter was the preferred god addressed in the sacrifice.

16. For a summary of the Decian persecution, see Sage, *Cyprian*, 165–265.

expected to carry this *libellus* and might be asked to show it as proof of good citizenship, in order to participate in commerce (cf. Rev 13:17).[17] Second, the enforcement of the edict was no longer left up to the provincial governors. Apparently, each city in the empire was expected to create a council to oversee the sacrifices, possibly led by a local magistrate, but presumably answerable to authorities in Rome. Some of these council members' signatures can be seen on the *libelli* that survive from this time.[18]

This is the situation in which Novatian found himself. He had been ordained a priest under the shadow of Septimius Severus's edict, which allowed Christians (and especially clergy) to be rounded up, arrested, tortured, and executed, simply for being members of the church. He would then see Decius come to power, finding himself in the lion's den at the very moment that a more dangerous lion took over the den.

Two things remain to be mentioned to begin to understand the social and political climate in Rome in the middle of the third century. They both have to do with the balance of power between those of greater and lesser authority within the structure of the culture. One is the patron-client relationship, the other is the legal adoption of adults to secure inheritance and succession.

In a society built on relationships of patronage, the relative authority of men in the empire was often defined by a relationship of patron and client. The patron, or wealthier party, relied on the client to run errands, do odd jobs, or even do the family "dirty work." The client might even be told how to vote in certain elections. In return, the patron provided a kind of insurance for the client, giving advice and helping with any trouble that might arise. In this relationship, the patron was seen as influential and important; the more clients he had, the more influence he had. The client, on the other hand, had a friend in high places. As we have seen, an important aspect of *Logos* Christology is the relationship of the Father and Son described as Sender and Messenger. Novatian continues this trend and expands on it, using it to describe the distinction between the persons of the Trinity while maintaining

---

17. Knipfing, "*Libelli* of the Decian Persecution," 356–57, 363–90. Perhaps it is the case that something similar was used during the reign of Domitian, as indicated in Rev 13. See Papandrea, *Wedding of the Lamb*, 156–59.

18. Knipfing, "*Libelli* of the Decian Persecution," 350–54. See the texts of the extant *libelli* in Knipfing.

both the ontological unity and equality of Father and Son and the hierarchy of authority that exists between them. It is possible that the emphasis on the Sender/Messenger relationship within the Trinity was articulated that way in part because of the influence of the patron/client relationship in Roman culture. In other words, the patron and client were understood to be equal in the sense that they were both Romans, but fulfilling roles in society at different places in the hierarchy, based on varying degrees of authority and influence. The early descriptions of the Trinity have some parallels to this, in the sense that the Father and Son are understood as ontologically equal (consubstantial), yet with an internal relationship to each other (the "economy") that meant that the Son comes with the Father's authority while at the same time submitting to it.

Roman law also allowed that an adult could be adopted by another man to create an heir. This happened with some regularity in cases where an emperor had no legitimate heir and/or wanted to choose his successor before he died. The successor would be adopted, and legally considered the son when the time came. Some of Novatian's opponents, the Adoptionists, seem to have taken this image and applied it to their description of the relationship between the Father and the Son. They did not accept the consubstantiality of the Father and Son, maintaining instead that the relationship between Father and Son was one of cooperating wills, so that the Son was "adopted" as a son of God (based on his obedient submission to the Father) rather than being the Son of God by nature. In this scheme, the *difference* between the adoptive father and the adopted son would be highlighted (they are not biologically related), and this would parallel the ontological difference between the God the Father and Jesus the Son. Thus the Adoptionists maintained that Jesus was the Son of God by adoption (by an act of will), but not by nature.

The Ecclesiastical Context

The time of Novatian is the time of the shift in the language of the Roman church from Greek to Latin. Novatian's Bible was a new Latin text (pre-Vulgate), specific to Europe.[19] This was also a time when the

---

19. Whereas Tertullian seems to have translated his quotations himself from Greek, Cyprian of Carthage had a Latin Bible, however this North African text was different

rule of one bishop per city was newly solidified in the larger cities. In Rome, the monoepiscopacy was assumed, but perhaps not yet considered safely entrenched, as some still thought it necessary to make a case for it.[20] Rome was a metropolitan see with sixty other episcopal sees in its area.[21] It could also have been the case that the boundaries of the sees were fluid and there was still no clear distinction of authority between bishops of neighboring cities (for example in the case of Hippolytus) and bishops of Rome. The neighboring bishops may already be functioning as advisors to the bishop of Rome, and those who were bold enough to oppose him might be able to gain their own rival following. In any case, the office of bishop of Rome was in some ways still tenuous, and the events of 250 CE would only make it seem less stable.

In the mid-third century, the church of Rome was comprised of just under fifty house churches. Cornelius tells us that there were forty-six priests (*presbyters*), forty-two acolytes, and fifty-two exorcists.[22] The city was divided into seven regions, each with a deacon and a subdeacon.[23] There were also lectors, ushers, deaconesses (for assisting in the baptism of women), and widows, whose ministry it was to pray and visit women whom the male clergy could not call upon.

---

from the one Novatian used. Novatian's Bible probably represents a second phase of translation into Latin, the North African one being the first. See Papandrea, *Trinitarian Theology of Novatian of Rome*, 8, 102–5. Novatian's Old Testament was translated from the Septuagint, and his New Testament may have included the *Shepherd of Hermas*. The Latin Bible that Novatian used, called the *Itala* (or the Italian version), was preferred by Augustine. See Augustine, *On Christian Doctrine* 2.15 (22).

20. The letter of Cornelius preserved in Eusebius's *Ecclesiastical History* seems to have a defensive tone on this point (6.43), however this is understandable given the situation of Novatian's election as a rival bishop of Rome. See Papandrea, *Trinitarian Theology of Novatian of Rome*, 358. Hippolytus may be evidence of multiple bishops in third century Rome; see Brent, *Hippolytus and the Roman Church*, 453–56. See also Jerome, *Illustrious Men* 61 (Jerome calls Hippolytus a bishop, but does not know where, cf. Eusebius, *Ecclesiastical History* 6.20.2); and Hippolytus, *Refutation of All Heresies* 9.6–7, in which Hippolytus refers to Victor (bishop 189–199 CE) as *a* bishop of Rome.

21. Cyprian of Carthage, *Epistle* 55. See also the letter of Cornelius preserved in Eusebius, *Ecclesiastical History* 6.43.

22. Eusebius, *Ecclesiastical History* 6.43. The exorcist, as an office of the church, seems to have had a role in the interrogation before baptism, and probably evolved into, or was absorbed by, the office of catechist.

23. *Catalogus Liberianus*, in the Chronograph of 354, s.v. *Fabius*. See also Papandrea, *Trinitarian Theology of Novatian of Rome*, 8–14.

There were as yet no church buildings, in the sense of structures built specifically for the purpose of worship. However, at this time some houses and apartments were being modified to make them more functional as worship spaces, incorporating baptismal fonts, so that the idea of interior consecrated space is emerging, that is, space dedicated to Christian assembly and used only for worship. Exterior consecrated space was already established at the cemeteries or in the catacombs.[24] The number of Christians in Rome in the middle of the third century has been estimated as high as 30,000.[25] However, this estimate is certainly too high if we are to accept the numbers of clergy above. The number at this time is much more likely to have been around 10,000.[26] This would be about two hundred Christians per house church, which would be manageable, especially when we realize that many people were worshipping outside the city at the cemeteries much of the time.[27] Also, it may have been that the early Christians assumed a synagogue model in which it was not necessarily the case that they felt obligated to attend worship every time there was a gathering. Therefore, if we assume the total population of Rome was about one million at the time, the Christians in Rome were approximately 1 percent of the population.

Novatian the Priest and Theologian

Novatian (Novatianus) was probably born around the turn of the third century. He was most likely a Roman, in spite of some later attempts to associate him with the east.[28] Cyprian, bishop of Carthage, said that Novatian had been a Stoic philosopher before his conversion to Christianity, however Novatian's apparent Stoicism may simply be

24. See MacMullen, *Second Church*, 69–76.

25. Chadwick, "Church of the Third Century," 5.

26. This is my own estimate based on Stark, *Rise of Christianity*. I come to the number 10,000 by starting with what appear to be five house churches in Paul's letter to the Romans, and assuming a 2 percent growth rate.

27. MacMullen, *Second Church*, 76–89.

28. It was said by some that he was from Phrygia, though this is unreliable and was probably based on the expansion and longevity of the Novatianist sect in the East and its apparent affinity with Montanism, which did come from Phrygia. In the fifth century, the historian Socrates Scholasticus said that there were still Novatianists in Phrygia. Since the Novatianists and Montanists were both moral rigorists, they may have seemed similar to the mainstream church, and may have even joined forces. See Daly, "Novatian and Tertullian."

the product of a standard Roman education.[29] He may have been a teacher of rhetoric before his conversion, and both Cyprian as well as his own rival Cornelius admitted his skill as a writer.[30] If Novatian did have a prior career as a teacher of philosophy or rhetoric, he probably intended to postpone his baptism until retirement, like many upwardly mobile men of the empire did. However, he apparently became very ill at some point in his thirties, and was baptized out of fear that he might die.[31] Once baptized, he was committed to give up his secular career, so he devoted his talents to the church, and was soon ordained a priest by bishop Fabian of Rome (bishop 236–250 CE).[32]

When the edict of Decius was issued, one of the first to be martyred was Bishop Fabian, who died on January 20, 250 CE. Since it would be too dangerous to elect another bishop right away, the church of Rome was without a bishop for over a year. Novatian was chosen to lead the

29. Cyprian of Carthage, *Epistle* 55.16–24, 60.3. See also Pacian of Barcelona, *Epistle* 2.14, where Pacian follows Cyprian. While Novatian may not have been a professional philosopher, the predominant philosophy that comes through his writing is Stoicism. In his treatise, *On Jewish Foods*, for example, we can see that he has read Seneca. In his treatise *On the Benefit of Purity*, he says, ". . . the greatest pleasure is mastery of pleasure itself," and ". . . your speech should be measured and your laughter contained. Laughter betrays an easygoing and dissipated spirit." Novatian, *On the Benefit of Purity* 11, 13. Therefore, it could be said that his background in Stoic thought contributed to his moral rigorism.

30. Cyprian, *Epistle* 55.24, 60.3. See also the letter of Cornelius in Eusebius, *Ecclesiastical History* 6.43.

31. Since Novatian was sick at the time of his baptism (a "clinical" baptism), he was apparently not baptized by immersion, but by affusion, or pouring. See Eusebius, *Ecclesiastical History* 6.43. Later, Novatian's enemies would claim that he was never confirmed, which would have disqualified him from ordination. However, even if true, it would have been easy enough for Fabian to confirm him just before his ordination, since it seems that baptism and confirmation were already becoming separate rites in Rome by this time. Rumors that Novatian was ordained against the wishes of the vast majority of the Roman church are certainly untrue and simply the result of his later enemies trying to discredit him and call into question the validity of his ordination. According to tradition, Fabian himself had been chosen for consecration as bishop of Rome by divine providence, when a dove landed on his head, which was taken by the people as an imitation of Jesus's baptism. Eusebius, *Ecclesiastical History* 6.29. In any event, if Fabian chose to ordain Novatian, the people would certainly have accepted his decision. Finally, Novatian would never have been chosen to lead the church of Rome after Fabian's martyrdom if he was ordained against the wishes of the people and the other clergy.

32. That Novatian would have been expected to give up teaching secular literature, see the *Apostolic Tradition* 2.16.9–24.

church as acting bishop and chair of the council of priests during this time. It is all but certain that Novatian was selected for this position because of his theological treatise, *On the Trinity*. Cornelius's (somewhat sarcastic) remark about Novatian as "this master of doctrine" nevertheless acknowledges that Novatian's ability as a theologian won for him the honor of being the spokesman for the Roman church. Thus we have to assume that the theology reflected in *On the Trinity* was considered orthodox in Rome at the time.[33] Furthermore, as I will demonstrate, it represents a Trinitarian theology and a Christology that was ahead of its time by the standards of later orthodoxy.

Novatian's *On the Trinity* is his *magnum opus*. It was clearly written before the persecution broke out, probably during the time that Novatian was a priest under Fabian, therefore in the late thirties or forties of the third century.[34] Its original title was probably *The Rule of Truth*, since this is how it begins, and since the Latin word *Trinitas* is not used. The document is, in essence, a commentary on the old Roman creed, the "Rule of Faith."[35] The writing style shows Novatian's education, but it also shows his desire to write for the common person. The Latin is not a high polished Latin, but a more popular style, which tells us that the document was meant to help the average Christian understand the faith, and it was probably used as a catechetical textbook.[36]

Novatian's methodology was to expand upon the creed by connecting the elements of the creed with passages from Scripture, and to exegete those passages for his audience in a way that would both interpret the Scriptures and explain the creed.[37] In addition, Novatian's

33. D'Alès, *Novatien*, 83–84.

34. Evidence that *On the Trinity* was written before the persecution includes the fact that in it Novatian attributes the rule of government to God's providence (*On the Trinity* 8.5). Also, Novatian quotes 1 Cor 12:3, that no one can deny Christ if they have the Holy Spirit (29.24). In this latter context, Novatian would never have passed up the opportunity to talk about the controversy over the lapsed if the issue had already arisen. Finally, the mention of reconciliation in *On the Trinity* 1.12 would not have gone by without some mention of the apostasy that occurred during Decius's persecution.

35. Novatian, *On the Trinity* 1.1. See Schaff, *Creed of Christendom*, 2:21. See also Dunn, "Diversity and Unity," 390.

36. For an outline of the contents of *On the Trinity*, see Papandrea, *Trinitarian Theology of Novatian*, 48.

37. Novatian rarely paraphrases Scripture, preferring rather to quote it from his new Latin Bible. Like his predecessors and contemporaries, he naturally assumed the infallibility of the Scriptures, including the apostolic writings of the New Testament.

agenda includes the refutation of the primary heresies of his time, adoptionism and modalism, so that there is an apologetic tone to the document, in which Novatian uses each of the heresies' favorite texts against the opposite heresy.

Novatian the Schismatic

Decius's edict brought a variety of responses from the Christians, often depending on their location in the empire. Some were martyred for their refusal to sacrifice. Others were imprisoned and tortured. But many Christians simply lined up to make the sacrifice, assuming that by mentally crossing their fingers they were doing no harm. They knew that God would know the faith in their hearts and that they did not really believe in the gods they pretended to honor by oath and sacrifice. They obviously had no idea of the controversy that would be caused when the persecution subsided and they wanted to return to the church. Called the *lapsed*, they were considered apostates who had excommunicated themselves by their actions. Many, including Novatian, felt it would dishonor the martyrs simply to receive them back into the fellowship when others had given their lives rather than deny the faith.

However, Cyprian of Carthage had gone into hiding, and some North African priests were readmitting the lapsed to communion in his absence. In this they were following the recommendation of the *confessors*, those who had witnessed to the faith before the Roman officials at the risk of their own lives, but who had not (yet) been martyred. Cyprian counseled patience while the persecution continued, but until he returned to Carthage, there was little he could do to stop the confessors from using their newfound charismatic authority (cf. Matt 13:11) to forgive the sins of the lapsed. Out of this controversy, two factions emerged. The *laxists* (for lack of a better name) advocated immediate and unconditional forgiveness and reconciliation of the lapsed. At the other extreme were the *rigorists*, of whom Novatian would become the leader. Both factions saw the majority (not to mention the other extreme) as overstepping boundaries and playing God. The laxists didn't

---

See *On the Trinity* 18.2, 24.6. Also consistent with early Christian exegesis, Novatian tended to interpret the New Testament literally (historically/grammatically) and the Old Testament non-literally, assuming that allegory is synonymous with a deeper spiritual or mystical meaning. See *On the Trinity* 6.2, 7.5; and Novatian's *On Jewish Foods*.

want to usurp God's authority to judge, while the rigorists didn't want to usurp God's authority to forgive the unforgivable sin.[38]

Novatian followed in the footsteps of previous moral rigorists such as Tertullian and Hippolytus.[39] When applied to the problem of the lapsed, rigorism assumed that God might forgive apostasy, but the church could not. In practice, this meant that the lapsed would remain in a state of excommunication until death was immanent.[40] After Novatian split from the Roman church, he did not grant the lapsed reconciliation even on their deathbeds. He believed that God *might* forgive them without the reconciliation of the church, but the church could not presume to offer forgiveness when God might not. No doubt the reality of those in the church who had been reconciled by the confessors, or

38. Pacian of Barcelona, *Epistle* 1.15. Pacian argued that to refuse reconciliation to the penitent is to "prejudge the future judgment of Christ." The point of the parable of the wheat and the weeds, then, is that permanent excommunication of the lapsed would be like weeding the fields when the master has commanded us to wait.

39. DeSimone, *Treatise of Novatian*, 8. See also Daly, "Novatian and Tertullian," 41, esp. note 5. Tertullian had apparently had a falling out with the Roman clergy over issues of discipline, among other things, and while Montanism is not what we would call a schism, Tertullian seems to have turned away from Rome in favor of an association with North African Montanism. Hippolytus was also critical of the Roman leadership, especially bishops Zephyrinus and Callistus, also over matters of discipline and reconciliation. According to Hippolytus, the Roman bishops were too lenient, reconciling those whom Hippolytus thought should not be reconciled.

40. Socrates Scholasticus, *Ecclesiastical History* 4.28, Cyprian of Carthage, *Epistle* 55.26–27. Novatian allowed no distinction between those who actually made the required sacrifice (apostates) and those who only acquired a *libellus* (called *libelliteci*). For him, obtaining and carrying a *libellus* was no better than making the sacrifice, especially in the case of one who had convinced a non-Christian to make the sacrifice. Even if the Christian was not present at the pagan altar, "the man who has issued the orders for the perpetration of crime is not free of guilt." Novatian, *Epistle* 1.3 (30.3). See also Novatian's *Epistle* 1.3, 7–8. In this letter, Novatian is speaking for the Roman council of priests, and does not have the freedom to say what he really thinks. Some authors, both ancient (Pacian of Barcelona) and modern (DeSimone), have criticized Novatian for changing his mind on the issue of reconciliation. However, in the letter he is clearly deferring to the council, which is probably following the advice of Cyprian. In the letter Novatian admits to the wisdom of the desire to "steer a middle course," however in the end he went to one extreme (rigorism) while the majority of the church looked for a middle way between the "indulgent treatment" of the laxists and the "inflexible cruelty" of the rigorists. Novatian's point in the letter is that even if some are to be reconciled because death was immanent, they should only be reconciled if their repentance was sincere and they showed their sincerity through penance. In other words, if one had not been doing the required penance when there was no danger of death, one should not be reconciled just because death seemed to be near.

those reconciled when they were thought to be mortally ill (but then recovered, ironically like Novatian himself), created a heightened sense of contrast with those who gave their lives rather than deny the faith. The situation could not help but beg the question whether the martyrs had died in vain. Ultimately Novatian considered that it would compromise the integrity of the church to reconcile the lapsed. For Novatian, the very presence of the lapsed within the church defiled the purity of the bride of Christ.[41]

Novatian believed that the denial of Christ was proof that one was not a Christian, because it demonstrated that a person did not have the Holy Spirit, based on the idea from 1 Corinthians 12:3, that one could not curse Christ when speaking with the Holy Spirit.[42] Denial of Christ was the opposite of being a confessor. If the confessors were invested with charismatic authority based on Matthew 13:11, then the lapsed were guilty of blasphemy of the Holy Spirit by not allowing the Spirit to speak for them. Novatian wrote that "the entire mystery of faith is contained in the confession of Christ," implying that the confession of faith is itself sacramental, and the denial of Christ is like defiling a sacrament, or at least undoing it.[43] After all, did Jesus not say that he would deny before the Father anyone who denied him (Matt 10:33; Luke 12:9)?[44] Therefore, denial of Christ was the unforgiveable sin (Matt 12:31–32).[45] As the unforgiveable sin, while it *might* be forgiven by God at his prerogative, it could not be forgiven by the church. Therefore, to reconcile the lapsed would be to usurp God's authority and contradict the Scriptures.[46]

---

41. Socrates Scholasticus, *Ecclesiastical History* 4.28, Cyprian of Carthage, *Epistle* 55.27.2–3. See also Novatian, *Epistle* 1.2 (30.2), where Novatian described the church as a ship, with moral discipline as its rudder.

42. Novatian, *On the Trinity* 29.24; *Epistle* 1.7 (30.7).

43. Novatian, *Epistle* 1.3 (30.3).

44. Ibid., 1.7 (30.7). See also Pacian of Barcelona, *Epistle* 3.13. The lapsed are those who disown Christ, they are trying to get into the wedding banquet without a wedding garment (Matt 22:11–13).

45. Novatian, *On the Trinity* 14.10; Papandrea, *Trinitarian Theology of Novatian*, 31. See also Ambrose, *On Penance* 2.4; and Jerome, *Epistle* 42.

46. Daly, "Novatian and Tertullian," 40. See also Ambrose, *On Penance* 1.2. For Novatian, evil exists because of the rejection of God's law, which implies that the rejection of Christ (God's *Logos*) is the ultimate evil (*On the Trinity* 1.9).

Thus for Novatian and his followers, the ultimate prooftext for refusing reconciliation to the lapsed was Hebrews 6:4–6. For those who have been enlightened but have fallen away, "it is impossible to renew them again to repentance, since they again crucify to themselves the Son of God and put Him to open shame."[47] In contrast, the opponents of this rigorism would point to the parable of the wheat and the weeds (Matt 13). For them, the church should not presume to weed out the lapsed. Assuming the impossibility of salvation outside the church, they reasoned that to refuse reconciliation would be to condemn a person to damnation. The concern was for the individual's salvation.

For the rigorists on the other hand, the concern was for the purity of the church. To excommunicate the impure is to safeguard the chastity of the bride of Christ, and the rigorists would argue that to reconcile the lapsed was doing them no favor, since it gave them false hopes and encouraged them to relax their penance. Novatian expected that the lapsed should endure lifelong excommunication, remaining on the periphery of the church doing penance with no hope of absolution or reconciliation in this life.[48]

When the church of Rome was finally able to elect a new bishop in 251 CE, it would have seemed that Novatian should be the obvious choice. He was without a doubt the pre-eminent theologian of the time, and he was the acting bishop of Rome. But ecclesiology trumped theology, and a pastor was elected over the theologian. Cornelius, who followed Cyprian and who apparently represented the majority of bishops on the issue of the lapsed, became the next bishop of Rome. The rigorists responded by consecrating Novatian as their bishop, and calling him the bishop of Rome in opposition to Cornelius. Novatian would write his shorter treatises as though they were episcopal letters from a bishop who had been removed from his flock.[49]

---

47. Ambrose, *On Penance* 2.2. See also Philaster (Philastrius) of Brescia, the anti-Arian contemporary of Ambrose's Arian predecessor. In his catalogue of heresies, *Diversarum Hereseon Liber* 41, Philaster says that it was because of the rigorist application of this text that the letter to the Hebrews almost wasn't included in the New Testament canon.

48. Cyprian of Carthage, *Epistle* 55.14.

49. Heine, "Cyprian and Novatian," 159. The three treatises were therefore written after 251, probably during 252–257.

After Novatian's consecration, his enemies started rumors meant to discredit him—that his clinical baptism was the result of a demon possession and exorcism, that everyone in Rome had objected to his ordination as a priest, and that during the persecution he had failed to perform his clerical duties out of fear.[50] None of this should be trusted.[51] Novatian tried to gain the support of other metropolitan bishops to assert himself as the legitimate bishop of Rome, but in the end they all sided with Cornelius. Many of his followers stuck with him, however, and the rigorist movement became a schism known as the *Novatianists* in the West and the *Katharoi* ("purists") in the East. The Novatianists began rebaptizing those who had been baptized by non-rigorist bishops during or after the persecution, apparently out of fear that the original baptism might have been performed by someone who had lapsed.[52] The documents *Against Novatian* and *On Rebaptism* would eventually be written against the new movement.

Both the Novatianists and their opponents in the church would have agreed that there could be no salvation outside the one true church. Both sides would also have agreed that the church should not allow the unholy to remain in it. The disagreement was over who the unholy were. For the Novatianists (the rigorists), the unholy are those who commit serious sins. And in fact, the Novatianists after Novatian cultivated an ever-growing list of serious sins that could not be forgiven. For the non-rigorist bishops on the other hand, the unholy are *unrepentant* sinners such as schismatics.[53] They would argue that the

---

50. See the letter of Cornelius preserved in Eusebius, *Ecclesiastical History* 6.43.

51. Papandrea, *Trinitarian Theology of Novatian*, 29–31. See also DeSimone, *Treatise of Novatian*, 3; Heine, "Cyprian and Novatian," 157; and Weyer, "Novatian and Novatianism," 534.

52. Cyprian of Carthage, *Epistle* 72.2. It seems that Novatian advocated rebaptism, however it must have been only a "provisional" baptism, since he would not have rebaptized those who were baptized before the persecution. The evidence of this is in the criticism that he himself was not rebaptized. It is not clear whether Novatian himself had a "Donatist" view of the sacraments (which would have assumed the sacraments were rendered invalid by a lapsed presider), though the later followers of Novatian may have. See Ambrose, *On Penance* 1.7, 2.2. The document *Against Novatian* (*Contra Novatianum*) seems to assume a Novatianist ecclesiology that sounds like Donatism. See Gregory, "Essay *Contra Novatianum*," 567–69.

53. On this point, see the Pseudo-Augustinian *Quaestiones veteris et novi Testamenti*. Pacian of Barcelona argued that the church is not defiled by sinners because only repentant/penitent sinners are reconciled. Only the unrepentant sinner could defile

real unforgiveable sin is to split the body of Christ, especially over a refusal to forgive sin (Matt 6:15). After all, had not even King David been forgiven?[54] Thus both groups would argue that the other group was usurping God's authority and contradicting Scripture.

The Catholic Church, represented by Cyprian in North Africa and Cornelius in Rome, attempted to take the middle way between the rigorists' refusal to reconcile the lapsed and the laxists' desire for absolution without penance.[55] Therefore the tradition of confession, penance, and reconciliation was solidified in the church as part of the aftermath of the persecution.[56]

At this point, it may prove helpful to give an outline of the timeline of events as they transpired during the controversy over the lapsed and the schism of Novatian:

- December 249: The emperor Decius issues the edict commanding sacrifice.[57]
- January 250: Cyprian of Carthage goes into hiding. He had been bishop for less than a year.
- January 20, 250: Fabian of Rome is martyred. The church of Rome could not formally deal with the question of the lapsed until it elected a new bishop, but the persecution prevented the election.[58]
- January 250: Novatian becomes acting bishop of Rome until an election can be held (fourteen months). As acting bishop and chair of the council of priests, Novatian is overseeing, and speaking for, a metropolitan church of about ten thousand Christians in almost fifty congregations. Many of these Christians had denied their faith by making the required sacrifices to protect their property and save their lives.[59]

---

the church, but the schismatic movements are defiled by the very fact of their schism. Pacian of Barcelona, *Epistle* 3.11.

54. Ibid., 1.10.

55. See the *Didascalia* for another example of the Catholic approach and condemnation of those who would refuse reconciliation. Many of the laxists were probably lapsed themselves, hence the desire for quick and easy reconciliation.

56. On the ongoing controversy over rebaptism, see Sage, "Cyprian," 295–335.

57. Burns, "On Rebaptism," 369.

58. Novatian, *Epistle* 1.5, 8 (30.5, 8).

59. Ibid., 2.1, 6 (31.1, 6).

- Summer 250: Novatian corresponds with Cyprian of Carthage on behalf of the Roman church.[60]

- In his *Epistle* 1 (number 30 in the correspondence of Cyprian), Novatian seems to be in agreement with Cyprian. It is best to wait until the persecution is over (when a new bishop of Rome can be elected), then deal with the question of the lapsed in consultation with the clergy and the "remaining faithful laity."[61] Novatian counsels against reconciliation at the present time because premature reconciliation could not guarantee the forgiveness of the lapsed if God is not willing to forgive. Not that the church is the enemy of the lapsed, but it is their physician, and it might be that distasteful medicine is their only hope for cure. The lapsed should not be fighting for reconciliation, as if they have a right to it, they should instead ask to return to the church in humility, showing the sincerity of their repentance by their tears.[62]

- In his *Epistle* 2 (number 31 in the correspondence of Cyprian), Novatian speaks for the Roman confessors (who followed him until it became clear that the other bishops were siding with Cornelius as the legitimate bishop of Rome).[63] At this point, the Roman confessors were in agreement with Novatian that apostasy is the unforgivable sin. The assumption seems to be that reconciling the lapsed would be a slap in the face to the confessors, especially those in prison, and would dishonor the martyrs.[64]

- In his *Epistle* 3 (number 36 in the correspondence of Cyprian), Novatian's rigorist position becomes more hardened as he points to Hebrews 6:4–6 as justification that the lapsed cannot be reconciled. Apparently, by this time, the lapsed are becoming even bolder in their assertion that reconciliation with the church is

---

60. DeSimone, *Treatise of Novatian*, 179.

61. Novatian, *Epistle* 1.5 (30.5). See also *Epistle* 2.6 (31.6). Note Novatian's concern for the opinions of the unlapsed laity. We must keep in mind that these had certainly lost friends and loved ones to martyrdom, and the reconciliation of the lapsed would call that sacrifice into question.

62. Novatian, *Epistle* 1.3, 6 (30.3, 6). See also *Epistle* 2.6–7 (31.6–7).

63. There is some doubt over Novatian's authorship of the second letter, however it is clear that the confessors sided with him at this point. The letter could be a response to Cyprian's *Epistle* 20, or possibly 28.

64. Novatian, *Epistle* 2.6–8 (31.6–8).

their right, based on their belief that they have already received forgiveness in heaven. They may have claimed the absolution of confessors who went on to become martyrs, but Novatian argues that the martyrs could not allow the reconciliation of the lapsed when they are martyrs precisely because they knew that they would have lost their own salvation if they had made the sacrifice. The only remedy is continued penance—this is the medicine—and premature reconciliation would be poison.[65] To discontinue penance would be to rule out all hope for salvation. At this point, Novatian is still giving lip service to the middle way, claiming the church should neither give in to the demands of the lapsed, nor give up hope that God might forgive them.

- Early 251: Decius dies in battle, and the persecution subsides temporarily.
- March 251: Cyprian returns to Carthage, and Cornelius is elected bishop in Rome.[66]
- Cornelius reconciles a group of apostates, which apparently provoked the Roman confessors to side with Novatian.[67]
- Novatian is consecrated bishop by three bishops from southern Italy. The move was apparently instigated by a North African priest named Novatus (who is often confused with Novatian in the early sources). Novatian claims he was forced into it, and accepted consecration reluctantly.[68]
- Novatian begins writing letters to other bishops to gain their support, hoping they will acknowledge him as the bishop of Rome over Cornelius. He accused Cornelius of having obtained a *libellus*

---

65. Ibid., 3.1–2 (36.1–2). This letter is a reply to Cyprian's *Epistle* 35.

66. Eusebius, *Ecclesiastical History* 6.43. Eusebius says that Cornelius was elected by sixteen bishops, however he may be projecting fourth-century practice onto the third century. It is probably the case that Cornelius was elected by the council of priests in Rome, and consecrated by bishops from the surrounding towns.

67. Cyprian of Carthage, *Epistle* 54.3, 55.5–6, 11, 25, 65.1–4, 67.3, 9; Novatian, *Epistle* 1.4 (30.4). See Burns, "On Rebaptism," 395; and Weyer, "Novatian and Novatianism," 534.

68. *Catalogus Liberianus*, in the Chronograph of 354, s.v. *Fabius* and *Cornelius*. Eusebius, *Ecclesiastical History* 6.45; Cyprian of Carthage, *Epistle* 52.2; Pacian of Barcelona, *Epistle* 3.15, cf. 2.3–4, 14.

during the persecution, and of being in communion with bishops who had sacrificed.[69] The latter point probably has some truth to it, based on Cornelius's reconciliation of the apostates. At first Cyprian was not sure whom to support. He may have wanted to side with Novatian based on his correspondence with Novatian and their apparent agreement on the issues.[70]

- April 251: A synod of Carthage excommunicated the rigorists, and ruled on the question of the lapsed based on varying degrees of severity. Those who apostatized by actually making a sacrifice would be expected to perform life-long penance, only to be reconciled at the end of their lives. Those who only acquired a *libellus* could be reconciled with shorter terms of penance.

- May 251: A synod of Rome comes to the same conclusions regarding the lapsed as the synod of Carthage, thus confirming that the church will adopt the middle way between the laxists and the rigorists. Sixty bishops from the area of metropolitan Rome attended the synod. Novatian and his followers were excommunicated, and the bishops who had consecrated him were deposed. The confessors and many others abandoned Novatian at this time, and aligned themselves with Cornelius as the legitimate bishop of Rome.[71]

- July 251: Novatian sent representatives to Carthage in an attempt to get Cyprian on his side, but his representatives were rebuffed. He may also have sent representatives to Alexandria, prompting Dionysius of Alexandria to write to Novatian to abandon his schism, and to other bishops advising them not to side with Novatian.[72] Cyprian and Fabius of Antioch confirm their communion with Cornelius.[73] There may have been another synod

---

69. Socrates Scholasticus, *Ecclesiastical History* 4.28; Cyprian of Carthage, *Epistle* 55.10.

70. Heine, "Cyprian and Novatian," 155, See also Harnack, "Novatian, Novatianism," 200.

71. Eusebius, *Ecclesiastical History* 6.43; Cyprian of Carthage, *Epistle* 55; Burns, "On Rebaptism," 374.

72. Eusebius, *Ecclesiastical History* 6.45, 7.8. See also Stevenson, *New Eusebius*, 232–37.

73. Novatian had thought that he and Cyprian were "united and of one mind in regard to discipline" (*Epistle* 1.1 [30.1]). No doubt he felt betrayed by Cyprian.

in Rome in the fall of 251, at which the excommunication of the Novatianists was reiterated.

- May 252: A certain Maximus was sent to Carthage and installed by the rigorists there as the "Novatianist" bishop of Carthage.

- 253: It has become clear that a resurgence of persecution is imminent. A synod of Carthage rules that those who sacrificed in the last persecution can be reconciled in the face of renewed persecution, in order to prevent them from giving up and sacrificing again.[74]

- 253: Cornelius is arrested and exiled, and dies in exile. Novatian may also have been arrested and exiled at this time.[75] Novatian may have written his three shorter treatises during his time in exile.

- 257: *Against Novatian* is written, possibly by Sixtus of Rome (bishop 257–258 CE).[76]

- Summer 257: The first edict of the emperor Valerian outlaws Christian assembly (including visitation of the cemeteries) on pain of death, and orders all Christian clergy to make the loyalty sacrifices or face exile. Lay Christians faced condemnation to the mines. The edict was not enforced consistently across the empire, however, if Novatian had not been exiled in 253 he was at this time.[77]

- Summer 258: The second edict of the emperor Valerian orders that all Christian clergy should be put to death. Lay Christians would be exiled with the confiscation of their property. Christians of the senatorial and equestrian classes would be stripped of their rank, and if they refused to deny the faith, they would be executed.

---

74. Cyprian of Carthage, *Epistle* 48, 49, 51, 52.

75. Eusebius, *Ecclesiastical History* 7.1; Cyprian of Carthage, *Epistle* 60.1–2. Cf. Novatian, *On Jewish Foods*, 1.

76. Harnack, "Novatian, Novatianism," 198. But see Gregory, "Essay *Contra Novatianum*," 566. Gregory prefers Ambrosiaster as the author, putting the document into the fourth century. Cf. *Against Novatian* 6, 13. Note that the author refers to Cyprian's writings.

77. Keresztes, "Two Edicts," 81–84. See Eusebius, *Ecclesiastical History* 7.10; and Papandrea, *Trinitarian Theology of Novatian of Rome*, 35.

Clergy who had been previously exiled were recalled and executed, including Cyprian, Sixtus, and Novatian.[78]

According to tradition, Novatian was martyred in Rome on June 29, 258.[79] In the early twentieth century, the tomb of a Novatianus was discovered in an anonymous catacomb at the first mile marker outside the walls of Rome on the Via Tiburtina.[80] An inscription on the tomb reads, "Novatian, the Most Blessed Martyr," and indicates that the monument and inscription were set there by a deacon named Gaudentius (see photograph below).[81] It is impossible to know whether this is the tomb of our Novatian, though it is probable.[82] There may have been a Novatianist church at this site (near San Lorenzo Fuori le Mura) until the fifth century, when the bishops of Rome suppressed the Novatianist churches.[83] In fact it was at this time, in the fifth century, that this particular catacomb fell into disuse, suggesting that it may have been a Novatianist catacomb.[84]

---

78. Keresztes, "Two Edicts," 84–95. See Socrates Scholasticus, *Ecclesiastical History* 4.28; Cyprian, *Epistle* 80.1f. Some have argued that Valerian's motivation was economic, i.e., to confiscate the property of the church or of wealthy Christians, however this could not have amounted to enough to affect the problems in the Roman economy.

79. Papandrea, *Trinitarian Theology of Novatian*, 35–38. Cf. Rocco, "La Tomba del Martire Novaziano," 335.

80. Rocco, "La Tomba del Martire Novaziano," 332–33.

81. DeSimone, *Treatise of Novatian*, 7.

82. Rocco, "La Tomba del Martire Novaziano," 332–33, 339–41. According to Anita Rocco, the monument is similar in structure to another tomb from the fourth century, which could indicate that it was the tomb of a later martyr. On the other hand, Novatian's remains may have been taken to the East for a time, or it could be the case that he was martyred in the East and his body was not returned to Rome until the fourth century. However, the most likely scenario is that Novatian was buried in the catacomb shortly after his death, and the site of his burial was embellished by faithful followers in the fourth century. Pacian would say that Novatian is disqualified from being called a martyr since he was a schismatic (based on 1 Cor 13:2–3), however this would not prevent his own followers from calling him a martyr. See Pacian of Barcelona, *Epistle* 2.14–15.

83. Leo of Rome, *Epistle* 12.6.

84. Rocco, "La Tomba del Martire Novaziano," 339.

Novatianists after Novatian

Later Novatianists extended refusal of reconciliation to all mortal sins, probably because they were accused of inconsistency in their forgiveness of some sins and not others.[85] They seem to have been pushed eventually to assert that all sins carried equal weight before God.[86] By the fourth century, there was a Novatianist treatise that claimed there should be no chance for repentance of any post-baptismal sin, and gave the church no authority to forgive mortal sin. It said that by reconciling sinners the church is destroyed.[87]

In 325 CE, the Novatianist bishop Ascesius was invited to the Council of Nicaea, where he signed the creed, confirming that the Novatianists were theologically orthodox, even if they were schismatics.[88] In fact, a canon of Nicaea decreed that the Novatianists should be allowed to keep their buildings and cemeteries, and stated that Novatianist clergy who returned to the Catholic Church could retain their status as ordained, as long as they agreed to reconcile those whom the Catholic bishops would reconcile. In effect, the Council of Nicaea recognized the Novatianists as Christian (orthodox), though not Catholic, creating the precedent of the possibility of separated Christians not in communion with the greater church. In spite of this, the Novatianists were persecuted at times by Catholic metropolitan bishops. In the East, the Novatianists (as Nicenes) would also have suffered along with the Catholic Nicenes under Constantius and his Arian bishops, though without the strength of numbers or the support from the West that the Catholics enjoyed.[89] Ironically, they may have gotten some reprieve under the emperor Julian "the Apostate."[90]

---

85. For Tertullian's list of mortal sins, see Tertullian, *On Modesty* 19. On 1 John 5:16 applied to the concept of mortal sin, see Ambrose, *On Penance* 1.10. See also Daly, "Novatian and Tertullian," 39. Note that, like the other rigorists, Novatianists condemned second marriages as a form of adultery.

86. Ambrose argued against this idea, blaming it on Stoicism. According to him, the church distinguishes sins by their severity. See Ambrose, *On Penance* 1.2–3.

87. See Pacian of Barcelona, *Epistle* 3, which is a refutation of this Novatianist treatise.

88. Socrates Scholasticus, *Ecclesiastical History* 1.10, 4.28. See also Papandrea, *Trinitarian Theology of Novatian*, 40–42.

89. Harnack, "Novatian, Novatianism," 201.

90. Cf. Socrates Scholasticus, *Ecclesiastical History* 7.

Ambrose of Milan is typical of those later bishops who wrote against the Novatianist movement. In his *On Penance*, he argued that the Novatianists had it backwards: in truth there is only one baptism but multiple opportunities for repentance, while they refused reconciliation but rebaptized. Therefore the real unforgivable sin is not the denial of Christ (for even Peter was forgiven of this) but splitting the body of Christ in schism.[91] In their claim of purity, the Novatianists were arrogant and misguided, since original sin prevented even the most holy from claiming purity ("not even an infant of a day old is pure").[92] Pacian of Barcelona would use Novatian's own image against him: if the church is a ship, then schism is shipwreck.[93]

In 383 CE, a council under the emperor Theodosius confirmed the orthodoxy of the Novatianists, and that they were allowed to have their own church buildings, as long as they were outside the city walls.[94] In the fifth century there was a Novatianist church in Constantinople, with a Novatianist bishop named Marcian. However Marcian converted to the Catholic Church and brought many Novatianists with him.[95] There is also a story of a fifth-century Novatianist bishop of Salasia returning to the Catholic Church with his whole community.[96] In the East, Cyril of Alexandria expelled all Novatianists from that city. The West saw the suppression of the Novatianist churches by the fifth-century bishops of Rome. They were already on the decline by the time of Pacian of Barcelona, but the Novatianists were declared heretics in Rome in 412 CE, and steadily pressured until their churches were closed.[97] For almost two centuries the Novatianists had been a movement with its own churches, clergy and even bishops, officially declared orthodox and legally allowed to meet, yet at times persecuted. They all but died out in the fifth century in the West, but survived in some parts of the East until the seventh century.[98] When Novatianists came over to the Catholic Church, it was decided that they did not need to be rebaptized.

91. Ambrose, *On Penance* 2.4.
92. Ibid., 1.1, 1.8 (based on the LXX version of Job 14:4).
93. Pacian of Barcelona, *Epistle* 2.7.
94. Socrates Scholasticus, *Ecclesiastical History* 5.10.
95. Wallraff, "Markianos-Ein Prominenter Konvertit."
96. Leo of Rome, *Epistle* 12.
97. On the decline of the Novatianist movement by the time of Pacian, see Pacian's *Epistle* 29.
98. In the late sixth century, Eulogius of Alexandria wrote a treatise against the Novatianists, demonstrating that he still considered them a presence there.

Entrance to Novatian's Catacomb, Rome.
Photo by the Author

Marker of the Tomb of Novatianus in a Catacomb in Rome:
Novatianus, the Most Blessed Martyr—(placed here) by the Deacon Gaudentius
Photo Pontifical Commission for Sacred Archaeology

3

Novatian: Master of Doctrine

The Problem of Christian Monotheism

THE LABEL "MASTER OF DOCTRINE" WAS GIVEN TO NOVATIAN BY HIS rival, Cornelius.[1] Although Cornelius meant it sarcastically, he acknowledges what everyone at the time knew, that if not for the schism Novatian would have been known as the foremost theologian of his time. In response to the heresies of the day, he had articulated Christology and the doctrine of the Trinity better than anyone else up to his time, making his *On the Trinity* both a summary of the state of the art of orthodox doctrine, and also forward looking. Essentially, Novatian's task in writing was to solve the problem of Christian monotheism. This is the basic question that had dogged the early Christians from the beginning: How do you justify calling yourselves "monotheists" when you worship Jesus?

The Adoptionists had attempted to solve the problem by concluding that God is one because Jesus is not God.[2] In other words, Jesus Christ was the *adopted* Son of God, not the Son of God by nature, and was therefore not really divine. But for the majority of bishops, this would not do because it rejected the divinity of Christ and because it created a practical disconnect between theology and liturgy, since Christ was in fact being worshipped. From Novatian's perspective, adoptionism had created an ontological gap between the Father and the Son by assuming a difference of substance. The Father and Son were not only distinct, they were separate, and different—one the Creator and

---

1. Eusebius, *Ecclesiastical History* 6.43.

2. Novatian considered the Adoptionists the heirs of the so-called Judaizers, seen in the letters of Paul. Novatian, *On the Trinity* 15.2.

the other created. This, for Novatian, was too much distinction, and not enough unity of Father and Son.

On the other end of the spectrum, the Modalists had tried to solve the problem by concluding that God is one because the Son is the Father incarnate.[3] In other words, the Father became the Son, which not only diminished the distinction between the Father and the Son, it also effectively diminished the humanity of the Son. This was also unacceptable because it left humanity without a savior who was truly one of us. From Novatian's perspective, modalism confused and conflated the Father and Son into one, thus implying that the modalist "Trinity" was not a Trinity at all.[4] So for Novatian, modalism has too much unity between the Father and Son, and not enough distinction.

Novatian's solution, building on the accepted conclusions of those who had come before him, was to find a middle way between the extreme distinction (separation) of the Adoptionists and the extreme unity of the Modalists.[5] His task was to describe the Trinity in such a way that the Father and Son would be unified enough to be one God, yet not so unified as to lose the humanity of Jesus Christ (which would mean the loss of humanity's hope of connection with the Divine and ultimately of salvation itself). In other words, Novatian had to answer the question how the Son can be *one* with the Father (John 10:30; 14:9) without being *the same as* the Father (John 14:28). The answer ultimately comes from Novatian's interpretation of the Christ hymn in Philippians 2.

Novatian's Interpretation of Philippians 2:6–11

We have seen that Novatian's predecessors understood the incarnation as a descent. That "the Word became flesh" meant that the divine *Logos* preexisted his human nature, and "descended" to humanity, a convic-

---

3. Novatian, *On the Trinity* 12.9. Here Novatian mentioned Sabellius by name, saying that Sabellius had taught that the Son is the Father.

4. It is important to keep in mind that Novatian does not use the word Trinity (*Trinitas*), so statements about his understanding of the Trinity are meant to be taken with the acknowledgement that Novatian is consciously talking about the concept of the Trinity, yet without using this specific Latin term. Both forms of monarchianism, in their solutions to the problem of Christian monotheism, were in effect rejecting the doctrine of the Trinity.

5. Novatian, *On the Trinity* 11.5, 9, 30.6. See Dunn, "Diversity and Unity," 396.

tion held in opposition to the Adoptionist assumption that Jesus was a mere man who was adopted into an elevated status as God's favorite. On the other hand, the descent of the *Logos* could not be seen as any kind of change that would compromise the immutability of the divine nature of the Son.[6] Therefore, the church had to accept the paradox of incarnation as *descent without change*.

To this end, a certain distinction had to be maintained between the divinity of Christ (which was generally assumed to be immutable) and the humanity of Christ (which had to be born, grow, suffer, and die). But though the reality of the two natures had been affirmed since the first century, it was not yet clear how the relationship between the two natures was to be understood. Just as there had to be a balance of unity and distinction between the Father and the Son, there would also need to be a balance of unity and distinction between the two natures of Christ. As both Tertullian and Hippolytus had shown, the two natures would have to be unified enough to conceive of the second person of the Trinity as one person (not two), but distinct enough to maintain the integrity of each nature, so that the suffering of the human would not compromise the immutability of the divine.[7] Thus the church also had to accept the paradox of a Christ who is both divine and human, one person in which the two natures are *distinct but not separate*.

For Novatian, the key to both of these paradoxes was Philippians 2:6–11 and the concept of *kenosis*, or the "emptying" of the *Logos* in the incarnation.[8] As Novatian saw it, Philippians 2:6–11 affirmed both natures and refuted both extreme heresies. In fact, Novatian is

---

6. Novatian, *On the Trinity* 4.4–7, 12, 15.7, 25.4. Novatian would have accepted his predecessors' assumption that immutability was part of the very definition of divinity. Mutability, on the other hand, would imply corruptibility and therefore mortality. Any change in the divine nature, including suffering, would imply the possibility of an end to the subject's existence. Therefore, immutability and impassibility go hand in hand, though as we will see, Novatian was able to conceive of a *communicatio idiomatum* that allowed the divine nature of Christ to *experience* suffering without undergoing change. Cf. Origen, *Against Celsus* 4.15.

7. Hippolytus, *Expository Treatise against the Jews* 3–4.

8. It should be noted that Origen interpreted the "emptying" of Phil 2:7 more as a reference to the cross than the incarnation, connecting the *kenosis* in v. 7 to what appears to be Paul's gloss on the hymn in v. 8. See Origen, *Against Celsus* 6.15. However, on other occasions, Origen seems to be following Hippolytus in speaking of the incarnation as an emptying of glory. See Origen, *On First Principles* 4.1.32, Novatian, however, focuses on the incarnation as a *kenosis*, not of glory, but of divine power.

the first theologian to fully recognize the importance of Philippians 2 for Christology and the doctrine of the Trinity. Previous writers had touched on this text in passing, but it was primarily to emphasize one nature (usually humanity) against a particular heresy (usually docetism).[9] Novatian, however, seems to see it as a cure-all, devoting what amounts to a complete chapter of his *On the Trinity* to the exegesis of this text. He shows how this one passage can be used to affirm both the divinity and the humanity of Christ.

Against the Adoptionists, Novatian used Philippians 2 to emphasize the divinity of Christ. The Adoptionists' Christ with his acquired elevated status, even if it constituted a form of quasi-divinity as in later Arianism, would not suffice. In fact, the opposite was true; divinity was the prior state of the *Logos*, and it was the human nature that was acquired.[10] Thus the phrase "form of God" in verse 6 is taken to mean the same thing Tertullian meant by using the term *substantia*, that the Son is of the same divine *substance*, or nature, as the Father.[11] This means that the Son is ontologically equal to the Father, or *consubstantial* with the Father, yet for the sake of the mission of salvation, the Son was willing to set aside the equal authority that was his by right of consubstantiality. Given that the Son begins in a state of equality with the Father, the descent of incarnation must be voluntary, since it includes the Son's humiliation and ends with the Son's death. The divine *Logos* emptied himself, he was not emptied by another, since divinity cannot be acted upon.[12] Thus for Novatian, the incarnation as descent necessarily requires a prior state of divinity, which further proves the full divinity of Jesus Christ.[13] The *kenosis*, then, is a voluntary relinquishing of the

9. See Tertullian, *Against Marcion* 1.20, 5.20.

10. Novatian, *On the Trinity* 23.5. The human nature was "assumed" (*susceptum*).

11. Ibid., 22.2. See also Papandrea, *Trinitarian Theology of Novatian*, 268–74. Note that Novatian does use the term *substantia* to refer to the essence of God's nature in *On the Trinity* 7.2, and to refer to the humanity of Christ in 11.1.

12. Cf. John 10:17–18. Although in this context Jesus is speaking of his death, not the incarnation, the principle is the same. For Novatian, this text proves Jesus's divinity, since only one who is divine could die voluntarily. Novatian, *On the Trinity* 21.2. See Papandrea, *Trinitarian Theology of Novatian*, 190–91.

13. By "full divinity" I mean consubstantiality; the divinity is not acquired and is not a lower level of divinity or a divinity of different quantity or quality from the Father. It is a divinity that is natural to the Son. See Novatian, *On the Trinity* 12.3 (since the Son is called "Emmanuel"—God with us—he is therefore God) and 20.7 (since the Son is called "Lord and God of all creation"—he is therefore God).

Son's equal status—not an emptying of divinity, or even glory, but of hierarchical status, which, as we will see, Novatian speaks of in terms of power or authority.[14]

The fact that Christ can grant immortality is further proof of his divinity, and proof that he has not been emptied of it, since he must have it in order to give it. Christ is said to offer eternal life (John 10:27–28), and since only God is eternal only God can offer eternal life (which for Novatian is synonymous with immortality), and therefore the Son is fully divine.[15]

Against Marcionites and other Docetics, Novatian used Philippians 2 to emphasize the humanity of Christ.[16] Not only is Christ the Son of

14. The *kenosis* cannot be an emptying of divinity because that would be a form of change, and would contradict the generally held assumption of divine immutability. For divinity to be emptied or diminished in any way would negate the prior divinity itself. Mutability was considered incompatible with divinity because it was connected to corruptibility and mortality. In other words, whatever can change can also decay and die. As we have seen, Novatian, like most of his time, would have assumed that divinity necessarily implied and included impassibility, incorruptibility, immortality, and eternality. To be divine is to be eternal, and to be eternal requires immutability. Novatian, *On the Trinity* 4.12, 5.5–6, 6.9, 25.4. Note that divinity must also be simplex, for anything that is composite is also corruptible, that is it can break down into its parts. Only that which is simplex is also immutable, impassible, incorruptible, immortal, and eternal. Change, on the other hand, is a kind of death, and implies an ultimate end to the existence of whatever is mutable. Therefore, mutability is mortality, so the divine (which is by definition eternal) must be immutable. Novatian, *On the Trinity* 4.4–7, 9–10. Note that change also implies a beginning to the existence of whatever is mutable. However, if God is understood to be eternal, then God can have no beginning. God must be infinite, in fact this is the very definition of God. Whatever is eternal and infinite is God, whatever is not is not God. The interrelationship between all of these concepts in the definition of divinity is what I call "The Divine Sweater," an interwoven unity of threads where if any one thread is pulled, the whole thing unravels.

15. Novatian, *On the Trinity* 15.7–9. Note that the difference between Jesus Christ and the rest of humanity is that mere humans are not immortal by nature. For Novatian, Adam was not inherently immortal. Unlike some other theologians of the early church, Novatian did not see the fall as the loss of something that belonged to humanity by nature. Rather, he implies that if Adam had been immortal by nature, he would have wandered the earth forever exiled from God's presence as a punishment for his disobedience. See *On the Trinity* 1.12. For Novatian, salvation seems to be a gift, rather than a restoration. Thus salvation requires divine intervention in a way that does affect a change in the nature of humanity (2 Pet 1:4).

16. General anti-Marcionite arguments in Novatian's *On the Trinity* include an affirmation of the goodness of creation and that evil is not part of creation, nor does it come from God. See 1.9, 4.1–3, ". . . evil is that which departs from God." Against gnosticism, Novatian maintains that the assumptions of divine omnipotence and

the Creator God (against a Marcionite or Gnostic rejection of the God of the Old Testament), but he is also truly human.[17] Just as the phrase, "form of God" demonstrates his divine nature and his equality with the Father, the phrases "form of a slave" and "likeness of humanity" demonstrate his human nature and his solidarity with the human race.[18] The term "likeness" does not imply anything less than full humanity. This is clear by the way that Novatian criticized the diminished humanity inherent in Docetic Christology.[19] Even a tangible but ethereal body, which some Gnostics believed Christ had, would not suffice since it would not make him one of us. And if he is not one of us, he cannot save us. Novatian's version of "what is not assumed is not saved" is expressed

---

omnipresence require monotheism, since by definition they leave no room for other deities. See 2.1–2, 4.9. Finally, against the Docetics' favorite verse, 1 Cor 15:50 (flesh and blood will not inherit the Kingdom), Novatian argued that it was the sin and guilt (*culpa*) of flesh that will not inherit the Kingdom, but that this is removed in baptism leaving God's good creation (humanity) without the guilt of sin. See *On the Trinity* 10.9. However, Novatian's terminology is not always consistent. Sometimes he uses the concept of "flesh" to mean human nature, at other times to refer to the human body specifically. For example, see *On the Trinity* 21.10–12, 22.5, where Christ is said to have taken off the flesh in the time between his death and resurrection. It is clear that Novatian does not mean to imply that he stopped being fully human during this time, only that he was out of his body. Later such language would be unacceptable as it would imply something close to Apollinarianism, however this is an example of the imprecision of Novatian's terminology and the fact there was as yet no generally agreed upon technical language for Christology.

17. Novatian, *On the Trinity* 9.1. By "truly human," or "full humanity" I mean that his humanity is not an illusion. Docetics and some Gnostics maintained that Christ only appeared to be human, but was in fact a phantom. Others, including some Gnostics, allowed for a tangible body of Jesus (an "ethereal" body) but still maintained that he was not fully human in the sense of being able to suffer and die. Thus "full" or "true" humanity includes mutability, and implies consubstantiality with the human race, which allows Christ to be in solidarity with humanity and also be the representative of humanity. See *On the Trinity* 11.1. The church ultimately rejected any Christology that left Christ less than fully human because he would not be able to be the representative of humanity.

18. Here "form" is not the same thing as "image." Christ is in the form of God, the rest of humanity is in the image of God, which for Novatian primarily means the human capacity for reason, which is for the purpose of imitating God in Christ. See Novatian, *On the Trinity* 1.8.

19. Novatian, *On the Trinity* 10.3–5. Novatian used the term *figura* to describe the way the Docetics described Jesus as human in appearance only, as opposed to the reality (*substantia*) of his humanity. In asserting the full humanity, Novatian is consistent with Tertullian; see *On the Flesh of Christ* 4; *Against Marcion* 20; *Against Praxeas* 7; and *On the Resurrection of the Flesh* 6.

as, "we would not know salvation in our [Christ] if we could not recognize the solid form of our body [in him]."[20]

If there were any remaining doubt, the blood that Christ shed on the cross also proves Christ's true humanity.[21] That the sacrifice of Christ was voluntary also assumes a human mind and will, distinct from the divine will. The Word did not simply become flesh, as though putting on a disguise, the Word became human, which is also, "the substance of flesh and body . . ." and "the slavery which comes from the faults of the fathers according to humanity."[22] What is required to refute the Docetics' diminished humanity is a full humanity, with all of its weaknesses, humiliation, and suffering—a humanity that is "that frail substance of flesh."[23] Therefore the *Logos* accepted more than just a human body, he accepted the human condition.

Thus Novatian used Philippians 2 to argue for both natures. The phrase "form of God" describes the divine nature, and demonstrates the unity and equality of the pre-existent *Logos* with the Father.[24] The phrase "form of a slave" describes the human nature and demonstrates the distinction between the Father and the Son. Therefore this one passage explains the paradox of John 10 and 14—that the Father and Son and *one*, but not *the same*. For Novatian, the reality of the two natures of Christ means that the person of Christ is both consubstantial with God ("form of God") and with humanity ("form of a slave . . . likeness of humanity"). To deny the humanity of Christ is to be anti-Christ (John 4:2–3). To deny the divinity of Christ is to blaspheme the Holy Spirit (Mark 3:28–30).[25]

However, in order to become human, there are some aspects of divinity that the *Logos* had to set aside. In other words, it would be impossible to be truly human and also be omnipotent or omnipresent, since weakness and limitation are part of the human condition. Prior theologians had apparently struggled with how to understand the *kenosis* in a way that would not diminish Christ's divinity. Tertullian

---

20. Novatian, *On the Trinity* 10.6.
21. Ibid., 10.7.
22. Ibid., 22.6.
23. Ibid., 24.2, see also 14.2–4.
24. Ibid., 15.1–2, 22.2–4, 7–8.
25. Cf. Ibid., 15.11–12.

had speculated that the incarnation was a reduction of divine majesty, or possibly glory.²⁶ However, at best this raises the difficult question of degrees of majesty, and at worst it runs the risk of implying a *kenosis* of divinity. For Hippolytus, the *kenosis* was an emptying of glory.²⁷ However, this seems to contradict John 1:14, and in the end was too vague to be useful as an explanation of the *kenosis*. Novatian was the first to attempt a thorough answer to the question, "Emptied of *what*?"

Novatian knew that Christ could not cease to be consubstantial with God in his incarnation. But full humanity required relinquishing certain assumed aspects of the divine, including omnipotence and omnipresence. The crucial question implied in Novatian's work is how the *Logos* could relinquish these divine aspects without relinquishing divinity itself or experiencing a change in the divine substance. In his solution to the question, he seems to place these aspects, not as attributes in the divine substance, but as properties in the divine persons. This means that the second person of the Trinity, the *Logos*, could temporarily set aside these aspects, or *powers* of divinity, without relinquishing divinity itself or diminishing the divine nature in any way—that is, without being any less divine.²⁸ In other words, for Novatian divine *power* is not synonymous with divine *substance*.²⁹ Therefore, Novatian explained the

26. Tertullian, *Against Marcion* 2.27.

27. Hippolytus, *Expository Treatise against the Jews* 3–4; and *Commentary on Genesis 49:21–26*. Origen seems to have followed Hippolytus.

28. Novatian, *On the Trinity* 2.8-12, 4.6, 11.4, 18.13-16, 31.10-11, 31.22. For Novatian, *powers* refers to effective/creative abilities. See *On the Trinity* 3.6-7. While his terminology overlaps the concepts of effective power and authority, this actually allows him to subordinate the power of the Son to the Father without assuming any ontological inequality. For a possible precedent of divine power as a property of the person as opposed to an attribute of divine substance, see Tatian, *Address to the Greeks* 5, 7.

29. This part of Novatian's solution would not be acceptable for later orthodoxy, since as Augustine would say, God's attributes (including the aspects in question) cannot be distinguished from God's substance. In fact, the doctrines of divine simplicity and inseparable operation, which Novatian accepts in general, when pushed to their logical conclusions, would not allow for the concept of divine attributes that are not also the very definition of divinity and inseparable from the divine substance. Novatian does admit that the divine powers have their ultimate source in the Father, just as the divine substance. See *On the Trinity* 20.8–9, 26.20. See also Ayres, *Nicaea and Its Legacy*, 239–40, 258, 262. Novatian's predecessors had defined the oneness of God in terms of one divine power, thus equating divine power with divine substance. They would have assumed that omnipotence, as well as omniscience and omnipres-

kenosis as an emptying of divine powers, which nevertheless allowed the Son of God to retain full divinity in his incarnation.

Novatian described the emptying in this way: ". . . for the power [*auctoritas*] of the divine Word to be received by humanity, he lowered and humbled himself for a time, pausing for the time being, not exercising his powers [*viribus*], while bearing the humanity which he received."[30] The *Logos* does not actually give up his powers, rather the emptying is a self-limitation in which he simply chooses not to use the powers in question. The terms *auctoritas* and *viribus* are more or less synonyms in Novatian's writing, so we cannot define these words by their context here, but what Novatian is saying is that for the divine nature to "become flesh" the *Logos* temporarily set aside the divine powers.

Since Novatian does not make a distinction between what we would consider the different concepts of "power" and "authority," the incarnation is ultimately also a *kenosis* of authority, in which the *Logos* sets aside his natural equality with the Father and voluntarily takes a subordinate position.[31] The issue of the subordination will be explored

---

ence, were attributes of divinity itself and inseparable from the one divine substance of the Trinity. See, for example, Hippolytus, *Against Noetus* 8. See also Hultgren and Haggmark, *Earliest Christian Heretics*, 148.

30. Novatian, *On the Trinity* 22.8 (my translation). It would be tempting to try to make a distinction between *auctoritas* and *viribus*, as though they refer to two different concepts, but elsewhere Novatian does not make such a distinction between the terms. Here he is saying that the divine attributes in question (omnipresence, etc.) are set aside in order for the divine nature to be circumscribed in the person of Christ. The author's translation of the entire *De Trinitate of Novatian* can be found online at www.Novatianus.info.

31. Novatian follows Tertullian in using *potestas*, *auctoritas* and *vis* as more or less synonymous. For Tertullian, *potestas* could translate both *dunamis* and *exousia*. Thus there is no real distinction between power (as efficient power) and authority (as relational power), since for God it is all the same. See Tertullian, *Apology* 48, and Kearsley, *Tertullian's Theology*, 15, 43n59. However, unlike Novatian, Tertullian does seem to assume that God's powers and God's nature are inseparable, which Augustine will later clarify and expand upon. For Tertullian, divine will is indistinguishable from divine power. See Tertullian, *Against Hermogenes* 15; *Against Praxeas* 10; and see also Kearsley, 16–19, 54, 140. Hippolytus seems to have followed Tertullian in saying that there is only one divine power, implying that is it synonymous with the divine substance. See Hippolytus, *Against Heresies* 8. Tertullian also implies that divine power is synonymous with divine glory, which creates a problem if the *kenosis* is an emptying of glory. See Kearsley, 21. Of course, Tertullian knows that Christ did not empty himself of divinity in the incarnation, but as long as he located omnipotence and omnipresence

in detail below. For now it is enough to say that while the Son of God comes with the authority of God from the perspective of the rest of humanity, the *kenosis* implies that he is in a hierarchically inferior position in relation to the Father.[32]

It is important to note that the *kenosis* is temporary, limited to the earthly life of Jesus. At the ascension the Son of God takes back his powers and, though he does not cease to be fully human (Novatian does not explain how this is possible), he is restored to his place of equality with the Father.[33] During his ministry, the miraculous signs of Jesus are accomplished, not by Jesus's own personal divine power, but by the power of God (or the Holy Spirit) within him.[34] Also during his

---

in the divine substance (making them part of the very definition of divinity itself), he was hard pressed to explain the *kenosis*, which is why Novatian emerges as the first theologian to take it on in any detailed way. Cf. Kearsley, 16, 69. Novatian shows that he understands *potestas* and *auctoritas* as synonymous by using them in a parallelism in *On the Trinity* 17.5; see also 20.8–9, 25.11, and 27.2. He also used *virtus* for God's creative power, in reference to the conception of Christ, in 24.4.

32. Novatian, *On the Trinity* 22.4. Technically, the hierarchy that is implied in the *kenosis* does not originate with the *kenosis*, since as we will see it is based on the logical priority of the Father as the First Cause and ultimate Source of the divinity, and in fact the very existence, of the Son.

33. Although for Novatian the *kenosis* and the incarnation are inseparable, technically speaking they are not synonymous. The *kenosis* is temporary, limited to the earthly life and ministry of Jesus, but ending with his exaltation at the ascension (Phil 2:9–11), at which time the Son is restored to his place of equality with the Father, the equality that he had previously been willing to let go of. The incarnation on the other hand, is not temporary, because Christ retains his human nature eternally in his post-ascension phase. See Papandrea, *Trinitarian Theology of Novatian*, 273. Although the *kenosis* is temporary, the logical priority of the Father as ultimate Source is eternal, and is a personal property unique to the first person of the Trinity as *unbegotten*.

34. Novatian, *On the Trinity* 29.10. Note that the word translated "miracles" is actually one of the terms Novatian uses for power, but this is precisely the point. The "powers" that Novatian's predecessors would have assumed were attributes of the divine substance, and part of the very definition of divinity (including omnipotence, omniscience and omnipresence), Novatian saw as properties of the divine persons. This is how the Son can set aside his own divine powers to become human, yet still have access to the divine power of the Holy Spirit to perform miracles. This would explain why in Matt 24:36 the Son is not omniscient. It would also explain how the disciples could be said to do even greater things than Jesus (John 14:12). After all, Peter walked on water, if only for a moment! Cf. Tertullian, *Against Praxeas* 27. Tertullian does anticipate Novatian in a way when he says that Jesus drove out demons by the Father's authority, not his own. See Tertullian, *Against Marcion* 4.8–9, 24; and Kearsley, *Tertullian's Theology*, 66. This is, of course, based on the biblical concept of the Kingdom of God, with the Son as the Father's ambassador (Matt 21:33–41). Novatian is apparently fol-

earthly life, the evidence of the *kenosis* can be seen in the fact that the divine Son of God was circumscribed, or localized (limited) in time and space.[35] In order to be in one place at a time, the divine *Logos* had to set aside omnipresence. In order to fully experience "the frailty of the human condition," the divine *Logos* had to set aside omnipotence, as well as omniscience (Matt 24:36).[36]

The conclusion at which Novatian is compelled to arrive is that the incarnation requires the subordination of the Son—not only submission to the Father, but submission to the state of humanity, since it would be impossible for Christ to be truly human while being omnipotent and omnipresent. Previous writers (especially Hippolytus) had assumed such a separation of the two natures of Christ that in effect, only the human nature experienced the human condition.[37] For Novatian, however, it is not that simple. For him, even the divine nature experienced the human condition, in ways that will be explored in detail below. For now, the point is that the incarnation demonstrates, and in some ways necessitates, hierarchy within the Trinity.

However, the basis for the hierarchy is not limited to the time of the incarnation, since Novatian saw that the submission of the Son that is manifest in the *kenosis*, while voluntary, is based on a logical priority of the Father over the Son. This priority is due to the fact that the Father alone (as unbegotten) is the First Cause and ultimate Source of all existence, including the existence of the Son and the Spirit.[38] The Son is eternal (there is no beginning to his existence) yet he is also begotten,

---

lowing the apologists, tapping into this relationship between a royal father and son (heir) to find a way to define the relationship between God as Father and Jesus Christ as Son that would allow for both equality and hierarchy.

35. Novatian, *On the Trinity* 11.4. On circumscription as the opposite of omnipresence, see 2.1–11, 4.9. See also Papandrea, *Trinitarian Theology of Novatian*, 324–26.

36. Novatian, *On the Trinity* 11.4–9.

37. For example, Hippolytus had said that it was only the human nature that was circumscribed, but this led to a problem when Hippolytus wanted to affirm that the pre-incarnate Christ was present in the Old Testament theophanies. How could the *Logos* appear to humans in the Old Testament without being circumscribed in time and space? Hippolytus's own answer, the manipulation of creation by the agent of creation, amounts to the theophanies being explained as little more than illusions. Novatian apparently felt this was not a satisfactory solution to the problem, thus he allows that both natures could be localized in time and space. As we will see below, this allows for the designation of Mary as *Theotokos*. See Novatian, *On the Trinity* 17.7, 18.1–2, 11.

38. Novatian, *On the Trinity* 2.3, 3.1, 9.1, 22.4, 31.1, 20. Cf. Ayres, 48.

or generated, so that there is a source of his existence. Thus the priority of the Father over the Son, while not chronological, does mean that the Son is not independent of the Father. The existence of the Son (and the Spirit) is contingent and dependent upon the Father.[39] Therefore the hierarchy within the Trinity is not an ontological or temporal hierarchy, but a logical priority that leads to the voluntary subordination of the Son to the Father's authority.[40] This is explained by Novatian's understanding of what I call the phases of the life of the *Logos*.

Kenosis and the Life of the Divine Word

The Greek apologists had speculated that the divine *Logos* (the Word) could be described as analogous to human speech. A word of speech begins its life as a thought in the mind of the speaker, and only subsequently is it emitted by the mouth. Thus some had attempted to say that the divine *Logos* was originally to be equated with the wisdom of God, existing eternally in the mind of God, but not "coming forth" from God until the creation of the universe, when the *Logos* became the agent of creation. However to varying degrees this had created two specific problems. One is a change in the *Logos*, by which the *Logos* goes from being *in* the Father to being *with* the Father at the point at which he goes from *thought* (wisdom) to *Word*. The other problem is an implied change in the Trinity, specifically that the personal distinction between the Father and the Son is not eternal but has its beginning at the "emitting" of the Word.[41] This implies that God is not eternally a Trinity at all—resulting in something like a form of modalism—but *becomes* a Trinity when the Word is emitted from the Father.[42] Both of these per-

---

39. Novatian, *On the Trinity* 27.12.

40. Novatian, *On the Trinity* 27.2, 12–13, 31.3, 6–15, 18–19.

41. As we have seen, even Tertullian described the generation as an event (albeit outside of time), at which the Son becomes distinct from the Father. See Tertullian, *Against Praxeas* 5–6. To be fair, at the time of Tertullian, it was enough to affirm the fact that the Son was eternal in the past, and thus Tertullian and others (including Origen) used the analogy of the Word beginning as a thought in the mind of God to demonstrate how the Word was eternal. However, this had the effect of diminishing the distinction between the Father and the Son, so that while it affirmed that the Son was eternally pre-existent, it did not go far enough by later standards, since it did not make the Son eternally distinct from the Father.

42. Of course this depends on what one assumes is happening with the Holy Spirit, but the point is that such a move from a kind of modalism to a Trinity would also

ceived changes would compromise divine immutability, and therefore must ultimately be unacceptable. Novatian accepted the idea that the life of the Divine Word may have distinguishable phases, however he knew that such an understanding could not imply any change over time, either in the Trinity or within the second person of the Trinity. In explaining these phases, Novatian at times falls back on the language of the apologists, but at times also advances forward-looking solutions to the question, and thus he lays the groundwork for what would become later orthodoxy.[43]

Phase 1: Eternal Generation

It would have been a given in the early church that Jesus Christ, as Son of God, was "begotten." He is called the "only-begotten" in the Johannine writings.[44] However, it remained unclear exactly what this meant, or how it could be explained in a way that did not raise difficult questions. Arius, building on Adoptionist Christology, would later interpret "begotten" to mean created. Novatian's orthodox predecessors equated the Son's "begottenness" with his generation from the Father, and interpreted the "only" in "only-begotten" as pointing to his uniqueness among humanity. In other words, while the rest of us may be adopted sons and daughters of God, he is the natural Son of God, the Son of God by nature. In fact, the generation of the Son meant that he was consubstantial with the Father. Novatian took what Irenaeus and Tertullian had said to its logical conclusion, presenting generation and consubstantiality as two sides of the same coin, generation necessarily resulting in consubstantiality. What is generated must be of the same substance as the one who generates.[45] In other words the divine Father, in generating the Son, would only generate one who was equally divine and of the same divine substance.

However, before Novatian, the *generation* (or, "begetting") of the Son was also referred to as the *procession* of the Son. The procession had

---

imply a change in the divine substance, thus coming back again to the problem of compromising divine immutability.

43. Note that Osborn says the same of Tertullian. Osborn, *Tertullian*, 134.

44. John 1:14, 18; 3:16, 18; 1 John 4:9.

45. Novatian, *On the Trinity* 11.7, 15.10, 16.7–9, 22.2–5, 23.3, 27.5, 31.3–5, 20. See Tertullian, *Against Praxeas* 8. See also Weedman, *Trinitarian Theology of Hilary*, 187.

been described as the "emitting" of the Word from the Father, when the Word goes from being a thought in the Father's mind to come forth as the agent of creation. But as we have seen, this effectively proposes a change in the divine *Logos* at which time the *Logos* goes from being *in* the Father to *with* the Father. Such a change would seem to negate divine immutability, and therefore the use of the concept of procession as synonymous with generation could not last.[46] Novatian is the first theologian to make a distinction between generation and procession, thus separating the concept of generation from that of the Word's agency in creation.[47]

By separating generation from procession, Novatian was able to explain generation as an eternal state of being, rather than as an event that took place to facilitate the Son's agency in creation. Novatian accepts that the Son "proceeded" from the Father to be the agent of creation, but quite apart from that there is a prior, and eternal, distinction between the Father and the Son that is a function of the generation. Since one does not generate oneself, the Son must be an eternally distinct

---

46. Eventually, the concept of procession would come to be applied to the Holy Spirit to describe the way in which the Spirit's existence is contingent and dependent on the Father, and that the Spirit is consubstantial with the Father, while maintaining a personal distinction between the Father and the Spirit. Thus we say that the Holy Spirit "proceeds" from the Father, or as the Western version of the creed affirms, from the Father and the Son.

47. Novatian did accept that there is a sense in which it could be said that the Word was emitted for the purpose of creation. However, he called this the *procession* of the Word, not the generation of the Word. See *On the Trinity* 15.6, 10, 21.4, 31.2–4. Novatian is making a distinction between *generation*, which is an eternal state of being, and *procession*, which is the extension of the *Logos* as agent of creation. The key to understanding this is in *On the Trinity* 22.4, where Novatian speaks of generation and procession as two different things, "he was generated [*genitus*] and extended [*prolatus*] from the Father." At first glance, this may seem like a redundancy, or some kind of parallelism, but it is not. We can see this because Novatian says that the *Logos* is always *in* the Father, rejecting the change in status that Theophilus implied. (Cf. Irenaeus, *Against Heresies* 2.30.9, 4.20.3, where Irenaeus says that the *Logos* is always *with* the Father.) In chapter 31 of *On the Trinity*, Novatian goes back and forth, speaking of the procession of the Word in verses 2 and 4, but the generation of the Word in verse 3. The use of the term *procession* for the Son would not catch on, since the term would come to be used exclusively for the Holy Spirit, but by finding a different way of describing the Word's agency in creation, Novatian was able to describe the generation of the Word in a way that made it an eternal state of being. See Papandrea, *Trinitarian Theology of Novatian*, 84–86. See also DeSimone's introduction to *On the Trinity* in DeSimone, *Treatise of Novatian*, 17.

divine person. That this distinction between Father and Son is eternal is a correction of earlier thought in which the *Logos* was understood as simply the wisdom of the Father.[48]

Therefore for Novatian, generation means both that the Son is of the same substance as the Father (against the Adoptionists), and also that the Son is eternally distinct from the Father (against the Modalists). Thus the one concept of generation includes both the unity and equality of the Father and Son, as well as the distinction. However, as we have seen, while the generation does not imply a chronological difference (the Father does not *temporally* precede the Son), it does imply a logical priority based on the causality of generation, and the resulting contingent nature of the Son's existence.[49] This relationship of dependency of the Son on the Father will be important for Novatian's Christology, as we will see below. However, for now it is important to note that in the separation of generation from procession, and in the close connection of generation with consubstantiality (which includes both eternal unity

---

48. Unfortunately, Novatian's language is not precise, and at times he falls back on the language of earlier *Logos* Christology. However, even if he inherited some terminology from Theophilus, he does not mean what Theophilus meant. The proof of this is in Novatian's definition of the generation of the Son as an eternal state of being, rather than an event. See Novatian, *On the Trinity* 31.3. Theophilus's way of preserving the oneness of God led to a lack of eternal distinction between Father and Son. Novatian emphasized that the Son's existence is derived, and he would say that while this emphasizes the unity of Father and Son, it also proves the eternal distinction.

49. Novatian, *On the Trinity* 31.14. The unity of God requires that the relationship between Father and Son cannot be chronological. Unfortunately, Novatian's terminology is not refined, so that he can use the word "born" (*nasci*) to refer to any one of the first three phases, including the incarnation. In general, the word means "to originate from another source," and this is the point. The Son has a source (the Father), but the Father has no source. See *On the Trinity* 14.5, 15.7, 26.20–21. See also Dunn, "Diversity and Unity," 407–8, however Dunn seems to be looking for more precision than Novatian's terminology exhibits, on the one hand, yet does not see that Novatian makes the distinction between generation and procession, on the other. Note that Novatian also used *genitum* to refer to the physical birth of Christ from Mary in *On the Trinity* 24.5. Novatian uses the term "born" to refer specifically to generation in *On the Trinity* 15.10 and 26.20. The point is that the use of this term does not imply a beginning to the Son's existence, only a dependence of existence. The Father has no origin, because he is not "born" of (generated from) another source, but the Son has an origin in that he has a source, the Father. This demonstrates the distinction between Father and Son against modalism. As a further example of the lack of precision in Novatian's terminology, he does say in *On the Trinity* 11.2 that the Father generated (*generare*) the Son, "before [*ante*] whom there was nothing except the Father." Here *ante* refers to the logical priority, not a temporal one.

and eternal distinction between Father and Son), Novatian has become the first theologian to articulate the doctrine of *eternal generation*, even if he does not quite name it as such.[50]

50. Novatian, *On the Trinity* 4.5-7, 17.3, 31.2-4, 31.3, 31.16. Other authors who acknowledge that Novatian was in fact the first to articulate eternal generation include DeSimone, *Treatise of Novatian*, 17; and Herbert Moore, ed., in Novatian, *On the Trinity* (1919), 18; as well as D'Alès, *Novatien*, 123-24; Simonetti, "Alcune Osservazioni," 778; and Barbel, *Christos Angelos*, 93. On the other hand, some authors have credited Origin as the first to have eternal generation. For example, see Ayres, *Nicaea and Its Legacy*, 22-24. Ayres says that since Origen equates the *Logos* with God's eternal wisdom, this constitutes a doctrine of eternal generation. While this does imply eternal coexistence, that is not the same thing as eternal generation. If it were, it would be found in several authors before Origen, including Tatian and Theophilus of Antioch, who described an eternal coexistence of the *Logos*/wisdom and Father, yet without the eternally distinct identity of the Son. For it to be true eternal generation, the Son has to be an eternally *distinct* divine person, since it is precisely the generation that constitutes the distinction, and as Tertullian pointed out, without distinction there is no equality. Like Theophilus of Antioch and the other *Logos* theologians, all Origen is really saying is that there was no time when the Word of God did not exist, which is not saying as much as eternal generation. See Origen, *On First Principles* 1.2.2-4, 1.2.8-9. Although Origen may have used the *language* of generation, he says in the same context that the same could apply to human beings. See Origen, *Homilies on Jeremiah* 9.4.5 (from the 240s CE), where Origen seems to approach the idea of generation as a state being. In reality, Origen is following Theophilus, so that generation is still an event, prior to which the *Logos* only exists as the Father's wisdom, though he seems to be saying that the generation is ongoing. Furthermore, for Origen, it is unclear how Christ's pre-existence is any different from the pre-existence of all human souls (note Novatian's critique of those who say that the *Logos* is eternal only in the sense of predestination in the Father's mind). Since Origen apparently believed in the pre-existence of all souls (probably influenced by Clement of Alexandria, *Exhortation to the Greeks* 1, where Clement mentions the pre-existence of human souls, though he probably means only by divine foreknowledge), he implied that humans are begotten by God just as Christ is, which diminishes the uniqueness of Christ. If one allows that he had a doctrine of eternal generation of the Son, one would also have to say that he had a doctrine of the eternal generation of all of humanity. In other words, for Origen, generation equals creation. See Origen *On First Principles* 4.1.1. Even Ayres admits that Origen did not believe the Son was from the essence of the Father, preferring to say that he was begotten of the Father's will. See Ayers, *Nicaea and Its Legacy*, 24, 27, 46; and Williams, 140-41. Cf. Origen *On First Principles* 1.2.6, 1.2.9. This should rule out any possibility that Origen had a doctrine of eternal generation, since eternal generation requires consubstantiality. It is only Novatian's understanding of generation, and not Origen's, that could later be used to refute Arianism. See Origen, *On First Principles* 1.3.5. We have seen that it is highly unlikely that there was any influence of Origen on Novatian, and in any case, the use of eternal generation language in *On First Principles* 1.2.2-4 comes from a post-Athanasian Latin translation by Rufinus. Although the language is post-Nicene, the theology is actually less sophisticated than Novatian. Eternal generation requires eternal distinction of persons, which Origen does not have; see *On First Principles* 4.1.30. In the end, it is likely that Rufinus

Even as late as Tertullian, generation is an event that implies a change in the Son that would compromise immutability.[51] The change could be described as going from internal to external relative to the Father, or at least as going from not yet generated to generated. For Novatian, however, the generation is an eternal state of being. There can be no "before" the generation of the *Logos*. Both the existence of the Son, as well as his personal distinction from the Father, are eternal. Novatian appears to be the original source for the famous Alexandrian motto, "Always a Father, always a Son."[52] The implication is that the existence of the Son (as Son, not simply as God's wisdom) must be eternal, otherwise there would have been a time when the Father was not a Father. Not only would this imply a change in the Son (going from non-existent to existent, or from within the Father to distinct from the Father), but the more problematic point is that it would imply a change in the Father (going from not a Father to a Father). Whereas the Fourth Gospel affirmed that the *Logos* was pre-existent, and Athenagoras and Novatian's other predecessors had clarified that the *Logos* was *eternally* pre-existent, Novatian went beyond his predecessors, and emphasized that the Son was also *eternally distinct* from the Father.

At this point it will be helpful to present a passage from Novatian. Note how Novatian compliments Irenaeus's affirmation that the Son is eternally *with* the Father by his own affirmation that the Son is eternally *in* the Father:

---

has projected eternal generation onto Origen in order to make him more palatable to the post-Nicene reader. Nevertheless, attributing eternal generation to Novatian has become somewhat controversial. See, for example, Ayres, *Nicaea and Its Legacy*, 71–75. Ayres maintains that Novatian does not have a doctrine of eternal generation. However Ayres has not discerned Novatian's subtle distinction between generation and source/origin. Ayres's translation uses the word "born" where it should be "caused," and "beginning" where it should be "source" or "origin." A beginning implies a temporal subordination, not unlike what Arius proposed, however what Novatian is describing is the Son's source, as generation from the Father, the First Cause. And this is precisely the point: the Son is not later in time than the Father, however the Son's existence is dependent on the Father because the Son is begotten (generated/caused) from the unbegotten (ungenerated/uncaused) Father. See Papandrea, "Between Two Thieves: Novatian of Rome," 62–64. The author's translation of the entire *De Trinitate of Novatian* can be found online at www.Novatianus.info.

51. Tertullian, *Against Praxeas* 5–6. See also Dunn, "Diversity and Unity," 406.

52. Novatian, *On the Trinity* 31.3. See Papandrea, *Trinitarian Theology of Novatian*, 337–39. See also DeSimone, *Treatise of Novatian*, 8, 43, 170; and Harnack, "Novatian, Novatianism," 198.

> Therefore, since he has been generated from the Father, he is always in the Father. However, I say "always" in this way; not that he is uncaused, but so that I might demonstrate that His existence is caused. But he who is before all time is said to have always been in the Father. For time cannot be attributed to the one who is before time. Truly he is always in the Father, otherwise the Father would not always be a Father.
>
> And yet the Father also precedes him, since it is necessary that he would be first in order to be the Father, because it is necessary that the one who knows no source should come before the one who has a source, so that the Son would be lower, while at the same time he knows himself to be in the Father, since he has a source, because he is generated. And although he has a source because he is generated, in a particular way he is like the Father in his generation through him, since he is generated from the Father, who alone has no source.[53]

In these two paragraphs, Novatian is describing the two sides of the coin that is generation. The first paragraph describes the fact that the Son is consubstantial and eternal (the unity of Father and Son). The second paragraph describes the fact that that Son's existence is contingent and dependent on the Father as the First Cause and one ultimate Source (the distinction between Father and Son). However, the "precedence" of the Father is not temporal, since if it were that would contradict the first paragraph.[54] Because the Son is divine, he cannot be anything other than eternal. The Son's generation was "before all time," which means more than simply before creation. Therefore, he cannot have a beginning to his existence.[55] In addition, to preserve divine immutability, he also cannot undergo a change, even a change in relationship relative to the Father. Therefore, for Novatian, it would not be enough that the

---

53. Novatian, *On the Trinity* 31.3. The translation and paragraph division is the author's. The author's translation of the entire *De Trinitate of Novatian* can be found online at www.Novatianus.info.

54. The very next paragraph goes on to say, "Therefore, when the Father willed, the Son proceeded from the Father." *On the Trinity* 31.4. This has been misunderstood as a continuing reference to generation, however as we will see below, Novatian has switched to speaking of procession as distinct from generation. Cf. Tatian, *Address to the Greeks* 26. Tatian had said that time does not move, rather we move through time just as we move through space. His point was that time itself is part of creation and does not apply to the *Logos* before creation.

55. Novatian, *On the Trinity* 23.3.

Logos be eternal as the wisdom of the Father. There must also be an eternal distinction of persons. Otherwise (and this is the problem with confusing generation with procession) it could appear that there was no Trinity before the generation/procession, and that God began as a modalist unity only to *become* a Trinity at the generation/procession of the Son.

All of Novatian's predecessors understood the generation as synonymous with (or at least concurrent with) the procession. Novatian, because he separated generation and procession, was able to advance the concept of generation so that it was no longer thought of as an event, but as an eternal state of being.[56] Since the Son is "always in the Father," he has an eternal and unchanging relationship with the Father, which includes both eternal unity and eternal distinction.[57] There is no mutability in either the Son or the Father, or in the Trinity for that matter, since the relationship between Father and Son never changes. The Son does not go from being *in* the Father to being *with* the Father. Rather the Son is always in the Father (and as Irenaeus had said, always with the Father).[58] Thus the eternal generation of the Son from the Father demonstrates both eternal consubstantiality and eternal distinction.

What Novatian is essentially doing is moving away from older *Logos* Christology language, which blurred the distinction of persons in the pre-incarnate and post-ascension phases of the life of the *Logos*. Although Novatian slips back into the older language at times, he understands the generation of the Son not as a change from being *in* the

---

56. Papandrea, *Trinitarian Theology of Novatian*, 337–42.

57. Novatian, *On the Trinity* 31.6–16. In my own original translation, I made the same mistake as is evident in Ayres's translation, where I used "beginning" where I should have used "origin." Verse sixteen should be translated, "his origin is his generation before all time." This clearly refers to the causality/derived existence of the Son, not a temporal beginning. See also *On the Trinity* 18.17. That the eternal pre-existence of the Son is not by predestination only, Novatian clarifies in 16.7–9. The author's translation of the entire *De Trinitate of Novatian* can be found online at www.Novatianus.info.

58. But cf. Ayres, *Nicaea and Its Legacy*, 71. Ayres does not see Novatian's distinction between generation and procession, which leads him to read this as basically the same thing Theophilus of Antioch was saying. However, in Theophilus's description the Son ceases to be *in* the Father in order to become *with* the Father. Novatian has corrected this, allowing for eternal generation as the eternal *in*. See also Ayres, 75, where Ayres comments that Hilary seems to have changed from "a two-stage Logos theory" to eternal generation by the time he wrote his *On the Trinity*. I would argue that this is the result of Hilary having read Novatian.

Father to being *with* the Father, but as an eternal state of being according to which the Son is always *in* the Father (eternally consubstantial) and always *with* the Father (eternally distinct from the person of the Father).[59] This is why Novatian can be said to be the first to articulate eternal generation, since true eternal generation requires eternal distinction.

Phase 2: Procession

Colossians 1:15 presented a problem since "firstborn of all creation" could be interpreted to mean that the Son of God was the first created thing, created at (or just "before") the creation of the universe. In order to argue for the pre-existence of the *Logos*, earlier theologians had interpreted "firstborn" as a reference to the Son's procession. However, as we have seen, since they had not yet made a distinction between the procession and the generation, this solved one problem by creating another. The Son's pre-existence was spared, but at the expense of his immutability. Since Novatian had made the distinction between generation and procession, he was free to interpret "firstborn" as procession without compromising eternal generation.[60] Thus the concept of being "firstborn of all creation" implies an active, not passive, role in creation, and for Novatian it is simply another proof for the pre-existence, and therefore divinity, of Christ.[61]

Novatian described the procession of the Son this way: "when [the Father] himself willed, the Word was brought forth [*natus*] from him as the Son," and, "when the Father willed, the Son proceeded [*processit*] from the Father . . ."[62] Thus there is a sense in which, unlike the generation of the Son, the procession of the Son is an event at which the Son acts as the agent of creation, "the substance of power extended

---

59. Novatian, *On the Trinity* 16.7–9. The fact that the Son is always *with* the Father is implied in *On the Trinity* 31.3 and possibly in 17.3. Since Irenaeus said this explicitly, it is safe to assume Novatian had it in mind.

60. Novatian, *On the Trinity* 15.6–10, 21.4–6. Cf. 22.4 and 31.2. Terms Novatian used for procession are *procedo, prolatus*, and as I have already noted, *natus*.

61. Papandrea, *Trinitarian Theology of Novatian*, 275–76.

62. Novatian, *On the Trinity* 31.2–4. Note that this does not imply that the Word was not the Son before the procession, since in the same passage Novatian says that the Father was eternally a Father.

[*prolatae*] from God" for the purpose of creation.⁶³ The fact that the Son is an "extension" of the divine substance demonstrates the consubstantiality of the Father and the Son (from the eternal generation) but the procession itself demonstrates (at least in Novatian's mind) the distinction between the Father and the Son.⁶⁴ The point is that, for Novatian, this extension does not compromise either the eternal consubstantiality or the immutability of the Son, because both are preserved in the eternal generation. The procession, then, is not a change in the Son's existence, or even a change in the relationship between Father and Son; it is merely an activity of both Father and Son, with the Father as Source and the Son as Agent.⁶⁵

To a certain extent, Novatian was limited by the writings of his predecessors who were considered orthodox. Therefore, at one point he does use the older language of "internal Word" and "emitted Word."⁶⁶ However, the difference between Novatian and predecessors such as Justin, Tatian, and Theophilus is that for Novatian, *Logos endiathetos* is not pre-generation, but assumes eternal generation. Thus the *Logos endiathetos* is the eternally generated (but not yet proceeded) Word, while *Logos prophorikos* is the generated and proceeded Word. Since as we have seen, christological terminology (especially in Latin) is just developing, Novatian may have felt that he was stuck with some of these concepts. This makes him sound a bit contradictory at points, but we can see that he was trying to redefine the terms by his rejection of

---

63. Novatian, *On the Trinity* 31.2.

64. In later orthodoxy, the concept of the Son as an "extension" of the Father would be rejected as leaning toward a kind of modalism that would emphasize the unity of Father and Son to the detriment of the distinction.

65. For Novatian, both unity and distinction are seen here as the unity of Father and Son is demonstrated in the shared activity (inseparable operation) and the distinction is demonstrated in the difference between Source and Agent.

66. Of course Novatian does not use Theophilus's terms, since they are Greek, and he is writing in Latin. However he does seem to accept the concepts they imply to the extent described above. These terms actually predate the theologians who first used them. They come from Stoic thought, which was part of Novatian's background and to a certain extent formed some of his assumptions about God. The concepts seem to have originated with Chrysippus (third century BCE) and come into Christian thought from Philo of Alexandria via the apologists. See Kearsley, *Tertullian's Theology*, 31. Note also that Osborn makes the same case for Tertullian, that he was bound by some older terminology, but advances beyond it even while sometimes using it. Osborn, *Tertullian*, 134.

the analogy of the *Logos* with a spoken word.⁶⁷ Therefore, even while pioneering some concepts, Novatian retains some outdated ways of expressing these concepts.

In any event, it is clear that Novatian was correcting the way the apologists had described the phases of the life of the divine Word, since their description lacked an eternal distinction of persons in the Trinity before the procession. Instead, as we have seen Novatian says that the Son is eternally ("always") *in* the Father.⁶⁸ The Son never ceases to be *in* the Father, which shows that the procession of the Son is not a change per se, but an activity required for creation, in which the Son as agent of creation is, "God proceeding from God."⁶⁹ Therefore, for Novatian, the procession assumes consubstantiality and demonstrates the distinction of persons. Thus, like the generation, it shows both the unity and distinction in the Trinity.

One last point must be made about the procession of the Son. Novatian believed that in the Old Testament theophanies, the proceeded *Logos* could become visible and tangible, and could thus be sent to humanity as a manifestation of God that was circumscribed in time and space. This could be accomplished as a foreshadowing of (in anticipation of) the incarnation. The point to note is that since the divine *Logos* could be circumscribed prior to the incarnation and the reception of a human nature, Novatian had no problem with the idea that the whole person of Christ was circumscribed in the incarnation, including the divine nature.⁷⁰

---

67. Novatian, *On the Trinity* 31.2.

68. Ibid., 31.3–4. The fact that the Son does not cease to be *in* the Father in order to be *with* the Father shows that there is no change in the Son's status.

69. Ibid., 31.5. Here Novatian anticipates the language of Nicaea, "God from God."

70. Papandrea, *Trinitarian Theology of Novatian*, 328. Other theologians, like Hippolytus, had placed the pre-incarnate *Logos* in the Old Testament theophanies, but had found (sometimes elaborate) ways to specifically rule out the circumscription of the divine nature. For Novatian, circumscribability does not negate consubstantiality because for him circumscribability (in the Son) or uncircumscribability (in the Father) is a personal property, not a divine attribute. Cf. Dunn, "Diversity and Unity," 396, where Dunn has not recognized that Novatian places circumscribability in the person rather than in the substance.

Phase 3: Incarnation

The incarnation is concurrent with, and made possible by, the *kenosis*. Although the *Logos* was able to be visible, tangible, and localized before the incarnation, the *kenosis* is neither the procession nor even the passion; it is the birth of Christ.[71] In the incarnation, the divine *Logos* acquired a human nature, which Novatian describes as, "the Word of God has put on the substance of flesh."[72] By this he means that the *Logos* has taken on not just the appearance of flesh, and not just a "garment" of flesh, but the *substance* (or nature) of flesh, that is, a full human nature. In the incarnation "the divinity of the Word is in him, mixed together [*permixta*] with matter" ("bodily substance").[73] We will explore Novatian's understanding of the relationship between the two natures in detail below, but for now it is enough to note that the incarnation is the point of meeting of the divine and human natures of Christ, and, through the person of Christ, the nexus of the reconciliation and ongoing relationship of humanity with God.

Phase 4: Exaltation

The fact that the divine nature pre-exists the human nature, and that the human nature is acquired, means that the incarnation is a descent. Therefore the exaltation of Christ, which is described in the latter part of the Christ hymn (Phil 2:9), is a restoration to the prior position of the *Logos* (John 6:62).[74] For Novatian, the exaltation takes place at Christ's ascension, even though the universal acknowledgment of his authority (Phil 2:10–11) waits until the final judgment. In the descent, the Word united with flesh (humanity), in the ascent, the Word takes flesh (humanity) to the heavenly realm.[75] As we will see, Novatian saw in this an image of a groom coming to wed his bride and then take her to his

---

71. Technically speaking, it would be the conception of Christ at the annunciation, however Novatian does not make this distinction. The birth of Christ and his reception of a human nature are treated as one event. See Papandrea, *Trinitarian Theology of Novatian*, 272–73, 328.

72. Novatian, *On the Trinity* 21.14, 20. See also 22.6, 24.5–7.

73. Ibid., 11.1.

74. Ibid., 13.4, 14.6.

75. Ibid., 14.16–17.

home. In this image, the groom is the divine nature and the bride is the human nature.

The name that is above every name is the name of God.[76] Though he has never ceased to be divine, he is proclaimed God when he takes up again what he had laid aside—the divine powers of omnipotence and omnipresence.[77] This means that neither the incarnation nor the exaltation imply a change in the divine Word that would compromise divine immutability. Though he acquires a human nature in the incarnation, the divine nature is unchanged. The exaltation also maintains an unchanged nature, since both natures are retained in the ascension. Thus it is clear that the exaltation does not diminish the distinction between Father and Son. Just as the Son is more than simply a thought in the Father's mind before the procession, he is not "reabsorbed" into the Father after the ascension.[78] The distinction of persons is eternal, maintained by the fact that the Father alone is the Source of generation and procession, as well as the fact that once the Son receives a human nature he retains it eternally. On the other hand, the exaltation is also not a reward for obedience or an elevation to a status not earlier held.[79]

The Relationship of the Father and Son: Dynamic Subordination

Consubstantiality: The Father and I Are One

As we have seen, Novatian believed that generation and consubstantiality are interdependent, such that each assumes and requires the other.[80]

76. Ibid., 22.10. It is not simply the name of Jesus (Phil 2:10), it is the confession that he is *Lord* (verse 11) that implies divinity.

77. Novatian, *On the Trinity* 14.7. For Novatian, Christ's omnipresence in his post-ascension state (based on Matt 18:20) further proves his divinity. Note that the divine name cannot be fully comprehended, since that would be a form of mental circumscription; *On the Trinity* 4.10.

78. In the past, Novatian has been criticized for having a doctrine of "reabsorption" after the ascension. However, this is a misunderstanding of Novatian's attempt to describe what would later be called *circumincessio*, or *perichoresis*. The passage in question is Novatian, *On the Trinity* 31.19–22. See Papandrea, *Trinitarian Theology of Novatian*, 344–49.

79. Novatian, *On the Trinity* 22.10. In asserting this, Novatian is simply following the anti-Adoptionist argument of his predecessors, especially Hippolytus.

80. Papandrea, *Trinitarian Theology of Novatian*, 329–36.

Nature must beget the same nature, so that "whoever is from God is believed to be God," and "whatever the Father is, the Son is . . ."[81] Because he is eternally in the "form of God" (Phil 2:6), and since form equals substance, there is an identity and equality of the substance of the Son with that of the Father.[82] Thus the consubstantiality of the Father and Son is affirmed, not least as evidence of the divinity of the Son against the Adoptionists.[83]

Consubstantiality assumes inseparable operation, the doctrine that all divine activity is accomplished by all three persons of the Trinity. More than just the agent of creation at some time in the past, the Word of God continually "does all of the Father's works."[84] Consubstantiality also requires appropriation, the conviction that whatever can be said of the Father must also be ascribed to the Son ("whatever the Father is, the Son is . . ."). However, there are exceptions to the doctrine of appropriation, which are required to maintain the distinction of persons and avoid modalism. For example, the Father cannot be circumscribed, but the Son can.[85] Novatian speaks of this in the context of the Old Testament theophanies as well as the incarnation. The Son may be visible, as the "angel" or messenger of the Father, however the Father could never be visible, for no one can see God and live (Exod 33:20; John 1:18).[86] Also, the Father alone is the ungenerated First Cause and Source of all being, while the Son's existence (though no less eternal) is derived. In other words, the Father is *unbegotten*, while the Son is *begotten* and *incarnate*. Therefore Novatian qualifies his statement, "whatever the Father is, the

---

81. Novatian, *On the Trinity* 11.7, 22.2–4, 27.5. Cf. Dunn, "Diversity and Unity," 405.

82. Novatian, *On the Trinity* 22.4. See also 31.2 and 31.20, in which the procession is described as the extension of the divine substance. Although the latter passage is disputed, it is clear that Novatian did not question Tertullian's understanding of a single divine substance shared by the three persons of the Trinity. See Dunn, "Diversity and Unity," 405.

83. Novatian, *On the Trinity* 15.10, 16.7, 31.3, 31.20.

84. Ibid., 12.2, 22.3, 27.7–9. Note that the doctrine of inseparable operation refutes the only distinction between persons of the Trinity that modalism allowed, the distinction of function.

85. Ibid., 18.2–3, 13, 31.10–11. Note that the incomprehensibility of the Father (as opposed to the Son) is a function of the Father's uncircumscribability, in that comprehension is a kind of mental circumscription.

86. Ibid., 18.8–9, 16, 19.3.

Son is . . ." by adding, ". . . although the distinction remains, so that the one who is the Son is not the Father, because the one who is the Father is not the Son."[87]

Voluntary Submission: *The Father Is Greater than I*

The divinity of the Son is *equal to* the divinity of the Father, however it is also *derived from* the divinity of the Father, as a function of the generation.[88] This means that there is a logical priority of the Father as the one and only Source of the divine substance, a priority that maintains the distinction of persons even while affirming the consubstantiality.[89] Novatian recognized that just as consubstantiality was required to refute adoptionism, some distinction of persons was also required to refute modalism.

The most famous modalist in Novatian's time was Sabellius, whom Novatian mentioned by name in *On the Trinity*.[90] Modalists, or *Sabellians*, interpreted John 10:30 and 14:9 as though the Son was the Father incarnate.[91] However, according to Novatian, Sabellianism makes the Father circumscribed in time and space.[92] In general, the blurring of the distinction between the Father and the Son would compromise the immutability of the Father and diminish the humanity of the Son. Therefore, Novatian described the relationship of the Father and the Son as "a union [*concordiam*] of partnership [*societatis*], not a unity of person."[93] In other words, the Father and Son are *one*, but not *the same*.

---

87. Ibid., 27.5.
88. Ibid., 22.5–6. See also Papandrea, *Trinitarian Theology of Novatian*, 270–71.
89. Novatian, *On the Trinity* 16.2–3, 6, 8.
90. Ibid., 12.9.
91. Ibid., 28.2, 28.30.
92. Ibid., 12.7.

93. Ibid., 27.3–4, 6. Note that the Father and Son as two persons counts as two witnesses (John 8:17–18). Novatian also used the analogy of Paul and Apollos as two persons with agreement of purpose, however the analogy breaks down in that they have different functions (planting/watering), which could end up sounding like the very modalism (as functionalism) that Novatian is trying to refute. In emphasizing the distinction of persons, this analogy could also make Novatian sound Nestorian. However, note that he could be interpreted as sounding Nestorian when he is arguing against the Modalists, and Apollinarian when he is arguing against the Adoptionists. This shows that he was working toward a balance of unity (consubstantiality and in-

Novatian, like his predecessors, assumed that any Old Testament conversation that seemed like God was talking to himself was in reality a conversation between the Father and the Son.[94] For Novatian, this was a proof of the distinction of persons and a refutation of modalism. Novatian tends to reserve the term "God" for the Father and use the term "Lord" for the Son, though he is not always consistent, perhaps because he does not want to create a dichotomy that would call into question the full divinity of the Son.[95]

At this point, Novatian has a bit of a problem. Taking the equal divinity of the Father and Son with the distinction between persons, it might appear as though we have lapsed into a form of polytheism. In fact, this would be Arius's critique in the fourth century—that it seemed like the theologians had turned Father and Son into divine Brothers, making two Gods. Therefore, just as the distinction of persons was required to refute modalism, Novatian perceived that some form of hierarchy was required to preserve monotheism.[96] Novatian's solution to this problem is to emphasize the logical priority of the Father as First Cause and ultimate Source. Since the Father alone is the one Source of generation and procession, the Father alone is the one Source of divine authority, which maintains the oneness of God. Therefore the Son is the "second person after the Father." He is God, but not a second God.[97] As the apologists and earlier theologians had before him, Novatian assumed a hierarchy within the Trinity in which the Father took the first position, the Son took the second position, and the Holy Spirit took the third position.[98]

The biblical basis for this hierarchical distinction between the Father and the Son is John 10:36—that the Son was "sanctified and sent

---

separable operation) with a distinction of persons, and that he also saw that the arguments of each extreme alternative Christology would cancel out the other extreme.

94. See, for example, Gen 1:26, "Let *us* make . . ."; Gen 19:24; Ps 110:1; and Isa 45:1 (with the standard patristic misinterpretation of Cyrus as Christ).

95. In *On the Trinity* 9.1, Novatian calls Christ, "our Lord God." In 10.3 he uses the term "Lord" to refer to the Father. In 18.22, he uses the word "God" to mean divine, in reference to Christ.

96. Novatian, *On the Trinity* 27.2, 13, 31.18–19.

97. Ibid., 26.2–3.

98. See, for example, Irenaeus, *Proof of the Apostolic Preaching* 51.

into the world" by the Father.⁹⁹ For Novatian, the fact that the Son was "sanctified" (*sanctificationem*) means that his divinity is derived from the Father by generation. The fact that the Son is "sent" means that he has voluntarily taken a subordinate position as a Messenger, in which he will defer to and enforce the Father's authority rather than his own. In deference to the logical priority of the Father as the ultimate Source of divinity and divine authority, the Son volunteered to be the Father's Messenger in the world (cf. Matt 21:37–38). Thus *sanctified and sent* means derived and subordinate.[100]

However, this subordinate position as the Father's messenger does not contradict the equality affirmed in Philippians 2:6. Novatian makes a subtle and innovative distinction between the divine substance and what he refers to as "origin." With regard to substance, the Father and Son are equal because generated existence necessarily results in consubstantiality. But with regard to "origin," the Father and Son are not equal, since the Son as generated has an origin (he is begotten) and a cause (the Father), but the Father has no origin and is uncaused (unbegotten).[101] The Father alone is unbegotten, or ungenerated, which gives the Father hierarchical priority. This causal priority gives the Father a higher authority, even though the Son's substantial equality means that he defers to the Father's authority voluntarily.[102] He could theoretically "cling to"

99. Novatian, *On the Trinity* 27.12. Novatian does not interpret *sanctificationem* as later Arians might, as though it means the Son's divinity is *received*, only that the Son's divinity is *contingent*. I am not entirely happy with my own translation of Novatian's use of this passage as "he receives holiness." Knowing what Novatian meant, it is difficult to find an English phrase that conveys the idea that the holiness (divinity) of the Son is dependent on that of the Father, without implying that there was some *event* in time at which the Son received holiness, and before which the Son either did not exist or existed without this holiness. The author's translation of the entire *De Trinitate of Novatian* can be found online at www.Novatianus.info.

100. Papandrea, *Trinitarian Theology of Novatian*, 271–72.

101. Novatian, *On the Trinity* 2.3. Note that the Father is, "outside the limit of time." Time is a limit, a constraint, so the Father's timelessness is a function of his uncircumscribability. See *On the Trinity* 2.5, 4.10, 31.11. As further evidence of Novatian's distinction between substantial (ontological) equality and hierarchy of authority, note that he says words may be able to express God's powers (*virtutem*), but not God's essence, *On the Trinity* 2.6–8. In the end, even contemplating God comes up short, as "the sharp mind suffers in every thought about God, and it is affected all the more by considering God to the point where it is blinded by the light of its own thought." *On the Trinity* 2.10.

102. Novatian, *On the Trinity* 27.12–13, 31.3, 18–19. See Papandrea, "'Between Two Thieves': The Christology of Novatian," 64–73.

his equality and challenge the Father's authority, but he chooses instead to empty himself and become the Father's Messenger in the world.[103]

The *kenosis* is Novatian's key to unlock the paradox of the relationship between the Father and Son, in which there is both equality and hierarchy. Unlike his predecessors, Novatian allowed that Christ could set aside divine *power* (i.e., refuse to cling to equality and empty himself), yet without relinquishing his divine *nature* (or substance).[104] Therefore the Son could remain "fully God" without being confused with the Father.[105] The fact that the Son's divinity (and his very existence) is generated means that his divinity is the same divinity as the Father and thus he is substantially (ontologically) equal to the Father, while at the same time it also affirms the Father's logical priority as the one and only First Cause and Source of all being.[106]

In order to refute the Adoptionists, Novatian had emphasized the unity of the Father and Son in terms of substantial equality. At the same time, he refuted the Modalists by emphasizing the distinction between the Father and Son in terms of the roles of Sender and Messenger.[107] However, describing the relationship between Father and Son in terms of these roles does not imply a modalist functionalism, since Novatian assumes inseparable operation.[108] Thus the roles of

---

103. Novatian, *On the Trinity* 31.22.

104. Ibid., 22.8. Tertullian did not distinguish divine substance from divine power, and in fact this aspect of Novatian's Christology would not catch on in the long term. However, Tertullian had said that Christ did not cast out demons by his own powers in *Against Marcion* 4.8–9, 24, and this is Novatian's implied answer to the question of how Jesus could perform miracles in his ministry if he had set aside his divine powers. The miracles he performed were done by the power of the Holy Spirit, the same Holy Spirit available to the apostles (cf. John 14:12).

105. Novatian, *On the Trinity* 23.3.

106. Ibid., 31.1, 3. The dependent and contingent existence of the Son (and, by implication, the Holy Spirit) relative to the Father is somewhat based on Tertullian's analogy of the Father and Son as the sun and its rays. As rays from the sun cannot be distinguished from their source (one cannot tell where the sun ends and the rays begin), yet the rays would not exist without the sun, the Son of God is both consubstantial with, and dependent on, the Father. See Tertullian, *Against Praxeas* 9, 14. Note that the Father's priority is a logical priority, not a chronological priority, so that there is no "time" before the generation of the Son. The generation is not an event, but an eternal state of being.

107. Novatian, *On the Trinity* 15.12–13, 16.2–3, 18.8f.

108. Athenagoras had compared the Father and Son to the Emperor and his heir, two persons who share one authority. Novatian's solution is more nuanced, however it could be influenced by Athenagoras.

Sender and Messenger are not really different "job descriptions" since both together accomplish the singular will of God, but rather the roles explain the relationship between the Father and Son, as well as the fact that the Father cannot be visible or circumscribed while the Son can be.

Novatian followed his predecessors in pointing to the Old Testament theophanies as tangible examples of the pre-incarnate *Logos* descended to the earth as the Father's Messenger. Since the Greek word for "angel" (*angelos*) simply means "messenger," any appearance of an "Angel of the Lord" could be the pre-incarnate Christ. Especially in those cases where the Angel of the Lord speaks for God in the first person, the implication is that this Angel of the Lord could not be a mere angel, in the sense of a created spiritual being. Based on the promises (or threats) made in the name of God, and on the fact that in a few instances the Angel of the Lord is apparently worshipped, it was concluded that this Angel must be divine.[109]

However, this Angel could not be the Father, since the Father is uncircumscribable, and so cannot be localized in time and space, let alone be tangible so as to eat and have his feet washed.[110] Therefore, given the interpretation that the Angel of the Lord is God but not the Father, the only possibility left is that this is a pre-incarnation manifestation of God the Son. Novatian does not clarify exactly how the Son can be circumscribed and tangible before the incarnation, but this is not the point. He has the luxury of accepting what his predecessors had already assumed. He simply emphasizes that when we are told in Scripture that no one can see God and live (Exod 33:20), it is a reference to the Father specifically (cf. John 1:18). Therefore if one is seeing God, it cannot be God the Father but must be God the Son, the only person of the Trinity who can be visible.[111] As we have seen, Novatian

---

109. Novatian, *On the Trinity* 18.19–20. The fact that Jacob wrestled with God (Gen 32:24–31) would have to mean that he had actually wrestled with Christ. See *On the Trinity* 9.3, 19.2, 7–8, 12–13. Note that the reference to Jacob striving "with God and with man" is interpreted as a reference to the two natures of Christ. Novatian calls the pre-incarnation appearance of the *Logos* to Jacob a "sacred mystery" (*sacramentum*). Later, at the blessing of Jacob's sons, his crossed hands is also called a "sacred sign" (*sacramentum*), and it is interpreted as a foreshadowing of the cross of Christ, *On the Trinity* 19.16–20.

110. Novatian, *On the Trinity* 17.7, 18.11, 16, 19.2–3.

111. Ibid., 18.2–3, 6f, 19.7, 13, 31.10. It is implied that the ability of the pre-incarnate *Logos* to be circumscribed, visible and tangible is still a function of the incarnation, even though it comes chronologically before the birth of Jesus. See 19.6.

has made uncircumscribability (i.e., omnipresence) and invisibility into personal properties rather than attributes of divine substance.[112] This means that the second person of the Trinity can set these properties aside and accept the limitations of circumscription and visibility without relinquishing his divinity.

The end result of speaking of the Son as "Angel" is that the roles of Sender and Messenger are parallel to uncircumscribability/circumscribability and invisibility/visibility.[113] The circumscribability and visibility of the Son, if not a direct result of the *kenosis*, are in some way a function of the incarnation, and therefore constitute a *descent* to the world of humanity.[114] The *Logos*/Angel/Christ is sent to humanity as Messenger. But as Messenger, he must necessarily take a subordinate position relative to the Sender, whose message he brings. The Father could never be called "Angel," but the Son can be (though only voluntarily).[115] This distinguishes the Father and Son on the level of person, rather than in terms of function, so that even the "roles" of Sender and Messenger are not really the point of the distinction; the point is the difference in personal properties (that the Son *can* be localized and visible while the Father *cannot*) and the relationship between the two, characterized by the voluntary submission of the Son to the authority of the Father.

Dynamic Subordination

In my 1998 doctoral dissertation[116] I coined the term "dynamic subordination" to describe Novatian's solution to the problem of Christian monotheism and the relationship of the Son to the Father. Novatian described the Son of God as ontologically equal (consubstantial) while also hierarchically subordinate to the Father. Both are a function of the generation, since generation results in the same substance but different origin.[117] The distinction also requires hierarchy to prevent the perception of polytheism, but the consubstantiality requires that the

---

112. Ibid., 18.13.
113. Ibid., 18.8.
114. Ibid., 19.6.
115. Ibid., 19.3.
116. Papandrea, James L. "'Between Two Thieves': The Christology of Novatian." The dissertation was later published in its entirety as *The Trinitarian Theology of Novatian of Rome: A Study in Third-Century Orthodoxy* (2008).
117. Novatian, *On the Trinity* 31.12.

hierarchy be voluntary on the part of the Son.[118] Against adoptionism, the subordination is not ontological because the generation of the Son results in consubstantiality. Furthermore, eternal generation necessarily includes coeternality. Against modalism, the person of the Son is eternally distinct from the person of the Father because the Son's eternal generation from the Father demonstrates an eternal distinction of persons. Eternal generation also necessarily implies a derived causality, resulting in the logical priority of the Father and the ability of the Son to set aside certain personal properties (or powers, including omnipotence, omniscience, and omnipresence/uncircumscribability/invisibility) in order to become human. The *kenosis*, as we have seen, is an emptying, or more precisely a temporary setting aside, of the Son's personal powers in order to experience the human condition. But it is also a voluntary submission to the will of the Father, taking on the role as the Father's Messenger, subordinate in authority to the Sender for the time of the *kenosis*.

The subordination of the Son to the Father is therefore not ontological (as it would be in the case of adoptionism); it is *dynamic*, meaning that it is a hierarchy of power or authority. It is an "arrangement of the order of power [*potestatis*]" relative to the authority (*auctoritate*) of the Father.[119] For Novatian, it is the (always voluntary) obedience of the Son to the Father that preserves the oneness of God, since the Father remains the one divine authority and the Source of the Son's power/authority.[120] Therefore, what Novatian's Greek predecessors had called the "economy" of the Triadic God, Novatian calls an "arrangement of order" (*ordine dispositae*), an administrative ranking that is both manifest externally (in the Old Testament theophanies and in the incarnation) and as internal relationships within the Trinity (in the voluntary obedience of the Son to the Father).[121] However, given the assumption

---

118. Ibid., 22.5–6, 12, 31.6–9. Novatian uses each point to prove the other in a kind of chicken-and-egg circular argument, but the point is that he is holding together the ontological equality with a hierarchy of authority.

119. Ibid., 27.2; see also 22.8. Note that for Novatian, there is not a strict distinction between power and authority. He uses the terms interchangeably.

120. Ibid., 31.15, 20. Note that the Son must be of lower rank than the Father because of the Father's logical priority. Logical precedence results in the right of higher authority (cf. John 1:15). See Papandrea, *Trinitarian Theology of Novatian*, 301.

121. To apply later distinctions of *economic* and *immanent* to the Trinity would be anachronistic. For the early theologians, the hierarchy of persons is called an *economy*,

of inseparable operation, the purpose of describing this ranking is not to assign different functions to the persons of the Trinity, but primarily to clarify that the unity of substance in the Trinity does not imply that the Father is the Son (modalism) and that the divinity of the Son does not imply that he is a second God (polytheism).[122]

Therefore *dynamic subordination* is a subordination of authority, not of substance. A subordination of substance (an ontological subordination) would be a form of adoptionism, while no subordination at all would be either modalism or polytheism. Novatian knew that the question was not *whether* the Son was subordinate to the Father, but *how*. Refuting the heresies that Novatian saw as a threat to orthodox doctrine required both a distinction of persons and a hierarchy of authority. But on the other hand, since his subordination is not ontological, Novatian also avoided adoptionism.[123] The unity and equality of the Father and Son is expressed in the doctrine of eternal generation, while the distinction between the persons is expressed in the dynamic subordination of the Son to the Father. By keeping this careful balance of unity and distinction within the Trinity, Novatian had brought pre-Nicene theology and Christology to its point of furthest development. He had successfully synthesized the orthodox theologians who had come before him, but even more, he had advanced doctrinal thought beyond them, and in doing so he anticipated the solutions of the ecumenical councils.[124]

---

which is both internal and external to the Trinity. Cf. DeSimone, "Holy Spirit," 68–69. In fact, there is both unity and distinction internally (in the relationships between the persons of the Trinity) and externally (in the Trinity's relationship with humanity). Internally, the unity is in the consubstantiality and the distinction is in the difference of source, that is, the difference between unbegotten (the Father is uncaused and has no source) and begotten/proceeding (the Father is the Source and the existence of the Son and Spirit is contingent and dependent on the Father). Externally, the unity is in the inseparable operation and the distinction is in the difference of omnipresence/circumscription (visibility). See Osborn, *Tertullian*, 121, 123. Note also that Osborn points out the "administrative" nature of the hierarchical distinctions in Tertullian.

122. DeSimone, "Holy Spirit," 68–69.

123. Novatian, *On the Trinity* 31.3. Note that the subordination is also not a temporal/chronological distinction.

124. Note that Brent makes the same claim for Hippolytus. Brent, *Hippolytus and the Roman Church*, 238.

Novatian's Trinity Anticipates Nicaea and Constantinople

To be clear, Novatian never used the word *Trinitas*, probably because it was not in his Bible. In the mid-third century, Trinitarian doctrine does not yet have a technical terminology. Novatian is of course influenced by Tertullian, and he does accept Tertullian's definition of one substance, three persons. However even this has not yet become standardized language.[125] At times Novatian seems to be willing to experiment with terminology, suggesting multiple synonyms to try to make the sheer volume of the words describe that which he knows cannot be described by human language.[126] Sometimes he seems to be throwing out words like spaghetti at a wall, to see what will stick. He appears to coin some new Latin terms, such as *se exanire* (for "he emptied himself") and *incarnatus* (for "incarnation").[127] However, it is impossible to know which of these apparently new Latin words were already in his Bible, or in the Roman creed.[128] For these and other reasons it is always problematic to try to assess a theologian by later standards of orthodoxy, and yet we can see that at least for the West (and as I will argue below, for the East as well) Novatian has paved the way for Nicene orthodoxy.

For Novatian, orthodoxy is the middle way between the extreme heretical positions.[129] He claimed that the true Christ (the orthodox Christ) was being crucified again between the two thieves of modalism and adoptionism.[130] The first two ecumenical councils of Nicaea (325 CE) and Constantinople (381 CE) dealt more specifically with Arianism, the fourth-century evolution of adoptionism. The Arians had emphasized the distinction between Father and Son to the point of an ontological separation, and thus (from the perspective of the orthodox) they had effectively dismantled the Trinity by denying the full divinity of the Son and proposing a Christology of ascent. After the Council of

---

125. Papandrea, *Trinitarian Theology of Novatian*, 58–61.

126. As I will explore below, Novatian applies terms related to marriage to the union of the two natures within Christ.

127. Novatian, *On the Trinity* 24.7.

128. Papandrea, *Trinitarian Theology of Novatiane*, 60–64.

129. Ibid., 361–65. Dunn later made this same observation, see Dunn, "Diversity and Unity," 396.

130. Novatian, *On the Trinity* 30.6.

Nicaea, the same arguments were applied to the Spirit, whose divinity was denied by some. While the stated question at issue at the Council of Nicaea was whether the Son was coeternal with the Father, the real question behind the question was whether the Son was to be described in terms of a Christology of descent or of ascent. A Christology of descent assumes that the *Logos* started out divine and acquired humanity in the incarnation (thus the *kenosis* of Phil 2). This was, of course, Novatian's understanding, and the position that would continue to be defined as orthodox after the council. A Christology of ascent assumes that Christ acquired divinity, and in the case of Arianism it was a lower degree of divinity than the Father. The Arian Christ was therefore *between* God and humanity, while the orthodox Christ was *both* God and human.

As we have already seen, Novatian's Christology includes both consubstantiality and eternal generation. Each assumes the other as the generation results in consubstantiality and the consubstantiality requires that the generation is eternal.[131] Novatian himself used the phrase "God from God," which would find its way into the creed.[132] The creed's famous *homoousios* (of the same essence/substance) was meant to affirm both the consubstantiality and the coeternal existence of the Father and the Son, in the same way that Novatian understood the two concepts to be interrelated. As Novatian had stated, whatever the Father is, the Son is (but the Son is not the Father).[133]

Novatian's *kenosis* Christology was an affirmation and explanation of the Christology of descent. In fact, for Novatian, the *kenosis* proves the Christology of descent, since the *Logos* starts out divine and acquires humanity when he does not cling to his equality with the Father.[134] Novatian notes that by the time of the incarnation, the *Logos* was already

131. Ibid., 15.10, 16.7, 31.3, 20.
132. Ibid., 22.5.
133. Ibid., 27.5.
134. Ibid., 14.17, 15.1-2, 22.6-8. See also 11.8, 13.4-5, 14.17. For the translation of Phil 2:6 with the sense of "cling to," see Grillmeier, *Christ in Christian Tradition*, 21. Defining the incarnation in terms of the *kenosis* means that the divine nature of Christ is prior to the human nature, that is, that Christ started out "filled" (cf. Col 2:9) and had to be "emptied" to become human. In other words, if he had to be emptied in order to become human, then he must have started out as more than human. If one assumes, as Novatian apparently did, that there could be no degrees of divinity, then "more than human" necessarily means divine. This is the meaning of the Son's original state as being in the "form of God."

accustomed to descending, since he had descended to humanity in the Old Testament theophanies.[135] Thus the *kenosis* assumes both natures in Christ, the divine nature being consubstantial with the Father and the human nature consubstantial with humanity.[136] For Novatian, this explains how the Son can be truly and fully divine without being confused with the Father, and without creating two Gods. The divine nature's consubstantiality with the Father ensures that there is only one God, and the human nature's consubstantiality with humanity demonstrates the distinction that the Son is not the Father. In other words, the consubstantiality of the divine nature refutes adoptionism (and Arianism), and the consubstantiality of the human nature refutes modalism (and later, by implication, monophysitism). That the pre-existence of the *Logos* is not by predestination only (an apparent concession of Arius), Novatian clarifies, "Christ has existed *in substance* before the creation of the world."[137] Therefore the *kenosis* and the Christology of descent are proof for Novatian of the full divinity of the Son, a divinity equal with the Father.[138]

With regard to the Holy Spirit, Novatian clearly taught the divinity of the Spirit. Because the primary heresies of his day were christological, it is natural that Novatian would not spend as much time on the Holy Spirit as he does on the Son (the direct discourse on the Holy Spirit is only one chapter in *On the Trinity*). Some have speculated that Novatian may have downplayed the role of the Spirit to avoid appearing as a Montanist.[139] However, this is not necessary, since Novatian says more about the Spirit than would have been required to refute the alternative Christologies of his own time.

---

135. Novatian, *On the Trinity* 18.2. Novatian also mentions the "descent" of the manna in the wilderness as a type of the incarnation (cf. John 6:51). *On the Trinity* 11.8, 14.14.

136. The consubstantiality of the Son's human nature with humanity is strongly implied in Novatian, *On the Trinity* 11.1.

137. Ibid., 16.6–7; emphasis mine. It is not clear at whom this clarification was aimed, though this does become an issue in the Arian controversy. It may have been a response to a precursor of Paul of Samosata, or possibly it was aimed at something Novatian heard from Origen. If Christ were pre-existent by predestination only, this would eliminate his uniqueness among humanity.

138. Novatian, *On the Trinity* 15.1–2, 22.7–8, 12.

139. Dunn, "Diversity and Unity," 403.

Like his predecessors, Novatian says that the Holy Spirit inspired the prophets and the apostles. This is important to refute a Marcionite separation of the Old and New Testaments. Novatian affirms, against this docetic rejection of the Old Testament, that it is the *same* Holy Spirit who inspired the prophets and the writing of the gospels.[140] The Spirit, "defined the sacred mysteries of the gospel . . ." and is "the revealer of divine things."[141] The Holy Spirit is therefore the "Spirit of Truth" (quoting John 15:26), who proceeds (*procedit*) from the Father.[142] In fact, Novatian implied that the Spirit also proceeds from the Son, anticipating the Western addition of *filioque* to the creed, and demonstrating how the anti-Adoptionist argument naturally leads to double procession.[143]

The divinity of the Holy Spirit is demonstrated in the Spirit's role in the regeneration of baptism. If part of the proof for the divinity of Christ is that he is able to grant eternal life, it is assumed that the Holy Spirit is also divine because he "works a second birth . . ."[144] In addition, the Holy Spirit is said to be the power behind healings and miracles (*virtutes*). Novatian is speaking specifically of healings and miracles in the church, though it is implied that the Spirit is also the power behind the miracles of Christ (since he has set aside his own personal divine powers in the incarnation).[145] Thus it is clear that Novatian treated the Holy Spirit as uncreated and consubstantial with the divine essence, yet a distinct divine person.[146]

Just as the Son is of equal divinity as the Father yet with a hierarchy of authority, so the Holy Spirit is "lower than Christ."[147] Just as the Father is the Sender of the Son, and the Son is the Father's Messenger,

140. Novatian, *On the Trinity* 29.6, 9.

141. Ibid., 29.9.

142. Ibid., 29.7.

143. Ibid., 29.6–11. This is based primarily on Jesus's words about the Holy Spirit in the Gospel of John. The Latin term *filioque* is translated "and the Son," and is included in the Western version of the Nicene creed as a way to emphasize the equality of Father and Son against adoptionism/Arianism.

144. Novatian, *On the Trinity* 29.16.

145. Ibid., 29.10. Note that Tertullian had said that the Son and the Spirit are the two hands of God, extensions of the divine substance. See Tertullian, *On Baptism* 1–2. No doubt Novatian assumed the consubstantiality of the Holy Spirit.

146. DeSimone, *Treatise of Novatian*, 17–18.

147. Novatian, *On the Trinity* 16.3.

so the Spirit is the Messenger of the Father and the Son, and thus the hierarchy is complete. Using the Roman patron-client relationship as an analogy, Novatian further describes the Holy Spirit as the patron (*patrocinio*) of believers.

Novatian's Christology Anticipates Ephesus and Chalcedon

The relationship of the two natures in the person of Christ was not yet the subject of major debate in Novatian's time, but it would become the focus of the controversies that led to the councils of Ephesus (431 CE) and Chalcedon (451 CE), the third and fourth ecumenical councils. While it may seem anachronistic to ask whether Novatian anticipated the decisions of these later councils, it is clear that the conclusions of later orthodoxy were built on the foundations of the orthodoxy of the second and third centuries. The fact that Christ had a human and a divine nature had been assumed by the major extant theologians since the second century, and indeed the assertion was based on first-century apostolic writings. As he did with consubstantiality, the Christology of descent, and the divinity of the Holy Spirit, Novatian passed on (in a newly clarified way) concepts that he inherited from his predecessors, including what would come to be called the *hypostatic* or personal union. And as he did with eternal generation, Novatian also pioneered concepts that would be important for refuting later alternative Christologies (heresies), specifically the concepts of *communicatio idiomatum* (the communication of idiomatic properties between the two natures) and *circumincessio* (also called *perichoresis* or "reciprocity").

In accepting Tertullian's term *persona* to describe the three persons of the Trinity, Novatian also accepted that the second person of the Trinity is *one* person. Yet this one person is both fully human and fully divine. Thus there are two *substances*, or natures, within the one person. Novatian described the human nature as "the frailty [*fragilitas*] of the body."[148] But this is more than the weakness of flesh, it is the fragile existence that is the human experience. In his humanity, Christ is in solidarity with us, because he is consubstantial with us.[149] The divine

---

148. Ibid., 14.4–5.

149. Ibid., 11.1. Novatian uses the term *substantia* to speak of the humanity of Christ.

nature of Christ, on the other hand, is, "the divinity of the Word," which "is not from this world."[150]

Where Novatian goes beyond his predecessors is in the way he describes the union of the two natures within the one person. This union is more than a mere juxtaposition, it is an interrelatedness in which the two natures affect each other, yet without compromising the immutability of the divine nature. For Novatian, the two natures are "humanity and God reciprocally associated."[151] The person of Christ is, "God in union [*sociato*] with human frailty [*fragilitas*]."[152] Rather than simply assign Scripture passages that speak of humiliation to the human nature and passages that speak of glory to the divine nature (as his predecessors had done), Novatian's understanding of the incarnation as a *kenosis* that included the circumscription of the divine nature allowed him to have all passages apply to the whole person of Christ.[153] Thus Novatian is the first extant author to articulate the doctrine of *communicatio idiomatum*.[154]

---

150. Ibid., 14.4–5.

151. Ibid., 24.11.

152. Ibid., 25.3.

153. Papandrea, *Trinitarian Theology of Novatian*, 313–18. Of course, Novatian does use certain texts to affirm the humanity against docetism and other texts to affirm the divinity against adoptionism, however he does not have the strict segregation of passages that earlier writers seemed to think was required to protect the immutability of the divine nature.

154. DeSimone, *Treatise of Novatian*, 43. See also Mattei, Novatien Précurseur," 460, 464–65. However, there is some evidence that Callistus of Rome was teaching an early form of *communicatio idiomatum*, which Hippolytus did not understand, and to which he objected, as it sounded to him like a form of modalism. See Hippolytus, *Refutation of All Heresies* 9.7. Some have claimed that Origen taught *communicatio idiomatum*, however although he did say that the human nature is made immutable by the divine nature, he never says that divine nature receives anything from the human nature (in fact this would contradict the very point he was trying to make in the passage in question). See Origen, *On First Principles* 2.6.6. Origen gets this from Clement of Alexandria; see *The Instructor* 3.1, where Clement says that the humanity is granted incorruption and immortality. But this is exactly the point. Novatian is the first to articulate a true *communicatio idiomatum*, since Clement's and Origen's *communicatio* only works in one direction, while Novatian's is a two-way *communicatio*. There is also the later question of whether *communicatio idiomatum* requires the communication of properties from one nature to the other nature, or whether it is enough to say that properties of each nature are communicated to the whole person of Christ (for example, see Kereszty, *Jesus Christ*, 268). However, it remains unclear what it would mean for the human nature to effect the whole person of Christ without also effecting

Although Novatian does not name it as such, he described the *communicatio idiomatum* as a mutual sharing between the two natures of Christ.[155] Of course Novatian follows his predecessors in describing the ways in which the divine nature "elevates" the human nature, and leads to the sanctification of the human nature. Novatian says, "gradually and by increments human frailty had to be brought up through the image toward that glory, so that at some time it might be able to see the Father."[156] Thus our own salvation (immortality) depends on the *communicatio* because the divine nature of Christ grants immortality and incorruptibility to the human nature on our behalf.[157] Novatian further states, "the frailty and limitation of the human condition is strengthened, improved and raised by him, so that at some time, one may also be able to see God the Father himself."[158] What he is saying is that the divine nature of Christ raises up the human nature of Christ and, because of his consubstantiality with humanity, he thereby also raises up humanity in general, so that a humanity that at one time could only see God the Son will someday see God the Father.

However, for a true *communicatio idiomatum* it is not enough that the divine nature affects the human nature; the human nature also affects the divine nature, although of course without compromising divine immutability.[159] For Novatian, the union of natures means that the divine nature experiences humility, "when he descends to injuries and insults, when he hears unspeakable things, experiences disgraceful things . . ."[160] Therefore, while the divine nature "loans" *immortalitas* to the human nature, it also "borrows" *fragilitas* from the human nature,

---

the divine nature. In any case it seems clear that Novatian's understanding is the most advanced, and more fully anticipates the Chalcedonian Definition.

155. Novatian, *On the Trinity* 13.5.

156. Ibid., 18.3. See Papandrea, *Trinitarian Theology of Novatian*, 67–71.

157. Novatian does not seem to have believed that Adam was created immortal, so that the immortality of the human is not a restoration to an original state, but an elevation to a new level at which a connection with the Divine is possible. Thus the very possibility of human contact with God has as its nexus the *communicatio idiomatum* in the person of Christ.

158. Novatian, *On the Trinity* 18.5.

159. That the *communicatio idiomatum* does not compromise the immutability of the divine nature. See Novatian, *On the Trinity* 24.7–11, 13.5, 18.5, 22.6, 9.

160. Ibid., 22.9. Here Novatian is building on Irenaeus and his understanding of the atonement as an exchange (cf. Gal 3:13–14).

a "frailty" that is a necessary part of the incarnation if the Word is to be fully human.[161] A few short samples of Novatian's text will suffice to demonstrate the point:

> ... through the mutual connection the flesh carries the Word of God and the Son of God accepts the weakness of flesh.... And for that reason, the frailty and limitation of human circumstance is strengthened, improved [and] raised by him ... by being born he received the substance of flesh and body, the slavery which comes from the faults of the fathers according to humanity. At that time he also emptied himself, since he did not refuse to take up the frailty of the human condition.... he empties himself when he descends to injuries and insults, when he hears unspeakable things, experiences disgraceful things, yet with such humility comes extraordinary fruit.... so that when the Son of Man clings to the Son of God in the nativity, he might hold, loaned and borrowed by the union itself, what he could not possess from his own nature.[162]

In the person of Christ, each nature receives something from the other: the human nature carries the divine Word of God, and thereby becomes the Son of God, while the divine nature "assumes the weakness of the flesh."[163] Since the incarnation is a *kenosis*, the divine *Logos* accepts the limitations of the human condition, including visibility and circumscription. That the divine nature is visible—far from being an emptying of glory—explains how "we beheld his glory" (John 1:14). That the divine nature is circumscribed lays the foundation for the understanding of Mary as *Theotokos* (Mother of God), since the whole person of Christ, including the divine nature, was circumscribed within the womb of Mary.[164] However, the point for Novatian was that

---

161. Ibid., 24.10.

162. Ibid., 13.5, 18.5, 22.6, 22.9, 24.10 (my translation). Note the language of loaning and borrowing, which allows the divine nature to *experience* the human condition without undergoing any real change that would compromise divine immutability. The author's translation of the entire *De Trinitate of Novatian* can be found online at www.Novatianus.info.

163. Ibid., 13.5, 24.7–11.

164. Novatian does not specifically anticipate the *Theotokos* controversy, however since the divine nature (the *Logos*) was able to be circumscribed in the Old Testament theophanies, it is no problem for Novatian to see the divine nature circumscribed in the incarnation. In fact, he assumed that at least by divine foreknowledge the human nature of Christ was also present in the Old Testament theophanies, so that in a way both

the whole person of Christ (not just the human nature) experienced the human condition.

Technically speaking, the Son of God became the Son of Man by *taking* flesh (active), while the Son of Man became the Son of God by *receiving* the Word (passive).[165] However it is important to note that in the transaction each nature "becomes" something it was not before. By the incarnation and the reception of the Word, the human nature (the Son of Man) became the Son of God.[166] By the descent and the *kenosis*, the Son of God received (*suscepit*) the Son of Man and "became flesh."[167] Thus "Son of God" actually refers to the whole person of Christ, both natures. Although Novatian does sometimes fall back on the earlier distinction of "Son of God" as the divine nature and "Son of Man" as the human nature, when he wants to be precise he refers to the divine nature as the "Word of God," so that the incarnation could be expressed as an equation: The Word of God (divine nature) plus the Son of Man (human nature) equals the Son of God (the person of Christ).[168]

The point is that the *communicatio idiomatum* is a union of the two natures that is more than mere juxtaposition (as Nestorianism would later imply) and yet is not the creation of an alloy (as monophysitism would later imply).[169] Novatian understood that the connection

---

natures are present and circumscribed in both cases, the pre-incarnate theophanies and the incarnation. See *On the Trinity* 19.13. The point is that by the *communicatio idiomatum*, the divine nature of the Son is circumscribable, which (though Novatian does not take this step) would allow the whole person of Christ to be circumscribed in the womb of Mary. It is important to note that although the title *Theotokos* is a title that refers to Mary, the controversy and its implications were really all about Christology.

165. Novatian, *On the Trinity* 23.7.

166. Ibid., 24.7–8, 10.

167. Ibid., 24.10. While Novatian accepts John 1:14 as evidence of the divine *Logos* taking up a full humanity, he does not use the language of "becoming" with reference to the divine nature, presumably to avoid the problem of contradicting the immutability of the divine nature. The use of such language here runs the risk of appearing to compromise immutability, but it is important to keep in mind that for Novatian, this "becoming" is not a change per se, but something that each nature "borrows" from the other. This idea of loaning and borrowing, though Novatian only seems to use these terms in passing, makes it possible to understand the *communicatio idiomatum* in a way that allows the divine nature to *experience* the limitations and humiliations of the human condition, without actually suffering change.

168. Papandrea, *Between Two Thieves*, 59–61.

169. Tertullian had clarified that the union could not imply a confusion of natures. See Tertullian, *Against Praxeas* 27. See also Osborn, *Tertullian*, 140.

of the divine with the human in the person of Christ is what made the reconciliation of the human race with God possible. He knew that a real union must be maintained to preserve that connection with the divine, but also that some distinction between the natures must be maintained so that full humanity is not lost (which would also result in the loss of the divine-human connection). Thus Novatian worked to describe a balance of unity and distinction, just as he did with the persons of the Trinity, now he does with the two natures of Christ. They are one but not the same, distinct but not separate. Just as dynamic subordination was the middle position between adoptionism and modalism, the *communicatio idiomatum* navigates the middle way between a Nestorian separation of natures and a monophysite confusion of natures.[170] The *communicatio idiomatum* also assumes that both natures together are the "second person after the Father," and so it affirms and requires a personal (*hypostatic*) union.[171]

Novatian described the union of the two natures in Christ as a marriage of humanity and divinity. We have seen that Novatian was not afraid to experiment with multiple synonyms to explain concepts, and in this case he used terms that would have been familiar from the context of Roman marriage. Marriage was described in Roman law as both a joining (*iunctio*) and a partnership (*consortium*).[172] This is how Novatian saw the two natures—unified and yet with a distinction that retained the integrity of each nature.[173] Just as the Trinity must be simultaneously *one* and *three*, the person of Christ must be simultaneously *one* and *two*.

---

170. Cf. Grillmeier, *Christ in Christian Tradition*, 401. The *communicatio idiomatum* almost becomes a doctrine of appropriation for the two natures of Christ, in the sense that what is proper to one nature can be said to be *experienced* by the other nature.

171. Novatian, *On the Trinity* 26.2–3, 31.5. See Papandrea, *Trinitarian Theology of Novatian*, 318–19.

172. Grubbs, "'Pagan' and 'Christian' Marriage," 363, 371–73, 378. Tertullian wrote of marriage in *To His Wife* 2, however he does not seem to have used the marriage terminology to describe the union of natures. Novatian may have gotten the idea from reading Tertullian. See Hunter, "Augustine and the Making of Marriage," 68–69.

173. In *On the Benefit of Purity* 5, Novatian described marriage as "a natural bond uniting both in complete harmony." Novatian describes the unity (a uniting bond) while maintaining the distinction of the two individuals (a harmony of both).

In *On the Trinity*, the descent of the incarnation is compared to a groom coming to claim his bride. The divine Word descends from his own realm to claim the human nature to which he is united. In the ascension, then, the divine nature takes the human nature back to his home, with the result that Christ does not cease to be fully human after his life and ministry on earth. The connection between the two natures is mutual (*connexoinem mutuam*), which reinforces the *communicatio idiomatum*.[174]

A survey of terms Novatian used to describe the union of the two natures reveals no less than seventeen Latin words, many of which would have been used to describe the marriage union as one that created a new unity but left the integrity of the two individuals intact:

- *Adhaeret* (cling to), *On the Trinity* 24.10–11.
- *Annectit* (tie, connect, bind), *On the Trinity* 24.8–10.
- *Assumit* (taking up), *On the Trinity* 24.8–10.
- *Concordia* (harmony, unity), *On the Trinity* 21.7–8, 24.10–11. Lactantius later used this term in reference to marriage.[175]
- *Concretum* (compounded), *On the Trinity* 24.10–11.
- *Confoederatum* (united), *On the Trinity* 21.7–8.
- *Confibulatio/confibulo* (clasp together, unite, bond), *On the Trinity* 23.7, 24.10–11. Novatian's use is the first extant appearance of this form.[176] It includes the connotation of interaction between the two natures that is assumed in the *communicatio idiomatum*.
- *Coniunctionem/coniunctum* (a joining/joined), *On the Trinity* 16.4, 21.7–8. Novatian also uses this term to speak of marriage in *On the Trinity* 10.5. Lactantius would also use it.[177]

---

174. Novatian, *On the Trinity* 13.5. Note that Novatian implies that in the post-ascension phase, the human nature becomes omnipresent, a further gift of the *communicatio idiomatum*, which balances the circumscription of the divine nature during the time of the incarnation.

175. Lactantius, *Divine Institutes* 3.22.9. See Grubbs, "'Pagan' and 'Christian' Marriage," 371, 396. See also Papandrea, *Trinitarian Theology of Novatian*, 90–93.

176. Loi, "La Latinità Cristiana Nel De Trinitate Di Novaziano," 151–52. See also Papandrea, *Trinitarian Theology of Novatian*, 92–93.

177. Lactantius, *Divine Institutes* 3.22.9, 6.23.17–30. See Grubs, "'Pagan' and 'Christian' Marriage," 396–98, and also 407 for the similar term *coniugi*. Tertullian used *coniungere*. Tertullian, *Against Praxeas* 8. See Osborn, *Tertullian* 142.

- *Connexum/connectens/connexione* (joined, connected, connection), *On the Trinity* 21.7–8, 23.7, 24.8–11.
- *Contextum* (united), *On the Trinity* 24.10–11.
- *Copularet* (join together), *On the Trinity* 23.7.
- *Foederis* (mutual unity), *On the Trinity* 24.10–11.
- *Iunctio/iunxit* (joined), *On the Trinity* 24.10–11. Marriage was considered a *dextrarum iunctio*, a joining of hands.[178] In Tertullian, divorce is *disiunxit*, from *disiungere*.[179]
- *Permixtio/permixta/permixtus* (mixture, combined), *On the Trinity* 24.8–10, 25.3–5. This term has the connotation of mutual interaction. For Novatian it meant not simply a juxtaposition, but also not a confusion or loss of distinction.[180]
- *Rapit* (take hold), *On the Trinity* 24.8–10. This is the same word Novatian's New Testament uses in Philippians 2:6 to describe the *kenosis*—that the Son did not *cling to* his equality with the Father but was willing to let go of it in order to become human.
- *Sociasse/sociata/sociavit/sociatum/sociato/sociatus* (combined, associated, united), *On the Trinity* 21.7–8, 24.8–11, 25.3–5.
- *Transducit* (drawn together), *On the Trinity* 24.8–10.

For Novatian, the incarnation *is* the union of the two natures. The incarnation is a mystery (*sacramenti*) and the union itself is a "mysterious sacred sign," which results in our salvation.[181] It is the "joining together" (*coniunctione*) of Word and flesh.[182] Both natures (or

178. Grubbs, "'Pagan' and 'Christian' Marriage," 371.

179. Tertullian, *On Modesty* 1. The context is Tertullian's complaint against those who would forgive "adultery" (as divorce was understood to rigorists such as the Montanists), thus for Tertullian, the disuniting of the marriage bond was grounds for excommunication.

180. Papandrea, *Trinitarian Theology of Novatian*, 95–97. But see Dunn, "Diversity and Unity of God," 398–99. Dunn thinks Novatian's phrase *connexione sua et permixtione sociata praestat* would not have been acceptable by Chalcedonian standards because he sees in it a confusion of the natures. However, see Mattei, "Novatien Précurseur," 463. Note that Novatian also uses this term to clarify that the two natures are not mixed up (*permixtam*) and are not confused (*confundens*).

181. Novatian, *On the Trinity* 23.8, 24.9–10.

182. Ibid., 14.4. That "flesh" means full humanity, as opposed to the human body only, see 14.2–4. The voluntary nature of the subordination of the Son to the Father

substances) are combined (*foederasse*) into one unity (*concordiam*), humanity and divinity joined (*iunctus*) and connected (*copulates*).[183] Yet the two natures are not so united that they cease to be distinctly two, since the two substances remain, and the person of Christ is "one harmony (*sociatum*) of both substances."[184] Here Novatian anticipates the Chalcedonian definition in that he clarifies that the two natures are one without being confused; mixed but not mixed up.[185] The natures are unified enough to allow for *communicatio idiomatum*, but not so unified that either nature is diminished. Thus the personal (*hypostatic*) union and the *communicatio idiomatum* go hand in hand because the union of natures is a mutual ("two-way") connection.

What the *communicatio idiomatum* is to the two natures of the person of Christ, *circumincessio* (*perichoresis*, or reciprocity) is to the relationship of the three persons of the Trinity. It is a mutual interrelatedness, often described as an orientation, or even motion, toward the Trinity. In other words, each of the three persons of the Trinity is oriented back toward the unity. This is manifest in *inseparable operation*, the assertion that no person of the Trinity acts alone. But even more than this, all activity of the Trinity, though it may be directed toward humanity, has as its ultimate goal a motion back toward and into the Trinity, presumably bringing humanity along, the end result of which is ultimate reconciliation. For Novatian, the Father is in the Son (John 14:10–11), but as we have seen the Son is also eternally in the Father.[186] The Father alone is the one Source of divinity, but the Son shares this same divinity by virtue of his generation and consubstantiality. Therefore all divine activity ultimately comes from the Father as the

---

implies that Novatian assumes a human will (rational soul) in Christ. In this he follows Hippolytus, who affirmed the human soul in Christ. See Hippolytus, *Against Noetus* 17; *Against Beron* 8.

183. Novatian, *On the Trinity* 13.3, 15.4–5.

184. Ibid., 24.11. As we will see below, this anticipates the language of Leo of Rome's *Tome* (the letter in support of Flavian), which contributed to the terminology of the Chalcedonian definition. See Leo I, *Letter* 28.5. Cf. Tertullian, *Against Praxeas* 27.

185. Novatian, *On the Trinity* 24.9.

186. Ibid., 31.3. Novatian's understanding of this "reciprocity" of the three persons of the Trinity can also be seen in his treatment of the Holy Spirit. The Holy Spirit is sent out by the Father (and the Son), but in the end everything is oriented back to the Father. For a possible influence on Novatian in the direction of *circumincessio*, see Athenagoras, *Plea for the Christians* 10.

one Source of authority, and the Son's obedience to the Father means that all divine activity is oriented back toward the Father as First Cause.[187]

In summary, Novatian's *On the Trinity* assumes or explains the major concepts important to Nicene-Constantinopolitan orthodoxy: consubstantiality, eternal generation, Christology of descent, and the divinity of the Holy Spirit. Novatian also anticipated the solutions to the christological problems that led to the councils of Ephesus and Chalcedon: the *hypostatic* union, the circumscription of the divine nature, *communicatio idiomatum, circumincessio*, and the balance of unity and distinction in the person of Christ such that the two natures are in union without confusion.

It is important to note the key distinctions that Novatian made, which are essential to understanding his theology. First, Novatian made the distinction between the generation and the procession of the Word, which allowed him to describe generation as an eternal state of being, not an event. In other words, the *Logos* does not go from being *in* the Father to being *with* the Father, rather the *Logos* is eternally *in* the Father and never ceases to be *in* the Father or changes status relative to the Father in any way. Second, Novatian made the distinction between substance and origin, which allowed him to describe the Son as unified with the Father by consubstantiality, yet distinct from the Father by a non-temporal dependency. Third, Novatian made the distinction between divine substance and divine powers (or attributes, conceived as personal properties), a distinction that would not be acceptable to later theologians such as Augustine (they saw it as incompatible with divine simplicity), but which nevertheless allowed Novatian to describe the *kenosis* as an emptying of divine power that did not diminish divine substance. Finally, these distinctions allowed Novatian to solve

---

187. Novatian, *On the Trinity* 31.20–22. For Novatian, holding the Father alone as the one Source of divinity and the one divine authority maintains the oneness of God. Although the conclusion to Novatian's *On the Trinity* has been interpreted by some as describing a kind of "reabsorption" of the Son into the Father (which would amount to a post-ascension modalism), Novatian is actually describing what would later be called *perichoresis*. For Novatian, it is simply a requirement of monotheism that there is only one Source (the Father) and that the other divine persons defer to the one Source. See DeSimone, *Treatise of Novatian*, 18; and Papandrea, *Trinitarian Theology of Novatian*, 362–64. See also Ayres, *Nicaea and Its Legacy*, 246, where Ayres gives his own definition of *perichoresis*. Note that Novatian's description does qualify according to Ayres's definition.

the problem of Christian monotheism by holding both an ontological equality and a dynamic subordination (or hierarchy of authority) of the persons of the Trinity.

Furthermore, in describing the union of the two natures of Christ in terms of a marriage, and especially in pioneering the doctrine of *communicatio idiomatum*, the fact that the divine nature "borrows" frailty from the human nature means that the divine nature can experience the suffering of the human condition without compromising divine immutability. Had Novatian lived in the fifth century, no doubt he would have said that Christ was being crucified yet again, this time between the two thieves Nestorius and Eutyches. Just as he did with the persons of the Trinity in response to adoptionism and modalism, Novatian balanced unity and distinction in the union of the two natures, and navigated the middle way.

4

Novatian's Ongoing Legacy

IT HAS LONG BEEN RECOGNIZED (BUT OFTEN MORE RECENTLY FORgotten) that Novatian was "at least a hundred years ahead of his contemporaries."[1] In spite of comments to the contrary in some patristic surveys, his work was clearly "an improvement over that of Tertullian and Hippolytus."[2] Specifically, we have seen that Novatian was the first extant author to articulate eternal generation and *communicatio idiomatum*, but in other ways, too, he was ahead of his time. In this chapter I will suggest some places where we can see the influence of Novatian in later theologians by focusing on these two doctrines, along with some other unique features of Novatian's thought, such as the importance of Philippians 2 for a two-natures Christology.

However, it would be impossible to prove dependence on Novatian, for several reasons. First, we may claim for Novatian that he "pioneered" certain doctrines that would become important later for defining orthodoxy. But since there were certainly documents before and during the time of Novatian that are no longer extant, some by theologians whose very names have been lost to history, it is impossible to prove that Novatian himself invented anything. This is partly because he does not name these doctrines as such, and sometimes he speaks of them as though they are taken for granted. Of course, part of Novatian's agenda would have been to write as though he was merely relating accepted tradition, so that even if he was conscious of his role as a doctrinal pioneer he would not want to be thought of in that way,

---

1. Jurgens, *Faith of the Early Fathers*, 247, also quoted in DeSimone, *Treatise of Novatian*, 14.

2. Weyer, "Novatian and Novatianism," 535. Even Weyer did not fully appreciate the extent to which Novatian anticipated later orthodoxy; still, he recognized that Novatian was at least moving theology and Christology forward toward the councils.

since often "pioneer" was synonymous with "heretic." Indeed, many of these ideas may already have been "in the air" in Novatian's time, and whether or not he was the first to articulate them in a document that would come to be accepted, he may have learned them from his predecessors. So while Novatian's *On the Trinity* may be the first *extant* document to demonstrate these doctrines, we will never know if he was passing along something he was taught, clarifying (or perhaps correcting) a prevailing view, or truly articulating something new. The *communicatio idiomatum* is a case in point. As we have seen, it is possible that Callistus of Rome taught (or approached) a version of *communicatio idiomatum*, which Hippolytus either misunderstood as a form of modalism or simply rejected, contributing to Hippolytus's critique of Callistus.[3]

Another reason that dependence would be difficult to prove is that Novatian's schism meant later writers would never attribute anything positive to Novatian. After the schism, his *On the Trinity* continued to be read, yet his readers knew him as a schismatic, and many considered him a heretic, if only on principle.[4] Eventually, *On the Trinity* continued to be read under other names, including Tertullian and Cyprian.[5] In the end, the document survived only because it was attributed to other, less scandalous writers. Still, on close examination Novatian has emerged as our best possibility for a theological and christological missing link between Irenaeus, Tertullian, and Hippolytus on the one hand, and Athanasius, Augustine, and Leo on the other.[6]

---

3. Hippolytus, *Refutation of All Heresies* 9.7.

4. Jerome, *Apology against Rufinus* 2.19. Jerome tells his readers that there was already some confusion over the authorship of Novatian's work. See also Jerome, *Lives of Illustrious Men* 70. Although Jerome knows the true authorship of *On the Trinity*, he confused Novatian with Novatus. Note that many of the ancient writers refused to acknowledge the distinction between schism and heresy, on the principle that dividing the body of Christ was the end result of heresy anyway, and was at least as bad.

5. DeSimone, *Treatise of Novatian*, 7. See also Jerome, *Apology against Rufinus* 2.19, where Jerome mentions that Rufinus thought that *On the Trinity* was by Tertullian.

6. Cf. Osborn, *Tertullian*, 116. See also Ayres, *Nicaea and Its Legacy*, 236. Ayres defines pro-Nicene orthodoxy as including eternal generation, inseparable operation and appropriation. Novatian has all of these elements almost a century before Nicaea.

Western Theologians Who Show Evidence of Influence from Novatian

Hilary of Poitiers

Novatian's influence on Hilary of Poitiers (c. 300–368) has been widely noted. It is clear that Hilary had read Novatian, and that many aspects of Hilary's own *On the Trinity* are based on concepts which Novatian advanced.[7] Hilary follows Novatian in emphasizing Philippians 2:6–11 as his primary christological text.[8] Hilary has the concepts of inseparable operation, appropriation, and eternal generation, though the latter is not as fully developed as it is in Novatian.[9] Hilary understands that generation must be an eternal state of being, but he does not seem to see that this requires an eternal distinction of persons.[10] Of course Hilary's version of eternal generation could have come to him from the east, which only further highlights the difficulty in tracing lines of

---

7. See for example the excellent book by Weedman, *Trinitarian Theology of Hilary*, 25–27, 33–39. Note that Weedman implies Hilary got his understanding of consubstantiality from Novatian. See also Ayres, *Nicaea and Its Legacy*, 67, 75. Both Ayres and Weedman acknowledge that Hilary's *On the Trinity* represents a change in his thinking from his earlier commentary on Matthew. Note that, in his early writing, Hilary has a progression of the Son going from *in* to *with* the Father, and in his *On the Trinity* this is rejected in favor of a Son whose status relative to the Father does not change. This is likely due to the influence of Novatian. For Novatian's influence on Hilary's exegesis, see Ayres, *Nicaea and Its Legacy*, 126–27. For example, Hilary on John 5:19 is influenced by Novatian. Cf. Hilary, *On the Trinity* 7.17–18; and see Papandrea, *Trinitarian Theology of Novatian*, 170–72. However, as Weedman points out, Hilary was also influenced by Athanasius, and as we will see below, Athanasius himself was influenced by Novatian (at least indirectly), therefore some of the influence on Hilary could have come indirectly through eastern writers.

8. On Hilary's use of Philippians 2, see Weedman, *Trinitarian Theology of Hilary*, 130–35. Note that Hilary follows Novatian in describing the human nature of Christ (the "form of a slave") in terms of "weakness." Hilary, *On the Trinity* 10.66.

9. Hilary, *On the Trinity* 7.7–18. On inseparable operation and appropriation in Hilary, see Ayres, *Nicaea and Its Legacy*, 369. By the time of Augustine, these two concepts were accepted as unquestionable tradition. See Augustine, *Epistle* 2.2.

10. For Hilary, the distinction of persons comes at the point of procession, or possibly even incarnation. But see Ayres, *Nicaea and Its Legacy*, 180, where Ayres points out that Hilary's concepts of generation and consubstantiality are interdependent, just as Novatian had understood them, though Ayres does not give credit to Novatian. Cf. Hilary, *On the Synods* 71. Note that Phoebadius of Agen (d. 392 CE) was also influenced by Novatian with regard to eternal generation. See Phoebadius of Agen, *Against the Arians* 15. See also Weedman, *Trinitarian Theology of Hilary*, 61.

dependency.¹¹ But Hilary's phrase "neither a solitary nor a diverse God" does seem to capture Novatian's concern for holding on to the paradox of unity and distinction.¹² In fact, for Hilary, heresies are seen as opposite alternatives to the one truth, resulting in a situation in which each heresy cancels out its opposite.¹³ This seems directly influenced by Novatian, who described adoptionism and modalism as extreme opposites, with orthodoxy in the middle ("between two thieves").¹⁴ After Novatian, orthodoxy is perceived as the middle way between the extreme alternatives.¹⁵

Ambrose of Milan

Ambrose of Milan (339–397) was heavily influenced by Hilary, so any influence of Novatian on Ambrose might very well have come indirectly through Hilary.¹⁶ However it is clear that Ambrose knew of Novatian and had probably read his *On the Trinity*, since he wrote the treatise *On Penance* against the Novatianist schism.¹⁷ Therefore it is worth noting that Ambrose seems to follow Novatian's sense of the *kenosis*, that in the incarnation Christ was "setting aside the *enjoyment* of his divinity" without setting aside the divinity itself.¹⁸

---

11. Hanson, *Search for the Christian Doctrine of God*, 430.

12. Ayres, *Nicaea and Its Legacy*, 181, Hanson, *Search for the Christian Doctrine of God*, 480ff. With regard to eternal generation, Hanson highlights Hilary's *On the Trinity* 3.3, 6.35, 9.36.

13. Hilary, *On the Trinity* 7.3–7, 7.39–40, 10.53–54. Note that for Hilary we must not accept only one side or the other, but must accept both aspects of apparently paradoxical truths.

14. Ayres, *Nicaea and Its Legacy*, 75. Note that for Hilary adoptionism is the unforgivable sin. Cf. Novatian, *On the Trinity* 14.10.

15. Ayres, *Nicaea and Its Legacy*, 181. Ayres recognizes this in Hilary, but says, "Hilary seems to be adopting an eastern polemical strategy emerging in [the post-Nicene decades]." But Hilary did not need to get it from the east, and it did not wait until after Nicaea to emerge, since it was an important operating assumption in Novatian.

16. For example, with regard to eternal generation, see Ambrose, *On Faith* 4.9.

17. This treatise is sometimes called *On Repentance*.

18. Ambrose, *Commentary on Luke* 10:56. However, Ambrose does not speak of the *kenosis* in terms of power, since he follows the majority of his predecessors in assuming that divine power is an attribute of divine substance, not a personal property as Novatian had conceived of it. For Ambrose, that the power is in the substance supports inseparable operation and appropriation. See Ambrose, *On the Holy Spirit* 1.12 (131), 2.10 (101).

Rufinus of Aquileia

Rufinus of Aquileia (345–410), like Hilary and Ambrose, was influenced by multiple writers of both the West and the East. In Rufinus's case, these include Athanasius and Cyril of Jerusalem. This makes it difficult, if not impossible, to pinpoint lines of influence.[19] Also, like Ambrose, Rufinus criticized the Novatianist schism, which at least means that he was aware of Novatian as a would-be bishop, and probably as a theologian, but would not want to count him among the orthodox.[20] On the other hand, he seems to have thought that Novatian's *On the Trinity* was written by Tertullian, which means that he probably read it as authoritative.[21] In fact, as a Western theologian who was for a time imprisoned in the East for being anti-Arian, Rufinus may be the one most likely to appreciate Novatian's theology as ammunition against Arianism. He could also appreciate Novatian's understanding of the necessary invisibility of the Father (as opposed to the visibility of the Son) as an argument against modalism.[22] Thus he has also inherited from Novatian (or from Hilary) the point of view that orthodoxy is the middle way between extreme alternatives that ultimately cancel each other out. However, the most striking connection to Novatian has to be Rufinus's understanding of eternal generation. In his *Commentary on the Apostles' Creed*, Rufinus describes the Son as eternally generated, yet not "unoriginately," echoing Novatian's distinction between consubstantiality and difference of origin. For Rufinus, then, eternal generation means both ontological equality and eternal distinction (hierarchy) based on the fact that the Son has a source (the Father) and the Father has no source.[23]

---

19. For example, Rufinus recognized the importance of Phil 2:6–11 for Christology. Is he following Novatian (thinking he is following Tertullian), or is he following Hilary?

20. Rufinus, *Commentary on the Apostles' Creed* 39.

21. Jerome, *Apology against Rufinus* 2.19.

22. Rufinus, *Commentary on the Apostles' Creed* 5.

23. Ibid., 4–6. As I have argued in the footnotes above, Rufinus has probably taken his own understanding of eternal generation and used it to "fix" certain passages in Origen's *On First Principles*, making it more consistent with post-Nicene orthodoxy. See Rufinus's preface to *On First Principles*, where he admits to having changed Origen's text to make it conform to fourth century expectations. See also Chin, "Rufinus of Aquileia and Alexandrian Afterlives," 630. Rufinus claims to have borrowed from Origen's other works, and that he was also making *On First Principles* conform with Origen's thought elsewhere, however, when it comes to eternal generation, Rufinus's

Augustine of Hippo

Augustine (354–430) was of course also influenced by those who came before him, including Hilary and Ambrose. In fact, by the time of Augustine, certain concepts such as inseparable operation and appropriation were either assumed to be unquestionable dogma, or Augustine took the final step to make them so.[24] Augustine solidified the importance of Philippians 2, referring to it about fifty times. And though Augustine would say that the divine substance and the divine power are essentially one, he borrows Novatian's language of *kenosis* of power when he says of the Son, "he was despised as though a mere man, as though of no power."[25] Thus in the incarnation the *Logos* voluntarily emptied himself to accept the weakness of humanity, and what Jesus did during his ministry was done by the power of the Holy Spirit.[26] Augustine follows Novatian in pointing to the phrase "form of God" in Philippians 2:6 as evidence of the Son's consubstantiality and equality with the Father.[27] On the other hand, as Augustine says, "the Son owes the Father his existence," thus demonstrating the distinction between Father and Son in terms of the difference of origin.[28] Therefore, like Hilary, Augustine has inherited Novatian's concern for the balance of unity and distinction in the Trinity, and the distinction between sub-

---

translation of *On First Principles* does not fit with what Origen says elsewhere, with the one possible exception being the passage in the *Homily on Jeremiah*.

24. This is especially true with inseparable operation and appropriation. See Augustine, *Epistle* 11.2; and compare Novatian, *On the Trinity* 27. See also Ayres, *Nicaea and Its Legacy*, 369. For other possible echoes of Novatian in Augustine, see *On Faith and the Creed*, Augustine's own *On the Trinity* (especially books 4 and 5, note 4.2 on *communicatio idiomatum*); *Sermon* 52 (2) on circumscribability; *Sermon* 117 (67) on eternal generation; and the *Handbook on Faith, Hope, and Love* (*Enchiridion*) 35 on the *hypostatic* union.

25. Augustine, *Sermon* 42.2. See also *Against Faustus* 3.6 and Augustine's *On the Trinity* 11. Note that Augustine clarifies that the Son was not emptied of divinity.

26. Augustine, *Sermon* 2.11; *On the Catechizing of the Uninstructed* 10.15 (cf. 1 Cor 9:22); *On the Trinity* 11. On the importance of the *kenosis* as voluntary, cf. Hilary, *On the Trinity* 7, 8.45.

27. Augustine, *On the Trinity* 7.

28. Augustine, *On Faith and the Creed* 9.18. See also Ayres, *Nicaea and Its Legacy*, 370. Augustine understood what Novatian had said, that the generation, which was a derived (received) and contingent (dependent) existence, proves both the ontological equality and the hierarchical distinction.

stance and origin.²⁹ Likewise, with regard to the personal (*hypostatic*) union of the two natures of Christ, Augustine echoes Novatian's balance of unity with distinction when he describes the person of Christ as "one person consisting of two substances" and "one person in both natures."³⁰

Leo of Rome

By the time we get to Leo I of Rome (bishop 440–461), there is enough distance after Novatian that no direct influence would be necessary.³¹ Leo is, of course, also influenced by Hilary, Ambrose, and Augustine, among others. However, he is worth mentioning here as the last stage of theological development in the West before the fourth ecumenical council of Chalcedon (451 CE). Leo is perhaps most famous for his *Tome*, and its contribution to the Chalcedonian definition. Leo's phrase "one person in both natures" is probably directly influenced by Augustine, but indirectly by Novatian, which highlights the importance of Novatian for later orthodoxy.³² In fact, Leo's description of the way that the two natures "came together," at which time "majesty took on humility, strength weakness, eternity mortality," is reminiscent of Novatian's descriptions of the union.³³ The fact that the divine nature is affected by the union ("majesty took on humility") in addition to the human nature being affected owes some debt to Novatian's clarification of a true (i.e., two-way) *communicatio idiomatum*. Thus the *communicatio idiomatum* becomes the middle way between an extreme

---

29. Augustine, *On the Trinity* 8, esp. 8.7.11.

30. Augustine, *Commentary on John* 99.1 (also called *Homilies, Lectures* or *Tractates on the Gospel According to John* 16.13); *Sermon* 294.9. Of course this concept can be traced from Irenaeus and Tertullian, but nevertheless the language seems to come to Augustine through Novatian. Note that this language will in turn influence the *Tome* of Leo.

31. The fact that Leo's thought includes consubstantiality and eternal generation is hardly surprising, nor can it be attributed directly to Novatian since we are well after the Council of Nicaea. However, it may be worth noting that Leo described the Son as "differing in nothing from the Father because he is God from God." Leo, *Epistle* 28.1–2. Cf. Novatian, *On the Trinity* 22.5, 27.5.

32. Leo, *Epistle* 28.5 (the *Tome*). Cf. Novatian, *On the Trinity* 24.11.

33. Leo, *Epistle* 28.3. Leo also sounds like Novatian when he says that "the one Son of God is both the Word and the flesh." Ibid., 28.5; cf. Novatian, *On the Trinity* 14.4, 23.7, 24.4–11. Leo describes the *kenosis* in terms reminiscent of Novatian when he says the incarnation was "that emptying of himself whereby the invisible one made himself visible." Leo, *Epistle* 28.3.

imminence of the Son (i.e., adoptionism or Arianism) and extreme transcendence (i.e., docetism or gnosticism). By virtue of the union of natures and the communication (loaning/borrowing) of properties between the two natures, the divine nature can experience the human condition, yet without compromising immutability. Therefore, in a way God knows what it's like to be us. Furthermore, the divine nature of Christ was circumscribed in the incarnation.[34] However, as Novatian had pointed out, Leo also clarifies that "both natures retain their own proper character without loss."[35] Each nature "does what is proper to it with the cooperation of the other."[36] Thus Novatian has, via Augustine and Leo, put his stamp on the Chalcedonian definition by impressing upon his successors the importance of the balance of unity and distinction (union without confusion) in the *hypostatic* union.

Eastern Theologians Who Show Evidence of Influence from Novatian

Dionysius of Alexandria

Dionysius of Alexandria (bishop 248–265) had corresponded with Novatian. He had received at least one letter from Novatian, which is no longer extant, but it is conceivable that Novatian would have defended himself from heresy in this letter, even though he could not deny having taken part in the schism. Dionysius's letter to Novatian, in which he attempts to talk him out of continuing the schism, is preserved in the *Ecclesiastical History* of Eusebius of Caesarea.[37] Although there is no way to know for sure if Dionysius of Alexandria learned anything

---

34. Leo, *Epistle* 28.4. As we have seen, this has implications for the *Theotokos* controversy (which was already in the past by this time), in which the question of the circumscription of the divine nature is implied in the description of Mary as "Mother of God." Note that Leo criticized Hilary for saying that the Son did not get his humanity from Mary. Leo corrected Hilary, connecting the human nature of Christ to Mary (Leo, *Epistle* 28.2).

35. Leo, *Epistle* 28.3. Cf. Novatian, *On the Trinity* 24.9. Neither nature is diminished by the union.

36. Leo, *Epistle* 28.4–5. That Leo assumed the person of Christ has two wills can be seen in his *Epistle* 165.8. Novatian's emphasis on the fact that the *kenosis* and the passion of Christ were voluntary supports orthodox Christology against an Apollinarian monothelitism.

37. Eusebius, *Ecclesiastical History* 6.45, 7.8.

from Novatian, the direct contact is certain. Also, we should keep in mind that Dionysius of Alexandria corresponded with Dionysius of Rome (bishop 260–268), who would have known Novatian, and would have read Novatian's *On the Trinity* before the schism, while it was considered the epitome of orthodoxy. We know that Dionysius of Rome corrected Dionysius of Alexandria on the doctrine of consubstantiality (and possibly eternal generation), so while we cannot say what else the Alexandrian bishop might have accepted from Roman theology, it is reasonable to speculate that Novatian's influence could have made itself felt in Alexandria through Dionysius of Rome, in spite of the schism.[38] Thus Novatian could have influenced Dionysius of Alexandria from two directions: directly, and indirectly through Dionysius of Rome. Furthermore, Dionysius of Alexandria would then become the avenue for Novatian to influence Alexander and Athanasius of Alexandria, and through them the rest of the east (not to mention those Westerners who traveled east, such as Hilary and Rufinus).

Alexander of Alexandria

In 324 CE, Alexander of Alexandria (bishop 313–328) sent a letter to Alexander of Byzantium, in which he outlined his perception of Arius's teaching, and contrasted it with his own. In his explanation of orthodoxy, Alexander said, ". . . it is necessary to say that the Father is always the Father. But He is the Father, since the Son is always with Him, on account of whom he is called the Father."[39] The implication is that the Son must be eternal or the Father would not always be a Father. This is the same point Novatian was making when he said, "Truly he is always in the Father, otherwise the Father would not always be a Father."[40] Alexander also seems to be following Novatian when he speaks of orthodoxy as the middle way between two unacceptable alternatives. He wrote, "For they ignorantly affirm that one of two things must necessar-

---

38. See Dionysius of Rome, *Against the Sabellians*; and Dionysius of Alexandria, *Epistle of Dionysius of Rome*. Dionysius had convened a synod in Rome that condemned the idea that the Son and Spirit are created. See Grillmeier, *Christ in Christian Tradition*, 156. On Dionysius of Rome's influence over Dionysius of Alexandria, see Ayres, *Nicaea and Its Legacy*, 93–94.

39. Alexander of Alexandria, *Epistle to Alexander of Byzantium* (Constantinople) 7. See also Athanasius, *On the Opinion of Dionysius* 15.

40. Novatian, *On the Trinity* 31.3.

ily be said, either that he is from things which are not, or that there are two unbegottens.... Between which two, as holding the middle place, the only begotten nature of God, the Word by which the Father formed all things out of nothing, was begotten of the true Father himself."[41]

Athanasius of Alexandria

The most famous opponent of Arianism was, of course, Athanasius of Alexandria (bishop 328–373). There are several points at which Athanasius could be said to exhibit influence from Novatian, however, by the time of Athanasius the influence is more likely to be indirect. Athanasius admitted to being influenced by Dionysius of Alexandria.[42] He also traveled to Rome, where he likely met Westerners who had been influenced by Novatian. Thus we arguably can see Novatian's fingerprints on Athanasius's understanding of eternal generation. In describing eternal generation in *Defense of the Nicene Council* (written after his sojourn in Rome), Athanasius contrasts Arian generation as an event, with eternal generation.[43] Athanasius believed, as Novatian did, that generation necessarily resulted in consubstantiality and that in turn results in appropriation, the conviction that what is said of the Father is also said of the Son.[44] Therefore the eternal coexistence of the Son is a function of eternal generation, and ensures divine immutability, since the Father is always a Father.[45] Thus, "Always a Father, always

---

41. Alexander of Alexandria, *Epistle to Alexander of Byzantium* (Constantinople) 11.

42. Athanasius, *On the Opinion of Dionysius* 12. See Hanson, *Search for the Christian Doctrine of God*, 72.

43. Athanasius of Alexandria, *Defense of the Nicene Council* (*De Decretis*) 5 (18). Note that Athanasius assumes Novatian's distinction between generation and procession, and between substance and origin. See also *Against the Arians* 4.1 and *Against the Nations (Heathen)* 47.2.

44. Athanasius, *Synodal Letter to the Bishops of Africa* (*Ad Afros*) 8, *Against the Arians* 3.4, *On the Councils of Ariminium and Seleucia* (*De Synodis*) 49. Cf. Novatian, *On the Trinity* 27.5.

45. Athanasius, *Against the Arians* 1.6 (17–18), 3.28, *Defense of the Nicene Council* (*De Decretis*) 5 (20). Cf. Novatian, *On the Trinity* 31.3. Note that Athanasius, like Novatian, connects the two concepts of "the Father is always a Father" and "the Son is always in the Father."

a Son." Athanasius also follows Novatian in connecting generation to inseparable operation.[46]

The Cappadocians

Finally the Cappadocians, who, like Leo, are far enough removed from Novatian to make any direct connection between them unnecessary. Nevertheless, it is worth mentioning that their conception of *circumincessio* (*perichoresis*) has echoes of the conclusion of Novatian's *On the Trinity*.[47]

In this brief survey of Novatian's successors who have benefitted from his work (while calling him a heretic), I have been able to give only a very cursory overview, without much regard for progression of thought within the careers of the more prolific writers, such as Augustine. Although in most cases a direct influence is impossible to prove, I could not end this study of Novatian without pointing out the places where later writers "sound like" Novatian. At the very least, among extant authors Novatian appears to be the pioneer of certain orthodox doctrines, such as eternal generation, *communicatio idiomatum*, and possibly *circumincessio* (*perichoresis*). I have also argued that Novatian is the first to recognize the importance of Philippians 2:6–11 for Trinitarian theology and Christology, and the first to connect the concept of the coeternal consubstantiality of the Son with the eternal fatherhood of the first person of the Trinity (i.e., "Always a Father, always a Son"). Yet it must be admitted that we cannot really know whether Novatian was the first to say anything, since so many teachers of the early church never wrote a treatise, and so many treatises do not survive today. The most we can say is that Novatian is the first *extant* writer to approach these doctrines that would only later be defined as doctrines per se and prove important for continuing orthodoxy. But we can also say that in the middle of the third century, Novatian (and those who made him acting bishop of Rome for over a year) believed that these concepts were already essential to orthodoxy, and to refuting

---

46. Athanasius, *Defense of the Nicene Council* (*De Decretis*) 3 (8). See also Gregory of Nazianzus, *Theological Orations* (the *Fourth Theological Oration*) 30.11.

47. Cf. Novatian, *On the Trinity* 31.19–22. On *perichoresis* in the Cappadocians, see Ayres, *Nicaea and Its Legacy*, 246. Though Ayres does not give credit to Novatian for explaining this before the Cappadocians, Novatian's understanding of the union of natures does qualify according to Ayres's own definition of the doctrine.

heresy. Thus, Novatian's influence is important, but not exclusive. The point is that Nicene, and even Chalcedonian, orthodoxy already existed in the West before the controversies of the East, and we can point to Novatian as the culmination and the state of the art for theology, not only for his own time, but leading up to Nicaea. I would like to suggest that Novatian's influence came to his successors through Dionysius of Rome and the other Western writers, including Rufinus, who thought he was reading Tertullian. These Western writers each took something from Novatian and passed it on, not only to the West, but to the East as well. In the East this began with Dionysius of Alexandria, who in turn influenced his successors in that see, but it also came through those Easterners who traveled west, such as Athanasius, and those Westerners who traveled east, including again Rufinus, who translated and corrected Origen.

Between Two Thieves

Novatian Was ahead of His Time

The idea that Novatian's theology was advanced compared to his predecessors and contemporaries has, in the past, been both challenged and championed.[48] By now it should be clear that this is in fact the case. In spite of the fact that he lapses into language reminiscent of earlier *Logos* Christology (so-called *Word-flesh*), he is forward-looking, marking a shift toward Nicene and Chalcedonian (*Word-man*) Christology.[49] Novatian was making a break from understanding the *Logos* in terms of human speech, so that the generation of the Word did not mean an "emitting." This allowed him to describe generation as an eternal state of being rather than an event at which the Word "proceeds" from

---

48. In addition to those who recognize Novatian as the pioneer of eternal generation (see chapter 3, footnote 50 above), those who agree that Novatian was in fact ahead of his time include De Labriolle, *History and Literature of Christianity*, 172–73; Mohrmann, C. "Origines De La Latinité Chrétienne À Rome," in Études *Sur Le Latin Des Chrétiens*, 3:165; Grillmeier, *Christ in Christian Tradition*; and Hazlett, ed., *Early Christianity*, 151.

49. Grillmeier, *Christ in Christian Tradition*, 133. Novatian's insistence on the full humanity of Christ against the Modalists, and the fact that the humiliation of Christ was voluntary, anticipate the Chalcedonian Definition's refutation of Apollinarius (monothelitism) and Eutyches (monophysitism). See Papandrea, *Trinitarian Theology of Novatian*, 302–5.

the Father. Still, his use of the older language betrays that he was not consciously trying to innovate. For him, orthodoxy (the Truth) was the "genuine tradition and catholic faith."[50] What he wrote was not an attempt at a systematic theology, but a response to the perceived threat of heresy.

Novatian recognized that the "monarchians" on both sides were trying to argue for the oneness of God, but that their conclusions either left Christ without a divine nature (in the case of the Adoptionists, or "dynamic monarchians") or that Christ is actually God the Father incarnate (in the case of the Modalists, or "modalistic monarchians").[51] The orthodox Christ was in the middle, between these two thieves, who would steal either his divinity or his humanity in order to preserve the monarchy of God.[52] But Novatian cautioned, "one is not to lean toward one part and avoid the other part, since whoever will have excluded some portion of the truth will not hold the complete truth."[53] The danger is in accepting only one of Christ's natures and rejecting the other.[54] Novatian's genius, if it can be called that, is in his ability to bring the two together, balancing the unity and distinction. For him, orthodoxy requires both natures, and in this he anticipates even Anselm of Canterbury's *Cur Deus Homo?* (*Why the God-Man?*), since one nature alone will not lead to salvation.[55]

In solving the problem of Christian monotheism, Novatian found the key in the *kenosis*. The oneness of God is preserved and expressed in the consubstantiality of the three persons, shown in the fact that the Son is originally in the "form of God." Specifically, the generation of the Son from the Father means that the Father and Son are one.

---

50. Novatian, *On the Trinity* 30.2.

51. Ibid., 30.3.

52. Ibid., 30.6. See Novatian, *Epistle* 1.8 (30.8). Novatian explicitly states that he wants to "steer a middle course." Ironically, this comment was in reference to the controversy over the lapsed, not over theology.

53. Novatian, *On the Trinity* 11.5.

54. Ibid., 11.9–10.

55. Ibid., 12.2. Note that in chapter 10 (arguing against docetism), Novatian says that Christ must be truly human in order to be the Savior of humans, while in chapter 11 (arguing against adoptionism), Novatian says that Christ must be divine in order to be the Savior. Specifically, salvation results from *both* Christ's human nature (as representative of humanity) *and* the individual's belief in his divine nature. In *On the Trinity* 4.9 Novatian even anticipates Anselm's ontological argument for the existence of God.

Monotheism is also preserved by the fact that the Father alone (as First Cause) is the one ultimate Source of divine authority. At the same time, the emptying of the Son in the incarnation demonstrates the distinction between Father and Son, so that while they are *one*, they are not *the same*. Finally, the *kenosis* of power, or dynamic subordination, prevents the distinction between Father and Son from creating the impression of two Gods. In choosing not to cling to his equality, the Son voluntarily and temporarily traded omnipotence, omnipresence, and omniscience for a fragile human existence.[56]

Therefore, Novatian overcame two theological problems, which was necessary to pave the way for the ecumenical councils, and he did it in a way that (as far as we know) no one before him had. First, by making the shift from generation as an event to generation as an eternal state of being (separating generation from procession), Novatian was able to show how the Father and Son are eternally equal (consubstantial), but also maintain the eternal distinction of persons. This preserves the immutability of the divine, since the persons of the Trinity do not go through a change at the point of generation or procession. This, in turn, would be important for Nicene theology, because Arianism proposed a mutability of the Son by which he is created and later elevated to a qualified divinity, a *received* divinity of lesser degree than the Father. To counter this, the bishops of the council needed consubstantiality and eternal generation.

Second, in allowing the divine nature to receive something from the human nature in the *communicatio idiomatum*, Novatian conceived of a way of describing the union of natures that allowed for real (personal) union and for a divine connection to humanity that does not need to shield the divine from the realities of the human condition, but also does not compromise the divine immutability that was so important.[57] Therefore, both in terms of the Trinity and the two natures of Christ, Novatian was looking for the orthodox "middle way" by finding the balance of unity and distinction. The three persons of the Trinity, as well as the two natures in Christ, are one but not the same, distinct but not separate.

---

56. Novatian, *On the Trinity* 22.6.

57. Even as late as Athanasius, some authors claimed that when Christ said he did not know the day or the hour of his return, his divine nature actually did know.

Novatian Was behind the Times

As much as Novatian was ahead of his time in terms of his Christology, he would prove to be behind the times with regard to his ecclesiology. When the church forged a solution to the problem of the lapsed, Novatian dug in his heels and watched as the majority of the church moved into the future without him. He and his followers represented a conservatism that looked back to a time when the church was young enough (and perhaps naive enough) to demand near perfection in the behavior of its members. However the majority of the church, led by bishops such as Cyprian and Cornelius, came to the conclusion that the lapsed should be reconciled (with penance), and schism was actually a sin worse than apostasy.[58] Therefore the controversy surrounding Novatian's schism represents a crossroads in the church, a corporate decision point.

The bishop of any given city had authority over both doctrine and discipline. In addition, the bishop controlled the catacombs, so that excommunication meant that one could not be buried with the rest of the Christian community, and certainly not near the martyrs. To be out of favor with the bishop was to be out of favor with the body of Christ. Consequently, by the time of Novatian it had become clear that there could be only one bishop per city, not only for the sake of consistent doctrine, but for the very unity of the church itself. Novatian's challenge of Cornelius for the office of bishop of Rome called the question. Would the lapsed be welcomed with open arms, or excommunicated? In the end, a third option emerged as the outcome. A middle way was found, by which the lapsed would be reconciled, but with penance. However, rather than embrace the ecclesiological middle way, Novatian refused to budge. The church was divided in schism, with a majority accepting the inevitability of reconciliation with the lapsed, while a minority followed Novatian in founding a separate sect. This sect would at times be persecuted by representatives of the majority, however officially it would be recognized as Christian, but not Catholic.[59] While on the one

---

58. Burns, "On Rebaptism," 386. Cf. Cyprian, *On the Unity of the Catholic Church*.

59. Socrates Scholasticus, *Ecclesiastical History* 2.38, 5.22, 7.11. See also Pacian of Barcelona, *Epistle* 1.1–8, 2.3–4. Although Pacian did consider Novatianists heretics, lumping them with other rigorists like the Montanists, to him their heresy was that they rejected the sacrament of penance. Pacian defined *catholic* as "everywhere one," so that it has the connotation of both unity and universality. In the end, he recognized that

hand it may be seen as positive that the church was able to conceive of some measure of diversity within the body of Christ, on the other hand the fact that Novatian had created something that might be called the first "denomination" outside the Catholic Church set a precedent of solving disagreements by mitosis.

The Relevance of Novatian's Schism for the Contemporary Church

In a way, historic rigorism, such as was found in the Montanists, the Novatianists, the Donatists, and to some extent in Tertullian and Hippolytus, is a kind of precursor to contemporary fundamentalism. Similarities include a very high moral expectation with little room for failure after baptism, coupled with the conviction that little or no distinction should be made between different types of sin.[60] In addition, the fact that other Christians differ with regard to discipline leads to an isolationism that forces the members of the rigorist sect to keep themselves separate, not only from the "secular world," but from other Christians outside the sect as well.[61] This is based on a particular ecclesiology that assumes that impurity taints purity, rather than the other way around.[62] In other words, while the majority of the church would take the view that the church should be inclusive, since the purity of some might save the others, the rigorist factions attempted to maintain a church of the perfected, for fear that the imperfect would infect the perfect.[63] This results in the rejection of the sacrament of penance and

---

there were those who called themselves Christian, but who were not Catholic. Note that the eighth canon of the Council of Nicaea recognized Novatianists as theologically orthodox, and allowed that clergy who came from the Novatianist movement into the Catholic church could retain their status as clergy, provided they agreed to reconcile those whom the Novatianists would not reconcile.

60. Novatian, *Epistle* 1.3 (30.3). See also Daly, "Novatian and Tertullian," 36.

61. There is also a tendency to see those within the faction as the only truly faithful Christians left in the world. It is possible that Novatian's use of the phrase *faithful Christians* in his *On the Spectacles* is used in this way, though DeSimone argues that it simply means baptized Christians as opposed to catechumens. See DeSimone's introduction to *On the Spectacles*, 115. See also the *Didascalia* 15, which advocates that anyone who prays with the excommunicated is thereby excommunicated themselves.

62. Daly, "Novatian and Tertullian," 39.

63. The controversy over the lapsed led to a controversy over baptism in which Stephen of Rome (bishop 254–257 CE) opposed Cyprian of Carthage. The question was whether those returning to the church from a schismatic sect should be rebaptized.

reconciliation, a rejection which seems to be based on the rigorist conviction that only God can forgive sin (and he probably won't).[64] Thus for the church, purity purifies the impure, so all should be included so that as many as possible might be saved (cf. Matt 13:24–30).[65] For the rigorist factions, on the other hand, impurity taints the pure, and those who have fallen should be cut off to save the perfected (cf. John 15:2).

With regard to Scripture, the rigorists tended to see the apostolic writings as exhaustive, and even though the New Testament canon was coming to its present form over time, Novatian believed that where Scripture is silent, it does not allow that which it does not mention.[66] Likewise, there is a certain strain within fundamentalism, that also assumes Scripture condemns whatever it does not specifically allow.[67] By contrast, the mainstream church has historically accepted the possibility that Scripture is not exhaustive, and that it allows what it does not explicitly condemn.[68]

On the other hand, Novatian was not a biblical literalist. Like the other patristic writers, Novatian interpreted the Old Testament non-

---

Stephen thought that they only needed to be reconciled (i.e., reconfirmed, with the imposition of hands) in the church, but that their baptism (as long as it was done in the name of the Trinity) was valid, even if it was performed in a separate sect. Stephen's view would eventually prevail. See Burns, "On Rebaptism," 398. Later, Augustine would solidify the church's ecclesiology in the controversy with the Donatists. For Augustine, the church must be like Noah's ark (containing both the clean and the unclean). He used the parable of the wheat and the weeds as an example of how the church must not attempt to "weed out" the sinners, or try to create a church within a church.

64. Those who called Novatian a heretic, as well as a schismatic, did so on the grounds that his sect rejected the sacrament of penance/reconciliation. This was further perceived as a rejection of apostolic succession, which conveyed the power of the keys (the power of absolution) to the bishops.

65. It must be kept in mind that even when the church can be perceived as most inclusive, reconciliation depends on repentance, so that an unrepentant sinner would remain excommunicated.

66. Novatian, *On the Spectacles* 3.

67. For example, the long debate over which musical instruments are appropriate for worship is connected to this question. During the reformation, some groups took to smashing organs with an axe because they are not mentioned in Scripture. More recently, the often painful debate over whether drums sets and electric guitars are acceptable for praising God would have been answered for us if only John had mentioned them along with harps in his vision of heaven (Revelation 4–5).

68. One interesting exception to this is polygamy. While not prohibited in Scripture, it has been universally condemned throughout the history of the church.

literally, in order to find the message for the Christian church.[69] He used typology and allegory to interpret passages that would otherwise have little meaning for Gentiles. For example, in his *On Jewish Foods*, he says that the Old Testament dietary laws would present a contradiction if taken literally because God created the unclean animals and commanded Noah to save them.[70] Therefore he interprets the dietary laws not as literal food restrictions, but as warnings about sinful behavior. In other words, if the Scripture forbids eating pork, it really means that we should not act like pigs.[71] And if the Scripture forbids eating an animal with a single hoof, it is because only one testament of Scripture is not enough. Whereas Jews accept only the Old Testament, and Marcionites only the New Testament, both testaments (the double hoof) are required for salvation.[72] It would be interesting to know how Novatian would have interpreted the book of Revelation since, even though he might not have interpreted the images literally, he may have followed the trend of the other rigorists in interpreting Revelation according to a dispensationalist view of history, ending with a literal millennium.[73]

---

69. For example, see Novatian, *On the Trinity* 6.1–5, 7.5. Novatian points out that anthropomorphisms of God in the Old Testament are not to be taken literally since they describe God, "according to the faith of the time, not as God was, but as the people were able to grasp him." So the wings and the feet of God mentioned in Psalm 139 represent God's omnipresence. The eyes and ears of God represent omniscience. Thus it is clear that the Old Testament as a whole cannot be taken literally, opening the possibility that other parts can be allegorized, such as the dietary laws.

70. Novatian, *On Jewish Foods* 2–3. The assumption is that since everything God created is good (Gen 1:31), nothing that is part of creation can be considered unclean in and of itself.

71. Ibid., 3.15. Likewise, one should not eat a weasel because weasels are thieves, and theft is a sin, so the prohibition against eating weasels is actually a warning against breaking the commandment, "Thou shalt not steal."

72. Ibid., 3.7–11.

73. There is no indication in the extant works of Novatian as to how he would have interpreted Revelation. Nevertheless, there is some as yet unexplored connection between rigorism and dispensationalism. Irenaeus and Tertullian followed Papias in his interpretation of Revelation that was based on 2 Pet 3:8 ("with the Lord one day is like a thousand years"; cf. Ps 90:4). The interpretation, in a nutshell, runs as follows: since creation is described in Genesis 1 as taking place over six days, with a seventh day of rest, the six days of creation are interpreted as six thousand years of human history—four thousand before the coming of Christ and two thousand after, with the seventh thousand years as a millennial Sabbath. Both Irenaeus and Tertullian were also sympathetic associates of the Montanists. It is not clear whether the dispensational interpretation was a feature of Montanism taken up by Irenaeus and Tertullian, or whether the influ-

The point is that though Novatian was not a biblical literalist, he could at times over-allegorize the text to the point of finding his own rigorist agenda there. Thus the Scriptures become a manual of prooftexts for the support of an argument, without regard for the original context of the documents.

Therefore, although Novatian found the middle way between the heresies with his Trinitarian theology and his Christology, he was not able (or refused) to do the same with his ecclesiology. This is ironic, since he specifically stated that he wanted to "steer a middle course" at the beginning of the controversy over the lapsed.[74] With the laxists on one side, and Novatian and the rigorists on the other, the majority of the church (represented by Cornelius and later Stephen of Rome) did navigate the *via media*. When the mainstream church found the balance between a kind of universalism and a kind of isolationism, Novatian chose the latter and was left on the fringe.[75] Ecclesiologically, he had become one of two thieves on either side of the church's Christ, the merciful Christ of the sacrament of reconciliation.[76] Thus Novatian did not follow his own advice, but the rest of the church did—against him. Novatian's legacy, then, is a double-edged sword. We can learn from his theology, and we can learn from his mistake. We can accept his Christology as orthodox, especially for his time, and at the same time we can reject his ecclesiology as one that divides the body of Christ.

---

ence went the other way, however it seems to be the case that this dispensationalist interpretation of the book of Revelation was not the interpretation of the majority of the church. See Papandrea, *Wedding of the Lamb*.

74. Novatian, *Epistle* 1.8 (30.8).

75. Note that, as applied to the sacraments, the laxists would have accepted the lapsed without condition, while the rigorists would not have accepted them at all. Certainly, the laxists would have claimed that their Christ was the most merciful, yet the church could not abide the way that unconditional reconciliation would seem to disrespect the martyrs and confessors. The middle way of the catholic church was to accept them within the discipline of the sacrament of reconciliation. There is an interesting parallel here with Anselm's *Cur Deus Homo?* in which he argues that it would be unjust for God to forgive sinners without condition, and unmerciful for God to leave sinners unforgiven. In the Eucharist, sacramental universalism is manifest in an open communion table, while the other extreme of isolationism is manifest in a table open only to members of the immediate congregation.

76. Novatian's opponents claimed that he believed in a Christ without mercy.

Conclusion

Novatian was the theological spokesperson for the Roman church in the mid-third century. His *kenosis* Christology would outlive his reputation as a theologian, and even outlive his schism, by having an impact on future theologians, and later conciliar orthodoxy. In addition, his understanding of orthodoxy as the middle way between the extremes endures, and though it probably comes from his own observation of the theological debates as they had played out before his time, it continued to play out that way long after he was gone. At the very least it is one helpful way of looking back on the development of doctrine in the early Church. Novatian saw truth as occupying a middle position between extreme alternatives, or perhaps as a balance that holds apparently paradoxical truths in tension rather than forcing a choice between them. Thus, with both the Trinity and with Christology, the answer is a balance of unity and distinction. Furthermore, the distinction itself maintains a balance, in that it cannot mean an ontological separation or substantial subordination, yet it also cannot mean a distinction in name (or function) only.

Within the Trinity, too much unity results in a confusion of persons, which is the hallmark of modalism (the Son is the Father and therefore he could not be fully human). On the other hand, too much distinction results in an ontological (substantial) separation between the persons, such as one finds in adoptionism, and later Arianism (the Son is not fully divine). Within the person of Christ, too much unity results in an overlap, or confusion of natures, which would later be manifest in Apollinarian monothelitism and Eutychian monophysitism (that there is only one will or one nature, and that divine). On the other hand, too much distinction results in a separation of natures, such as Nestorius would later be accused of, and which was perceived to threaten the *hypostatic* union of the person of Christ. In either case, too much unity leads to the loss of the humanity of Jesus, while not enough unity leads to the loss of his divinity. Either way, diminishing one nature or the other means that the connection between God and humanity in general is also diminished. Theologians like Novatian were convinced that to diminish either nature would ultimately make salvation impossible. So behind every theological or christological controversy one will eventually find a soteriological concern, motivating the urgency of the debate.

For Novatian, the balance is preserved by maintaining both natures in the person of Christ, and by emphasizing both the divinity of Christ as a person of the Trinity and the distinction of Christ as "second person after the Father." This balance is most clearly expressed by the concept of eternal generation, in which the unity is in the consubstantial divinity, and the distinction is the result of the second (and third) person's derived and dependent existence and dynamic subordination.

Appendix: Outline of Doctrinal Terms

- Divine Simplicity
  - This is a philosophical assumption shared by most early Christians (including Adoptionists).
  - Divinity is "simplex," which means that God is non-composite, does not have parts and cannot be divided.
  - Athenagoras explained that whatever is created, is necessarily made up of smaller parts and is therefore perishable, or corruptible. God, being uncreated, is not made up of smaller parts, therefore God is indivisible and incorruptible.[1] Thus divine simplicity is a function of uncreatedness.
  - Divinity is therefore incorruptible, since it would be impossible to break down into small components, being already perfect oneness throughout.
  - Divine simplicity goes hand in hand with monotheism, since more than one God would imply a division within the realm of the divine (it was partly the belief in divine simplicity that led early sdoptionists to assume that since God is one, Jesus could not be divine, thereby excluding him from the realm of the divine).
  - Therefore it is not appropriate to speak of the three persons of the Trinity as three "parts" of God, as if each person is only one third of God. Rather, it must be said that each person of the Trinity is fully God, fully divine.
  - Irenaeus, Tertullian and Novatian all understood the interconnectedness of divine simplicity with consubstantiality, inseparable operation and appropriation.[2]

---

1. Athenagoras, *Plea for the Christians* 6, 8.
2. Irenaeus, *Against Heresies* 2.17.3–7; Tertullian, *On the Flesh of Christ* 14, 18; *Against Praxeas* 17.

- Divine Immutability
    - Another widely held assumption, shared by philosophy and Hebrew thought alike, that the divine cannot change (Mal 3:6; Heb 13:8; Jas 1:17).
    - From the very beginning, the apologists affirmed that God cannot (or will not) change.[3]
    - Divinity is understood to be absolute perfection and the possibility of any change in the divine would imply either that the divine was once less than perfect and later became perfect, or that the divine could at some future point become less than perfect, therefore perfection (and perfect holiness) requires immutability.
    - Like divine simplicity, divine immutability assumes incorruptibility: what cannot change cannot degenerate, decay or die.
    - The apologists are unanimous in asserting that divine immutability also assumes eternality and uncreatedness: what cannot change could not have a beginning (or an end) to its existence, therefore the divine is uncreated and eternal.[4]
    - Divine immutability assumes omnipresence, since moving from place to place would be a kind of change (but see *circumscribability* below).
- Divine Impassibility
    - The divine cannot suffer, since suffering is a form of change, therefore immutability requires impassibility.
    - This means that it is only the human nature of Christ that suffers and dies on the cross (but see *communicatio idiomatum* below).
- Consubstantiality
    - All three persons of the Trinity are the same divine substance, or essence. This is the way the early theologians described the

---

3. Justin Martyr, *Dialogue with Trypho* 3; Athenagoras, *Plea for the Christians* 19.

4. Theophilus of Antioch, *To Autolycus* 2.4; Clement of Alexandria, *Exhortation to the Greeks* 6. See also Hippolytus, *Refutation of All Heresies* 1.1.

oneness of God and the unity of the Trinity, thus preserving monotheism.

- o The apologists and theologians all affirmed that God is one divinity:
    - ▫ Justin said that the one divinity is expressed as one divine power.
    - ▫ Athenagoras explained that the divine persons are "united according to power."[5]
    - ▫ Irenaeus further clarified that the persons of the Trinity share one and the same essence.[6]
    - ▫ Finally, Tertullian defined the Latin terminology of one substance, three persons.[7]
- o The bishops at Nicaea would add to the creed the words "of the same essence (consubstantial) with the Father" (Greek: *homoousios*) to express the equality and coeternality of the Father and Son against Arianism.
- o Consubstantiality goes hand in hand with divine simplicity, since it is assumed that there can be no division in the divine: any being that could be said to be of a different substance than God, is therefore not God (not divine).
- o There cannot be variations of divine substance, or different degrees of divinity (this is asserted against both gnosticism and Arianism).
- o Consubstantiality also goes hand in hand with generation, since the one who is generated must be of the same substance as the one who generates.

- Inseparable Operation
    - o All three persons of the Trinity are always unified in all divine activity.
    - o Inseparable operation follows from divine simplicity and consubstantiality.

5. Athenagoras, *Plea for the Christians* 24.
6. Irenaeus, *Demonstration of the Apostolic Preaching* 47.
7. Tertullian, *Against Praxeas* 25.

- Inseparable operation was assumed by Justin Martyr.[8]
- The theologians Irenaeus, Tertullian and Novatian all make it part of their arguments against modalism:
  - We cannot define or distinguish the persons of the Trinity by task or function, as the Modalists did: modalism said that the *only* distinction was by "mode" of activity, or function; the Son was simply the Father doing the work of Savior.
  - Orthodoxy maintains a real, eternal distinction between the persons, yet *not* one of function.
- In a practical sense, it is never appropriate to substitute modal (activity-oriented) terms for the Trinitarian formula:
  - For example, it would be invalid to baptize in the name of the "Creator, Redeemer, Sustainer," or anything that names the persons of the Trinity by function.
  - This is because it gives the impression that the Father is not also Savior (Exod 15) and that the Son is not also Creator (John 1:3) or Sanctifier/Sustainer. (Heb 1:3)
  - As Irenaeus said, the three *persons* of the Trinity are "the three articles of our seal" (of baptism).[9]

- Appropriation
  - Because of consubstantiality and inseparable operation, anything that can be said about one person of the Trinity can be said of the other two persons as well, including descriptions of divine activity.
  - Anything that can be said of the Trinity can be said of each of the persons and vice versa.
  - Scripture uses synecdoche to say, for example, that the Holy Spirit inspired the prophets, even though in reality it must be admitted that inspiration comes from all three persons of the Trinity (inseparable operation).

---

8. Justin Martyr, *Dialogue with Trypho* 56.
9. Irenaeus, *Demonstration of the Apostolic Preaching* 100.

- o Tertullian explained that any terms that could be used to describe the Father, such as "almighty," can also be used to describe the Son.[10]
- o Novatian said that since the Son is generated from the Father, "whatever the Father is, the Son is."[11]
- o There are a few exceptions to this rule: four relational terms that each apply to one person of the Trinity only:
    - Only the Father is *unbegotten*, since the Father alone is the First Cause, primary authority and ultimate Source (thus even the source of the existence of the Son and Spirit).[12]
    - Only the Son is *begotten*, or *generated*, which is defined as an existence that is derived and dependent/contingent, but not created. Generation is an eternal state of being, so that there is no time when the Son did not exist or the Father was not a Father. Eternal generation assumes an eternal personal distinction between Father and Son.
    - Only the Son is *incarnate*, i.e., only the Son became human.
        - However as Augustine would later clarify, because of inseparable operation, all three persons of the Trinity are at work in the incarnation.[13]
        - Also, as Novatian and later writers clarified, Divinity is able to experience the human condition (yet without change) by virtue of *communicatio idiomatum*.
    - Only the Holy Spirit *proceeds* from the Trinity, as God's gift to the Church and the world.
        - The use of this term for the Holy Spirit was not standardized until the fifth century, so that in the time before the ecumenical councils, the concept of procession is also used of the Son. However, eventually

---

10. Tertullian, *Against Praxeas* 17.
11. Novatian, *On the Trinity* 27.5.
12. Clement of Alexandria, *Exhortation to the Greeks* 5; Hippolytus, *Refutation of All Heresies* 10.28–29; Novatian, *On the Trinity* 2.3, 3.1, 9.1, 31.1, 31.20.
13. Augustine of Hippo, *On the Trinity* 1.9, 2.1.

this term came to be reserved for the Spirit, if for no other reason than the Spirit had no unique term to describe his relationship to the other two persons of the Trinity.[14]

- This relationship can be expressed as the Spirit proceeding "from the Father *through* the Son," or "from the Father *and* the Son" (both expressions are orthodox because of inseparable operation, however the latter version was a change in the creed made by the western church without the consent of the East).

- *Circumincessio* (also known as *perichoresis* or reciprocity)
  - This is a function of divine simplicity, consubstantiality and inseparable operation.
  - *Circumincessio* implies the mutual interexistence of the three persons of the Trinity, described as each person of the Trinity being "in" the other two persons (cf. John 14:10-11).
    - Athenagoras described the Holy Spirit as an emanation from the Father, moving in a cycle of flowing out from him and flowing back to him.[15]
    - Callistus of Rome also seems to have taught an early version of *circumincessio*, as evidenced by the way Hippolytus describes his teaching on the interrelationship of the Father and the Son (Hippolytus perceived this as a form of modalism).[16]

---

14. Later writers such as Augustine would point out that we cannot use the term *begotten* (generated) to describe the Spirit, since that would make the Spirit another Son of the Father. They defined generation as sonship, so that to use the term begotten of the Holy Spirit would create a situation where the Father has two Sons and Christ and the Holy Spirit would be brothers. Therefore, when we call the first person of the Trinity "Father," we must recognize that he is the Father of the Son, and he is our Father by adoption, but he is not the Father of the Holy Spirit. Technically, he is the Source of the Holy Spirit, and beyond that it remains a mystery to us.

15. Athenagoras, *Plea for the Christians* 10.

16. Hippolytus, *Refutation of All Heresies* 9.7; 10.23.

- Novatian stated that because of the generation of the Son and the consequent dependence of the Son on the Father, therefore the Son is always in the Father.[17]
- Novatian further explained that because of consubstantiality, all divine activity originates with the Father as the First Cause and Source of all being and is extended out through the Son (to be completed in the Holy Spirit, as later writers would say), and then moves back to the Father (cf. Isa 55:11), therefore the "majesty and divinity" of God moves in a cyclical pattern, going out to humanity, and returning back to the Father, the ultimate Source[18]

o The concept of *circumincessio* is meant to describe the fact that all divine activity is ultimately oriented back toward the Trinity: divine activity moves outward toward humanity, but always with the ultimate goal of moving back to return to the Trinity, orienting humanity toward the Trinity.

o No person of the Trinity ever moves out from the Trinity so as to be separated from the Trinity.

- The early theologians described the Son and the Spirit as light from the sun, or water from a spring (the Father being the sun and the spring). One cannot tell where the sun and the spring end and the light and the water begin.
- Also, the light and the water may go out from the sun and the spring, but they are never disconnected from the sun and the spring.
- However, for the image of the spring and the stream (for example) to truly be an image of *circumincessio*, we would have to include the water finding its way back to the spring.

---

17. Novatian, *On the Trinity* 31.3. Theophilus of Antioch had described the generation of the Logos as a movement from *in* the Father to *with* the Father, which implies an inherent change from a lack of distinction to a diminished connection. Novatian departed from Theophilus's meaning by maintaining both the eternal distinction between the Father and the Son, as well as the eternal connection.

18. Novatian, *On the Trinity* 31.20–21.

- Circumscribability
    - This term reflects the possibility of being "circumscribed," or enclosed within a place, in other words, to be able to be localized in time and space.
    - Circumscribability is the opposite of omnipresence, but paradoxically it is also a necessary condition of the incarnation.
        - Normally, it would be assumed that divinity cannot be circumscribed, because omnipresence was always thought to be part of the definition of divinity.[19]
        - This led some to say that only the human nature of Christ could be manifested in time and space, leaving the divine nature of Christ still omnipresent, even during the incarnation.
        - However, most of the apologists and early theologians identified Old Testament theophanies as appearances of the pre-incarnate Christ, assuming that while the Father could never be visible (Exod 33:20), the divine Word *could* be visible, and by implication, circumscribed (John 1:18, Col 1:15), even before the incarnation.[20]
        - Novatian would eventually solve the problem by explaining the incarnation as *kenosis*, or an emptying of divine powers (including omnipresence), which allowed that the *Logos* could temporarily set aside omnipresence, even in his pre-incarnate existence, in order to appear to people in the Old Testament.
        - Thus, as Tertullian had said, the whole person of Christ (including the divine nature) was circumscribed, not only in time and space, but also in the womb of Mary.
- Eternal Generation
    - Eternal generation goes hand in hand with consubstantiality

---

19. Theophilus of Antioch, *To Autolycus* 2.3.

20. Irenaeus, *Against Heresies* 2.1.2; *Demonstration of the Apostolic Preaching* 45. See also Novatian, *On the Trinity* 9.4, 18.19–20, 19.7–14, 26.3.

- Specifically, the Son is generated from the Father, but not in such a way that it implies a change or division in the divine substance.
- This term applies to the Son only, since we do not say that the Spirit is "begotten," or generated, rather we say the Spirit "proceeds," yet the principles are basically the same, so that it would be legitimate to say the Holy Spirit eternally proceeds.

○ While Christ is begotten (his existence is derived from, and dependent on, the Father), this "begottenness," or generation, is not an event, but an eternal state of being.

- Therefore, there was no time before the Son's generation, when the Son did not exist and the Father was not a Father.[21]
- There is also no time before the Son's generation when the Son existed only as the Father's thought or wisdom, *in* the Father with no real personal distinction.

○ While the New Testament documents affirm that Christ preexisted creation (Col 1:15–20; Phil 2:6–11; John 1:1–14), they do not clarify that his preexistence was eternal, thus the biblical witnesses leave open the possibility of "a time when he was not," as Arius had said.

- Athenagoras seems to be the first to articulate the Church's conviction of eternal preexistence.[22]
- Irenaeus would later hint that this includes an eternal distinction between the Father and the Son.[23]
- Novatian would put these concepts together to finally express the doctrine of eternal generation.[24]

○ Eternal generation is therefore the solution to Theophilus's inadequate (by later standards) concept of co-eternal preexistence, in which the Son always existed, but not as an eternally

---

21. Novatian, *On the Trinity* 31.3.
22. Athenagoras, *Plea for the Christians* 10.
23. Irenaeus, *Against Heresies* 2.30.9, 4.20.3.
24. Novatian, *On the Trinity* 4.5–7, 17.3, 31.2–4, 31.16.

distinct divine person. In other words, Theophilus had eternal preexistence, but not eternal distinction.

- o True eternal generation requires eternal distinction between the persons of the Trinity. To say otherwise ultimately results in a Trinity that goes from being less than three to fully three, which would compromise divine simplicity and immutability.[25]

- o Without eternal generation, the Trinity would not always be a Trinity.

- o Eternal generation is also the correction for Arius's concept of the preexistent but created Christ: the Council of Nicaea would affirm what the western theologians had taught, that to be generated is not to be created and that generation necessarily results in consubstantiality.

- o The Father and Son are distinct, but not separate: there is a balance of unity and distinction (generation results in both) between Father and Son, as indeed also with the Holy Spirit.

- *Communicatio Idiomatum*
  - o As *circumincessio* is to the persons of the Trinity, *communicatio idiomatum* is to the two natures of Christ: it is a way of describing the balance of unity and distinction, such that the two natures are distinct, but not separate.
  - o This concept describes the "communication" of idiomatic, or unique, properties between the two natures within the person of Christ.
    - ▫ It is not enough to say that each nature contributes something to the whole person of Christ, since this would still "protect" the divine nature from truly experiencing humanity.
    - ▫ It is also not enough to say that the divine nature affects the human nature without the communication also going in the other direction.[26]

---

25. Ayres, *Nicaea and Its Legacy*, 332.

26. Some writers, such as Origen, were so intent on preserving the immutability of the divine nature, they only had a one-way *communicatio*. The divine nature might give the human nature glory, but they stopped short of saying that the human nature had anything to contribute to the divine nature.

- *Communicatio idiomatum* means that each nature can "borrow" (i.e., *experience*) something that would normally belong to the other nature only, yet without implying any change in the divine nature.
- Specifically, the union of natures allows the divine nature to *experience* the "frailty of the human condition," including suffering, without actually undergoing change, likewise, the union of natures allows the human nature to be glorified.[27]

  o Novatian was the first to articulate a full two-way *communicatio idiomatum*, however a primitive version of the concept may already have existed in the Roman church in the time of Callistus. Hippolytus, who followed Tertullian in rejecting the possibility of *communicatio* from the human to the divine nature, complained when bishop Callistus taught an early version of the concept, Hippolytus claiming that it was a form of modalism.[28]

- *Hypostatic* union

  o This describes the union of the two natures within the one *person* (Greek: *hypostasis*) of Christ.

  - The point is that it is a real union that exists at the level of the very personhood of Christ.
  - This is more than simply a union of wills and yet this does not imply that either nature is changed or diminished by the union.

  o This terminology would not be standardized in the eastern church until the fifth century, however in the west, a personal union was already understood by the time of Novatian.

  - Tertullian said that the two natures were united, but not confused, an important distinction that would later be necessary to refute Eutyches's "one nature" Christology, known as monophysitism.[29]

---

27. Novatian, *On the Trinity* 13.5, 18.5, 22.9, 24.8–10.
28. Hippolytus, *Refutation of All Heresies* 9.7. See also *Against Beron* 1, 5–6.
29. Tertullian, *Against Praxeas* 27.

- Hippolytus clarified that the two natures were combined "into one person" (*hypostasis*), with a human rational soul (mind and will).[30] This is part of the refutation of later Apollinarian monothelitism.
- Finally Novatian, using language that anticipated Augustine and Leo of Rome, said that Christ is "both substances combined into one (person)," yet without any confusion of the natures that would diminish either one.[31] This language, via Leo, influenced the Chalcedonian definition.
  - The key to understanding the personal union and *communicatio idiomatum* is the *kenosis*.
    - The *Logos*, which is the divine nature in the person of Christ, emptied himself of divine powers (including such properties as omniscience and omnipresence) in order to become fully human.
    - Therefore, by virtue of the incarnation, the divine Word could experience human limitation and suffering, but without compromising divine immutability.
    - In addition, the union of natures goes beyond a mere juxtaposition, or cooperation of the human with the divine: the two natures of Christ are inseparable, yet neither one diminishes the other, nor do they create some other thing, such as a third nature.[32]

- *Theotokos*
  - This is the Greek term for "God bearer," meaning the one who gives birth to God (in English it is translated, "Mother of God").

---

30. Hippolytus, *On Christ and Antichrist* 4. See also *Against Beron* 1–2.

31. Novatian, *On the Trinity* 13.3, 24.9. Cf. Leo of Rome, *Epistle* 28.5 (the *Tome*), in which Christ is described as a "unity of person in both natures." In the East, credit is usually given to Cyril of Alexandria for defining the *hypostatic union*. Cyril had at first been closer to Apollinarius, or even Eutyches, in seeing the person of Christ as the result of a union of two natures, but after the union, some third thing (*tertium quid*) resulted, which was more fully divine than human. Eventually Cyril came to the middle, and with Leo, was instrumental in influencing the Chalcedonian definition in favor of the personal union, with its balance of unity and distinction of the two natures.

32. Tertullian, *On the Flesh of Christ* 8.

- Although it is a title that is applied to Mary, it is really a christological term. A controversy arose in the fifth century, surrounding the question of the union of the two natures in Christ, and whether they were united enough that it would be appropriate to say that the divine nature was circumscribed within the womb of Mary.
  - Based on the hypostatic union and *communicatio idiomatum*, the divine and human natures are so inseparably united that it is appropriate to say that Mary is not only the mother of the human nature of Jesus, but of the whole person of Christ, including the divine nature.
  - Since she is the one through whom the divine nature of Christ came into the world (the *Logos* became flesh), she can be called the Mother of God.
  - Tertullian had said that the Logos was circumscribed in Mary's womb, which is consistent with Novatian's concept of the whole person of Christ circumscribed in time and space.[33]
- The use of this term became an issue of major debate in the fifth century, leading to the ecumenical Council of Ephesus in 431 CE. At that council, it was determined that the term *Theotokos* was an appropriate title for Mary because it did in fact describe an orthodox understanding of the *hypostatic union*.

---

33. Ibid., 17, 19.

Other Works by the Author

The Wedding of the Lamb: A Historical Approach to the Book of Revelation (Eugene, OR: Pickwick, 2011)

Spiritual Blueprint: How We Live, Work, Love, Play and Pray (Liguori, MO: Liguori, 2010)

Pray (Not Just Say) the Lord's Prayer (Liguori, MO: Liguori, 2010)

"Between Two Thieves: Novatian of Rome and Kenosis Christology," in *Studies on Patristic Texts and Archaeology: If These Stones Could Speak . . . Essays in Honor of Dennis Edward Groh*, edited by George Kalantzis and Thomas F. Martin (New York: Edwin Mellen, 2009)

The Trinitarian Theology of Novatian of Rome: A Study in Third-Century Orthodoxy (New York: Edwin Mellen, 2008)

Forthcoming from the author:

How to Be a Saint: Discerning God's Will for Your Life (Liguori, MO: Liguori, 2011)

Romesick: Making Your Pilgrimage to the Eternal City a Spiritual Homecoming (Eugene, OR: Wipf & Stock, 2012)

Trinity 101 (Liguori, MO: Liguori, 2012)

For More Information about the Author:
www.JimPapandrea.com

Bibliography

Altaner, Berthold, and A. Stubier. *Patrology*. Translated by Hilda C. Graef. Freiburg: Herder, 1960.
Amann, Émile. "Novatien et Novatianisme." In *Dictionnaire de théologie catholique*, 11:816–49. Paris: Letouzey et Ané, 1931.
Ayres, Lewis. *Nicaea and Its Legacy: An Approach to Fourth-Century Trinitarian Theology*. Oxford: Oxford University Press, 2004.
Barbel, J. *Christos Angelos*. Theophaneia 3. Bonn: P. Hanstein, 1941.
Bardenhewer, Otto. *Geschichte der altkirchlichen Literatur*. Vol. 2. Darmstadt: Wissenschaftliche Buchgesellschaft, 1962.
Barnes, Timothy D. "Legislation against the Christians." *Journal of Roman Studies* 58 (1968) 32–50.
———. *Tertullian: A Historical and Literary Study*. Corrected ed. Oxford: Oxford University Press, 1985.
Baumstark, Anton. "Die evangelienzitate Novatians und das Diatessaron." *Oriens Christianus* 5 (1930) 1–14.
Bethune-Baker, J. F. *The Meaning of Homoousios in the "Constantinopolitan" Creed*. Texts and Studies 7.1. Cambridge, MA: Cambridge University Press, 1901.
Bettenson, Henry, editor. *Documents of the Christian Church*. 2nd ed. London: Oxford University Press, 1963.
Boeft, J. den. "Vergil im frühen Christentum: Untersuchungen zu den vergilzitaten gei Tertullian, Minucius Felix, Novatian, Cyprian und Arnobius." *Vigiliae Christianae* 56.3 (2002) 316–19.
Brent, Allen. *Hippolytus and the Roman Church in the Third Century: Communities in Tension before the Emergence of a Monarch-Bishop*. Supplements to Vigiliae christianae 31. Leiden: Brill, 1995.
Burns, J. Patout. "On Rebaptism: Social Organization in the Third Century Church." *Journal of Early Christian Studies* 1.4 (1993) 367–403.
Cantalamessa, Raniero. *La Cristologia di Tertulliano*. Paradosis: Studi di Letteratura e Teologia Antica 18. Fribourg: Edizioni Universitarie, 1962.
Cary, M., and H. H. Scullard. *A History of Rome Down to the Reign of Constantine*. 3rd ed. New York: St. Martin's, 1975.
Cayré, Fulbert. *Manual of Patrology and History of Theology*. Translated by H. Howitt. Vol. 1. Paris: Desclée, 1936.
Chadwick, Henry. "The Church of the Third Century in the West." In *The Roman West in the Third Century: Contributions from Archaeology and History*, edited by Anthony King and Martin Henig, 5–14. BAR International Series 109. Oxford: BAR, 1981.
Chin, Catherine M. "Rufinus of Aquileia and Alexandrian Afterlives: Translation as Origenism." *Journal of Early Christian Studies* 18.4 (2010) 630.

D'Alès, Adhémar. "Le corpus de Novatien." *Recherches de Science Religieuse* 10 (1919) 293–323.

———. *Novatien: Étude sur la théologie Romaine zu milieu du IIIe siècle.* Paris: G. Beauchesne, 1924.

Daly, C. B. "Novatian and Tertullian: A Chapter in the History of Puritanism." *Irish Theological Quarterly* 19 (1952) 33–43.

De Ste. Croix, G. E. M. "Why Were the Early Christians Persecuted?" *Past and Present* 26 (1963) 6–38.

———. "Why Were the Early Christians Persecuted?: An Amendment." *Past and Present* 27 (1964) 23–27.

———. "Why Were the Early Christians Persecuted?: A Rejoinder." *Past and Present* 27 (1964) 28–33.

DeSimone, Russell J. "Christ the True God and True Man according to Novatian *De Trinitate*." *Augustinianum* 10 (1970) 42–117.

———. "The Holy Spirit according to Novatian *De Trinitate*." *Augustinianum* 10 (1970) 360–87.

———. "Novatianists." *Encyclopedia of the Early Church*, edited by Angelo Di Berardino, translated by Adrian Walford, 2:604–5. New York: Oxford University Press, 1992.

———. *The Treatise of Novatian the Roman Presbyter on the Trinity: A Study of the Text and the Doctrine.* Studia Ephemeridis Augustinianum 4. Rome: Institutum Patristicum Augustinianum, 1970.

Diercks, G. F. "Note sur le traite *De Trinitate* de Novatien." *Sacris Erudiri* 19 (1969–70) 27–32.

———. "Novatien et son temps." In *Novatiani Opera*, 8–13. Corpus Christianorum, Series Latina 4. Turnholt: Brepols, 1972.

Dölger, Franz Josef. "Zum oikiskos des Novatianus: Klausnerhäuschen oder versteck?" In *Antike und Christentum: kultur- und religionsgeschitchtliche studien*, 6:61–64. Münster: Aschendorff, 1940.

———. "Die taufe des Novatian." In *Antike und Christentum: Kultur- und religionsgeschitchtliche studien*, 2:258–67. Münster: Aschendorff, 1930.

Dunn, Geoffrey D. "The Diversity and Unity of God in Novatian's *De Trinitate*." *Ephemerides Theologicae Lovanienses* 78.4 (2002) 385–409.

———. *Tertullian.* The Early Church Fathers. London: Routledge, 2004.

Eusebius of Caesarea. *Ecclesiastical History.* Translated by John E. L. Oulton. Vol. 2. Loeb Classical Library. Cambridge, MA: Harvard University Press. Reprint, 1980.

Favre, Raphaël. "La communication des Idiomes dans l'ancienne tradition Latine." *Bulletin de Littérature Ecclésiastique* 37 (1936) 130–45.

Ferrua, A. "Novaziano Martire." *La Civiltà Cattolica* 95.4 (1944) 232–39.

Frutaz, A. Pietro. "Novaziano, Cimitero detto di." *Enciclopedia Cattolica* 8 (1952) 1974–76.

Geweiss, Josef. "Zum altkirchlichen Verständnis der Kenosisstelle (Phil. 2.5–11)." *Theologische Quartalschrift* 128 (1948) 463–87.

Ginoulhiac, Jacques Marie Achille. *Histoire du dogme catholique: Pendant les trois premiers siecles de l'eglise et jusqu'au Concile de Niceé.* Vol. 2. 2nd ed. Paris: Auguste Durande, Libraire, 1866.

Goodspeed, Edgar J. *A History of Early Christian Literature*. Rev. by Robert M. Grant. Chicago: University of Chicago, 1966.

Gregory, Caspar René. "The Essay *Contra Novatianum*." *American Journal of Theology* 3 (1899) 566–70.

Grillmeier, Aloys. *Christ in Christian Tradition*. Vol. 1: *From the Apostolic Age to Chalcedon (451)*. Translated by John Bowden. 2nd rev. ed. Atlanta: John Knox, 1975.

Hagemann, Hermann. "Novatians angebliche Schrift van der Trinitat." In *Die römische Kirche und ihr Einfluss auf Disziplin und Dogma in den ersten drei Jahrhunderten*. Freiburg: Herder, 1864.

Hallman, Joseph M. *The Descent of God: Divine Suffering in History and Theology*. Minneapolis: Fortress, 1991.

Harnack, Adolf von. *History of Dogma*. Translated by Neil Buchanan. Vol. 2. Theological Translation Library 2.8. Boston: Roberts, 1907.

———. "Novatian, Novatianism." *The New Schaff-Herzog Encyclopedia of Religious Knowledge*, 197–202. Grand Rapids: Baker, 1952.

Hatch, Edwin. *The Organization of the Early Christian Churches*. Bampton Lectures 1880. 2nd ed., rev. London: Rivingtons, 1882.

Heckel, Hartwig. "Vergil im frühen Christentum: Untersuchungen zu den vergilzitaten bei Tertullian, Minucius Felix, Novatian, Cyprian und Arnobius." *Zeitschrift für Kirchengeschichte* 115.1–2 (2004) 207–9.

Heine, Ronald E. "Articulating Identity." In *Cambridge History of Early Christian Literature*, edited by Frances Young, Lewis Ayres, and Andrew Louth, 200–221. Cambridge: Cambridge University Press, 2004.

———. "Cyprian and Novatian." In *Cambridge History of Early Christian Literature*, edited by Frances Young, Lewis Ayres, and Andrew Louth, 152–60. Cambridge: Cambridge University Press, 2004.

Hultgren, Arland J., and Steven A. Haggmark, editors. *The Earliest Christian Heretics: Readings from Their Opponents*. Minneapolis: Fortress, 1996.

Hurtado, Larry W. *Lord Jesus Christ: Devotion to Jesus in Earliest Christianity*. Grand Rapids: Eerdmans, 2003.

———. *One God, One Lord: Early Christian Devotion and Ancient Jewish Monotheism*. Philadelphia: Fortress, 1988.

Janin, R. "Les Novatiens orientaux." *Echos d'Orient* 28 (1929) 385–97.

Jeffers, James S. *Conflict at Rome: Social Order and Hierarchy in Early Christianity*. Minneapolis: Fortress, 1991.

Jordan, Hermann. "Melito und Novatian." *Archiv für lateinische Lexikographie* 13 (1904) 59–68.

———. "Die rhythmische Pros aim apostolischen Symbol und in den Novatian zugeschrieben Schriften." In *Rhythmische Prosa in der altchristlichen lateinischen Literatur*, 33–74. Leipzig: Dieterich'sche, 1905.

Kearsley, Roy. *Tertullian's Theology of Divine Power*. Rutherford Studies in Historical Theology. Carlisle: Paternoster, 1998.

Keilbach, Gulielmus. "Divinitas Filii eiusque Patri subordinatio in Novatiani libro *De Trinitate*." *Bogoslovska Smotra* 21.3 (1933) 193–244.

Kelly, J. N. D. *Early Christian Doctrines*. 5th, rev. ed. London: A. & C. Black, 1977.

Keresztes, Paul. "Two Edicts of the Emperor Valerian." *Vigiliae Christianae* 29 (1975) 81–95.

Kereszty, Roch. *Jesus Christ: Fundamentals of Christology*. Rev ed. New York: Alba House, 2002.

Knipfing, John R. "The Libelli of the Decian Persecution." *Harvard Theological Review* 16 (1923) 345–90.

Koch, Hugo. "Zum Ablativgebrauch bei Cyprian von Karthago und andern Schriftstellern (Novatian)." *Rheinisches Museum für Philologie* 78 (1929) 427–32.

———. *Cyprianische Untersuchungen*. Arbeiten zur Kirchengeschichte 4. Bonn: Marcus and Weber, 1926.

———. "La Lingua e lo stilo di Novaziano." *Religio* 13 (1937) 278–94.

———. "Il martire Novaziano." *Religio* 14 (1938) 192–98.

———. "Novatianus: Römischer Priester und Gegenbischof." *Pauly-Wissowa* 17 (1936) 1138–56.

———. "Novaziano, Cipriano e Plinio il Giovane." *Religio* 11 (1935) 1321–32.

Kriebel, Martin. "Studien zur älteren Entwicklung der abendländischen Trinitätslehre bei Tertullian und Novatian." Dissertation, Universität Marburg, 1932.

La Penna, A. "De quodam Nouatiani codice, qui in Bibliotheca Perisiensi Sanctae Genouefae adseruatur." In *Maia: Rivista di letterature classiche*, 7:137–40. Bologna: Cappelli, 1955.

La Piana, George. "The Roman Church at the End of the Second Century." *Harvard Theological Review* 18 (1925) 201–77.

Labriolle, Pierre Champagne de. *The History and Literature of Christianity from Tertullian to Boethius*. Translated by Herbert Wilson. London: Routledge and Kegan Paul, 1968.

Lampe, Peter. *Die stadtrömischen Christen in den ersten beiden Jahrhunderten: Untersuchungen zur Sozialgeschichte*. WUNT 2.18. Tübingen: Mohr/Siebeck, 1987.

Langen, Joseph. "Die Kirchentrennug Novatians." In *Geschichte der römischen Kirche bis Zum Pontifikate Leo's I*, 1:289–314. Bonn: M. Cohen, 1881.

Laurentin, A. "Jean 17:5, et la prédestination du Christ à la glorie chez S. Augustin et ses prédécesseurs." In *L'Evangile de Jean: Études et problèmes*, edited by M. E. Boismard, 225–48. Recherches bibliques 3. Bruges: Desclée de Brouwer, 1958.

Lietzmann, Hans. "Ein Gnostiker in der Novatianuskatakombe." *Rivista di archeologia cristiana* 11 (1934) 359–62.

Loi, Vincenzo. "La Latinità Cristiana nel De Trinitate di Novaziano." *Rivista di Cultura Classica e Medioevale* 13 (1971) 136–77.

———. *Origini e Caratteristiche della Latinità Cristiana*. Supplements to Bollettino dei Classici 1. Rome: Academia Nazionale dei Lincei, 1978.

Loofs, Friedrich. "Das altkirchliche zeugnis gegen die herrschende Auffassung der Kenosisstelle (Phil. 2, 5–11)." *Theologische Studien und Kritiken* 100 (1927) 1–102.

Lupiere, Edmondo F. "Contributo per un'analisi delle citazioni veterotestamentarie nel *De Trinitate* di Novaziano." *Augustinianum* 22 (1982) 211–27.

Lupiere, Edmondo F. "Novatien et les Testimonia d'Isaïe." In *Studia Patristica*, edited by Elizabeth A. Livingstone, 17:211–27. Oxford: Pergamon, 1982.

MacMullen, Ramsay. *The Second Church: Popular Christianity A.D. 200–400*. Writings from the Greco-Roman World Supplement Series 1. Atlanta: Society of Biblical Literature, 2009.

Marucchi, Orazio. *Christian Epigraphy: An Elementary Treatise with a Collection of Ancient Christian Inscriptions, Mainly of Roman Origin*. Translated by J. Armine Willis. Cambrige: Cambridge University Press, 1912.

Mattei, Paul. "Novatien précurseur à la fois D'apollinaire et de Nestorius? Équivoques rétrospectives et portée réelle de la formule christologique dans le *De Trinitate*." In *Chartae caritatis: Études de Patristique et d'antiquité en hommage à Yves-Marie Duval*, edited by Benoît Gain, Pierre Jay, and Gérard Nauroy, 449–66. Collection des etudes Augustiniennes, série Antiquité 173. Paris: Institut d'Études Augustiniennes, 2004.

Mohlberg, L. C. "Osservazioni storico-critiche sulla iscrizione tombale di Novaziano." *Ephemerides litugicae* 51 (1937) 242–49.

Mohrmann, Christine. "Novatianus." In *Encyclopedia Britannica*, 571. Chicago: Britannica, 1960.

———. "Les origines de la Latinité Chrétienne à Rome." *Vigiliae Christianae* 3 (1949) 67–106, 163–83.

———. "Les origines de la Latinité Chrétienne à Rome." In *Études sur le Latin des Chrétiens*, 3:103. Rome: Edizioni di Storia e Letteratura, 1965.

Nautin, Pierre. *Lettres et écrivains chrétiens des IIe et IIIe siècles*. His Patristica 2. Paris: Éditions du Cerf, 1961.

Novatian. *La Trinità*. Edited and Translated by Vincenzo Loi. Corona Patrum 2. Torino: Società Editrice Internazionale, 1975.

———. *De Trinitate*. In *Novatiani opera*, edited by G. F. Diercks. Corpus Christianorum, Series Latina 4. Turnholt: Brepols, 1972.

———. *De Trinitate*. In *Nouatiani Presbyteri Romani opera quae extant omnia*, edited by E. Welchman. Oxonii, 1724.

———. *De Trinitate*. In *Novatiani Presbyteri Romani opera quae supersunt omnia*, edited by J. Jackson. London, 1728.

———. *De Trinitate*. In *Novatiani Romanae urbis presbyteri De Trinitate liber*, edited by W. Yorke Fausset. Cambridge Patristic Texts. Cambridge: Cambridge University Press, 1909.

———. *De Trinitate*. In *Patrologiae Cursus Completus: Series Latina*, edited by J. P. Migne, vol. 3. Paris: Migne, 1886.

———. *De Trinitate: Über den dreifaltigen Gott*, edited by Hans Weyer. Testamonia 2. Düsseldorf: Patmos, 1962.

———. *On the Trinity*. In *Ante-Nicene Christian Library: Translations of the Writings of the Fathers Down to A.D. 325*, edited by Alexander Robers and James Donadson, vol. 13. Edinburgh: T. & T. Clark, 1880.

———. *On the Trinity*. In *Ante-Nicene Fathers*, vol. 5. Buffalo, NY: Christian Literature Pub. Co., 1926.

———. *On the Trinity*. In *The Treatise of Novatian On the Trinity*, edited by Herbert Moore. Translations of Christian Literature, ser. 2, Latin Texts. New York: MacMillan, 1919.

———. *On the Trinity.* In *The Trinity; The Spectacles; Jewish Foods; In Praise of Purity; Letters.* Translated by Russell J. DeSimone. The Fathers of the Church: A New Translation, 67. Washington, DC: Catholic University of America Press, 1974.

Orbe, Antonio. *Hacia la primera teología de la processión del Verbo.* 2 vols. Estudios Valentinianos 1. Rome: Pontificia Universitatis, 1958.

Osborn, Eric Francis. *Tertullian, First Theologian of the West.* Cambridge: Cambridge University Press, 1997.

Papandrea, James L. "'Between Two Thieves': The Christology of Novatian as 'Dynamic Subordination,' Influenced by His Historical Context and His New Testament Interpretation." PhD diss., Northwestern University, 1998.

———. "Between Two Thieves: Novatian of Rome and Kenosis Christology." In *Studies on Patristic Texts and Archaeology: If These Stones Could Speak . . . : Essays in Honor of Dennis Edward Groh,* edited by George Kalantzis and Thomas F. Martin, 51–73. Lewiston, NY: E. Mellen, 2009.

———. *The Trinitarian Theology of Novatian of Rome: A Study in Third-Century Orthodoxy.* Lewiston, NY: E. Mellen, 2008.

Pelikan, Jaroslav. *The Christian Tradition: A History of the Development of Doctrine.* Vol. 1: *The Emergence of the Catholic Tradition (100–600).* Chicago: University of Chicago Press, 1971.

Pelland, Gilles. "Un passage difficile de Novatien sur I Cor. 15:27–28 (*De Trinitate*)." *Gregorianum* 66.1 (1985) 25–52.

Pellegrino, Michele. *Letteratura latina cristiana.* 2nd ed. Universale studium 48. Rome: Editrice Studium, 1963.

Peterson, Erik, "Novaziano e Novazianismo." In *Enciclopedia Cattolica*, 1976–80. 1952.

Petitmengin, Pierre. "Une nouvelle édition et un ancien manuscrit de Novatien." *Revue des études Augustiniennes* 21 (1975) 256–72.

Photius of Constantinople. *The Ecclesiastical History of Philostorgius, as Epitomized by Photius, Patriarch of Constantinople.* Translated by Edward Walford. In 1 vol. with *The Ecclesiastical History of Sozomen, Comprising a History of the Church, from A.D. 324 to A.D. 440.* Bohn's Ecclesiastical Library. London: H. G. Bohn, 1855.

Pollard, T. E. "The Exegesis of John 10:30 in the Early Trinitarian Controversies." *New Testament Studies* 3 (1956–57) 334–49.

Pollmann, Karla. "Vergil im frühen Christentum: Untersuchungen zu den Vergilzitaten bei Tertullian, Minucius Felix, Novatian, Cyprian und Arnobius." *Zeitschrift für antikes Christentum* 7.1 (2003) 167–68.

Prete, Serafino. "L'antico Testamento in Novaziano: *De Spectaculis.*" *Augustinianum* 22 (1982) 229–37.

Quarry, J. "Nouatiani *De Trinitate* liber: It's Probable History." *Hermanthena* 10 (1899) 36–70.

Quasten, Johannes. *The Ante-Nicene Literature after Irenaeus.* Vol. 2 of *Patrology.* Westminster, MD: Newman, 1953.

Rocco, Anita. "La Tomba Del Martire Novaziano a Roma." *Vetera Christianorum* 45 (2008) 323–41.

Rusch, William G. *The Trinitarian Controversy.* Sources of Early Christian Thought. Philadelphia: Fortress, 1980.

Sage, Michael M. *Cyprian*. Patristic Monograph Series 1. Cambridge, MA: Philadelphia Patristic Foundation, 1975.
Saller, Richard P. *Personal Patronage under the Early Empire*. Cambridge: Cambridge University Press, 1982.
Schaff, Philip. *The Creeds of Christendom*. 3 vols. New York: Harper, 1877.
Scheidweiler, F. "Novatianstudien." *Hermes* 85 (1957) 58–86.
Sherwin-White, A. N. "The Early Persecutions and Roman Law Again." *Journal of Theological Studies* 3 (1952) 199–13.
Simonetti, Manilo. "Alcune osservazioni sul *De Trinitate* di Novaziano." In *Studi in onore di Angelo Monteverdi*, 2:771–83. Modena: Società Tipografica Editrice Modenese, 1959.
———. "Ilario e Novaziano." *Rivista di Cultura Classica e Medioevale* 7 (1965) 1034–47.
Socrates, Scholasticus. *The Ecclesiastical History of Socrates, Surnamed Scholasticus, or the Advocate*. Bohn's Ecclesiastical Library. London: H. G. Bohn, 1853.
Stelzenberger, Johannes. *Die Beziehungen der frühchristlichen Sittenlehre zur Ethik der Stoa: Eine moralgeschichtliche Studie*. Munich: M. Huebner, 1933.
Stevenson, James, editor. *A New Eusebius: Documents Illustrating the History of the Church to AD 337*. London: SPCK, 1987.
Tertullian. Evans, Ernest, editor and translator. *Adversus Praxean Liber: Tertullian's Treatise against Praxeas*. London: SPCK, 1948.
Vagaggini, Cipriano. "Subordinazionismo." In *Enciclopedia Cattolica*, 1465. 1953.
Van den Eynde, D. "L'inscription sépulcrale de Novatien." *Revue d'histoire ecclésiastique* 33.1 (1937) 792–94.
Vogt, Hermann Josef. *Coetus Sanctorum: Der Kirchenbegriff des Novatian und die Geschichte seiner Sonderkirche*. Theophaneia 20. Bonn: P. Hanstein, 1968.
———. "Novatian." *Encyclopedia of the Early Church*, edited by Angelo Di Berardino, translated by Adrian Walford, 603–4. New York: Oxford University Press, 1992.
Vööbus, Arthur. *The Didascalia Apostolorum in Syriac*. 2 vols. Corpus Scriptorum Christianorum Orientalium 401–2, 407–8. Louvain: Secrétariat du CSCO, 1979.
Walker, G. S. M. *The Churchmanship of St. Cyprian*. Ecumenical Studies in History 9. Richmond, VA: John Knox, 1968.
Wallraff, Martin. "Markianos—ain prominenter Konvertit vom Novatianismus zur Orthodoxie." *Vigiliae christianae* 52.1 (1998) 1–29.
Weedman, Mark. *The Trinitarian Theology of Hilary of Poitiers*. Supplements to Vigiliae Christianae 89. Leiden: Brill, 2007.
Wehofer, Thomas. "Zur decischen Christenvervolgung und zur Charakteristik Novatians: Ein Beitrag zur Kirchengeschichte des 3 Jahrunderts." In *Ephemeris Salonitana*, 269–75. Split: Arheoloski Muzej, 1993.
———. "Sprachliche Eigenthümlichkeiten des classischen Juristenlateins in Novatians Briefen." *Wiener Studien* 23 (1901) 269–75.
Weyer, Hans. "Novatian and Novatianism." In *New Catholic Encyclopedia*, 10:534–35. New York: McGraw Hill, 1967.
Weyman, Carl. "Neue Traktate Novatians." *Archiv für lateinische Lexikographie und Grammatik* 11 (1900) 467–68.
———. "Novatian und Seneca über den Frühtrunk." *Philologus* 52 (1893) 728–30.

———. "Die Tractatus Origenis de Libris Ss. Scriptararum ein Werk Novatians." *Archiv für lateinische Lexikographie und Grammatik* 11 (1900) 545–76.

Williams, Rowan. *Arius: Heresy and Tradition*. Rev. ed. Grand Rapids: Eerdmans, 2002.

Young, Frances M., Lewis Ayres, and Andrew Louth, editors. *The Cambridge History of Early Christian Literature*. Cambridge: Cambridge University Press, 2004.

Subject Index

Adoptionists/adoptionism/
  dynamic monarchianism,
  12–13, 15–17, 20, 24–25, 29,
  31, 33–34, 41, 43–46, 53, 58,
  73–76, 85, 87, 96–98, 101,
  104–6, 108–9, 111, 115, 120,
  124, 128, 133, 140, 143, 148
Against Novatian (Contra
  Novatianum), x, 62, 67
agent of creation, 7, 10, 13, 21, 34,
  39, 42, 83–84, 86, 92–94, 97
Alexander of Alexandria, 129–30
Ambrose of Milan, x, 60–62,
  69–70, 124–27
Angel (of the Lord)/Christ as
  Messenger, 8, 21, 30, 43, 97,
  102–3
Anselm of Canterbury, 25, 133, 139
Apollinarius/Apollinarianism/
  monothelitism, 40, 78, 98,
  128, 132, 140, 154
appropriation, 30, 97, 115, 122–24,
  126, 130, 143, 146
ascension of Christ, 12, 27, 31, 37,
  43, 82, 91, 95–96, 116, 119
ascent, christology of, 16, 95, 106–7
Athanasius of Alexandria, 122–23,
  125, 129–32, 134
Athenagoras, 10–13, 19, 48, 89,
  101, 118, 143–45, 148, 151
Augustine of Hippo, 5, 28, 33, 54,
  80–81, 115, 119, 122–23,
  126–28, 131, 137, 147–48

baptism/rebaptism, 2–3, 16, 24,
  54–56, 62–63, 65–66, 69–70,
  78, 109, 135–37, 146, 159
Beryllus of Bostra, 16

Chalcedon, Fourth Ecumenical
  Council of (451 CE), 40,
  110–21, 117–19, 127–28,
  132, 154, 161
circumscription/circumscribability,
  xi, 8, 14, 20, 38, 41, 81, 83,
  94, 97–98, 102–4, 111,
  113–14, 116, 119, 126, 128,
  150, 155
Clement of Alexandria, 19, 31, 88,
  111, 144, 147
communicatio idiomatum, 6, 32,
  41, 75, 110–12, 114–16,
  118–20, 122, 126–27, 134,
  144, 147, 152–54
confessors, 59–60, 64–66, 139
Constantinople, Second
  Ecumenical Council of (381
  CE), 106–10
consubstantiality/essence/sub-
  stance, 8–9, 11, 13, 19–20,
  23–24, 27–33, 36–37, 41,
  43, 46, 53, 57, 73, 76, 78–82,
  85–88, 90–98, 100–101,
  103–10, 112–13, 118–19,
  123–27, 129–31, 133–34,
  143–46, 148, 150–52, 154
Cornelius of Rome, x, 54, 56–57,
  61–67, 73, 135, 139
corruptibility/incorruptibility, 23,
  41–42, 75, 77, 111–12, 143

Subject Index

Cyprian of Carthage, x, 51, 53–56, 58–68, 122, 135–36, 159, 161–62, 164–65

Dionysius of Alexandria, x, 66, 128–30, 132
Dionysius of Rome, 129, 132
Docetics/docetism, 2–4, 6, 17, 21–22, 24–27, 31–32, 35, 42–46, 76–79, 109, 111, 128, 133
dualism, 3, 6, 35
dynamic monarchianism. *See* Adoptionists.
dynamic subordination, ix, 96, 105, 115, 120, 134, 141, 164

Ebionites, 1–5, 15, 24–25, 43–46
economy. *See* hierarchy.
Ephesus, Third Ecumenical Council of (431 CE), 110, 155, 119
Epiphanius of Salamis, x, 23, 26
essence. *See* consubstantiality.
eternal generation, xi–xii, 14, 23, 34, 88–89, 91–93, 104–5, 107, 110, 119, 121–27, 129–31, 134, 141, 147, 150–52
Eucharist, 2–3, 6, 26, 47, 50, 139
Eusebius of Caesarea, x–xi, 16, 25, 48–50, 54, 56, 62, 65–67, 73, 128, 160, 165
Eutyches/monophysitism, 40, 108, 115, 120, 132, 140, 153–54

First Cause, 31, 36, 39, 82–83, 89–90, 97, 99, 101, 119, 134, 147, 149

Gnostics/gnosticism/gnosis, 2–4, 6, 17, 19, 21, 22–26, 31, 33, 35–36, 40, 43–46, 77–78, 128, 145, 162

hierarchy (within the Trinity), 9, 11, 20, 30–31, 33, 36–37, 82–84, 99–101, 103–5, 110, 120
Hilary of Poitiers, 85, 91, 123–29, 165
Hippolytus, 7, 17–18, 22, 26, 32, 34–42, 46, 54, 59, 75, 80–81, 83, 94, 96, 105, 111, 118, 121–22, 136, 144, 147–48, 153–54, 159
hypostatic (personal) union, 32, 41, 110, 115, 118–19, 126–28, 140, 153–55

Ignatius of Antioch, 2–6, 9, 11, 22
immutability/mutability, 5–6, 8, 12–14, 17, 23–24, 32, 34, 38–39, 44, 75, 77–78, 85–86, 89–90, 92–93, 96, 98, 111–14, 128, 130, 134, 144, 152, 154
impassibility/passibility, 5, 8, 20, 24, 41, 44, 75, 77, 144
inseparable operation, 9, 18, 21, 24, 30, 43, 46, 80, 93, 97, 101, 105, 122–24, 126, 131, 143, 145–48
Irenaeus of Lyons, xii, 4, 8, 11, 13–14, 17–26, 28–31, 34, 44–45, 51, 85–86, 89, 91–92, 99, 112, 122, 127, 138, 143, 145–46, 150–51, 164

Jerome, x–xi, 54, 60, 122, 125
Justin Martyr, 6–11, 13, 19, 22–23, 93, 144–46

kenosis/kenosis christology, ix, xi, 9, 23, 45, 75–77, 79–84, 95, 101, 103–4, 107–8, 111, 113–14, 117, 119, 124, 126–28, 133–34, 140, 150, 154, 157, 160, 162, 164

Subject Index   169

lapsed, 57–66, 99, 133, 135–36, 139
laxists, 58–59, 63, 66, 139
Leo of Rome, 68, 70, 97, 118, 122–23, 125, 127–29, 131, 133, 135, 137, 139, 141, 154, 162
Logos christology, 9, 34–35, 42–43, 45–46, 52, 87, 91, 132
Logos endiathetos, 12–13, 93
Logos prophorikos, 12, 14, 93

Marcion/Marcionites, 3, 26, 31–33, 42, 45, 76–78, 80, 82, 101, 109, 138
martyr/martyrdom, 4, 7, 19, 48, 50, 56, 58, 60, 63–65, 68, 135, 139
Modalists/modalism/modalistic monarchianism, 15, 17–18, 20, 25–29, 31–33, 35–37, 39–41, 43–46, 58, 74, 84, 87, 91, 93, 97–99, 101, 104–5, 108, 111, 115, 119–20, 122, 124–25, 132–33, 140, 146, 148, 153
monarchianism. *See* Adoptionists or Modalists.
monism, 17, 35
monophysitism. *See* Eutyches.
monotheism, 7, 15, 17, 38, 46, 73–74, 78, 99, 103, 119–20, 133–34, 143, 145, 161
monothelitism. *See* Apollinarius.

Nestorius/Nestorianism, 41, 98, 114–15, 120, 140, 163
Nicaea, First Ecumenical Council of (325 CE), 37, 42, 69, 80, 88–89, 91, 94, 106–7, 119, 122–24, 126–27, 129, 131–32, 136, 145, 152, 159
Noetus, 17–18, 34–40, 46, 81, 118
Novatianists/Katharoi, x, 55, 62, 67, 69–70, 135–36, 160

omnipresence, 8, 38, 41, 78, 81–83, 96, 103–5, 116, 134, 138, 144, 150, 154
On Jewish Foods (De Cibis Iudaicis), ix, 56, 58, 67, 138
On Rebaptism, 62, 65–66, 135, 137, 159
On the Benefit of Purity (De Bono Pudicitiae), ix, 56, 115
On the Spectacles (De Spectaculis), ix, 47, 136
Origen, xi–xii, 37, 40, 51, 75, 80, 84, 88–89, 108, 111, 125–26, 132, 152, 159, 166

Pacian of Barcelona, x, 56, 59–60, 62–63, 65, 68–70, 135
patripassionism. *See* Modalists.
patronage/patron-client, 52–53, 110, 165
Paul of Samosata, 16–17, 108
perichoresis/circumincessio/reciprocity, 11, 37, 41, 96, 110, 118–19, 131, 148–49, 152
persecution, 4, 19, 36, 48–52, 57–58, 62–67, 162, 165
Philo, x, 6–7, 10, 12, 15, 17, 19, 23, 43, 55–56, 93, 143–44, 162, 164–65
Polycarp of Smyrna, 5–6, 19
power (divine)/authority, xi, 8–9, 11–13, 16, 19, 28, 30, 36, 39, 41–43, 75, 77, 80–82, 92, 96, 100–101, 104, 109, 119, 124, 126, 134, 145, 150, 154, 161
Praxeas/Against Praxeas, 18, 26–34, 78, 81–82, 84–85, 89, 101, 114, 116, 118, 143, 145, 147, 153, 165

recapitulation/typology, 22, 108, 138
resurrection, 2–3, 5, 7, 10, 44, 46, 78

Rigorists/rigorism, 55–56, 58–59, 61–62, 64, 67, 69, 117, 135–39,
Rufinus of Aquileia, x–xii, 88, 122, 125, 129, 132, 159

Sabellius/Sabellians. *See* Modalists.
salvation/soteriology, 2–3, 5, 25, 43–44, 46, 61–62, 65, 74, 76–77, 79, 112, 117, 133, 138, 140–41
simplicity (divine), 23, 29, 46, 119, 143–45, 148, 152
Socrates Scholasticus, x, 55, 59–60, 66, 68–70, 135, 165
Stephen of Rome, 136–37, 139
subordination, ix, xi, 8, 81, 83–84, 96, 104–5, 115, 117, 120, 134, 140–41, 164
substance. *See* consubstantiality.
syncretism, 4

Tertullian, xii, 8–9, 11, 13, 17–18, 22, 25–39, 41, 45, 48, 50–51, 53, 55, 59–60, 69, 75–76, 78–82, 84–85, 88–89, 93, 97, 101, 105–6, 109–10, 114–18, 121–22, 125, 127, 132, 136, 138, 143, 145–47, 150, 153–55, 159–62, 164–65
Theophilus of Antioch, 5, 8, 11–15, 17, 21, 23–24, 33–34, 36, 38, 86–88, 91, 93, 144, 149–52
To Novatian (Ad Novatianum), x

via media (middle way/balance), 1, 32–33, 37–38, 41, 59, 63, 65–66, 74–75, 98–99, 105–6, 115–16, 119–20, 124–29, 134–35, 130, 133, 139–41, 152, 154

wisdom, 7, 12–14, 20, 38–39, 43, 45, 59, 84, 87–89, 91, 151